A Tax Guide to
Conservation Easements

A Tax Guide to
Conservation Easements

C. Timothy Lindstrom

ISLANDPRESS

WASHINGTON · COVELO · LONDON

   Lindstrom, Timothy C.
    A tax guide to conservation easements / by Timothy C. Lindstrom.
      p. cm.
    ISBN-13: 978-1-59726-387-0 (cloth : alk. paper)
    ISBN-10: 1-59726-387-7 (cloth : alk. paper)
    ISBN-13: 978-1-59726-388-7 (pbk. : alk. paper)
    ISBN-10: 1-59726-388-5 (pbk. : alk. paper)
    1. Conservation easements—United States. I. Title.
    KF658.C65L567 2008
    343.7305'3—dc22   2007045270

Keywords: Land conservation, land trust, estate planning, land
conservation finance, tax benefits, Land Trust Alliance, fee interests,
transfer of development rights, purchase of development rights,
bargain sale

Contents

Preface

A basic knowledge of federal tax law is essential to virtually all land trust personnel—to lawyers, appraisers, and accountants dealing with conservation easements, and to the landowners who grant them. In putting this book together, every effort has been made to make the information accessible and understandable. The federal tax law relating to conservation easements is relatively self-contained, however, it is complex. It is also evolving.

During the writing of this book, the Internal Revenue Service (IRS) was engaged in a newly vigorous and widespread examination of conservation easements and land trusts. A few cases resulting from that examination have already made their way through the courts and are discussed in this book; others are still wending their way through the judicial process and won't be reported until after this book is published. In addition, Congress is now considering revisions to the existing tax law relating to conservation easements. Final action on those proposals had not occurred before this book went to press. There will inevitably be additional legislation, as well as administrative rulings and actions by the IRS, and judicial decisions, about which no one yet knows. In other words, this book is a snapshot of a moving picture.

This book began as an outline for a continuing legal education lecture in Virginia and has grown over the years to its current form. It existed previously as *A Simplified Guide to the Tax Benefits of Donating a Conservation Easement* and, more recently, as an article in the *Wyoming Law Review*. As time passed and the law evolved, it became necessary to eliminate the word "simplified" from the title. The text now extends beyond conservation easement contributions to noncharitable, or only partly charitable, transactions involving conservation easements, so "donating" has also been dropped from the title.

The book is intended as a resource tool, a reference the reader can pull off the shelf to answer a specific question. While truly dedicated readers may sit down and read the entire work, it is intended to be read in bits, as needed. The book is written so that in reading about one topic, the reader will be alerted to related topics where possible. To some extent that results in repetition, but I believe some repetition is justified to avoid the need for constant page flipping to piece together the whole story. Nevertheless, no one reading a portion of this book should forget that the individual components of tax law are highly interconnected and that you cannot understand the general from the particular.

The material presented here is densely informative rather than prosaic. I have used examples extensively to illustrate the technical matters covered. Because I am dealing with a topic that has had little attention from the courts so far, few examples can be drawn from real life. The hypothetical examples provided are intended to represent the types of situations in which many land trusts and landowners may find themselves. For illustrative purposes, the examples are often simplified from (or made more complex than) what would likely be actual conservation transactions. **The examples and the conclusions drawn in them are not intended as formal legal opinions.**

This book deals with federal tax law, although it incidentally mentions some state tax incentives for voluntary land conservation. Extensive treatment of state tax law relating to conservation easements is beyond the scope of this book.

While the basic principles covered here are unlikely to change dramatically in the near future, critical details are likely to change. Let the reader beware of the need to double-check the currency of the information presented here.

Finally, and perhaps most important, this book is not a substitute for competent and knowledgeable legal counsel. Not only is the law covered by this book rapidly changing, as already noted, it is largely untested in court. While the examples and opinions given in this book are (hopefully) logical, they are often without benefit of any definitive statement of the law. It is entirely possible that there will be definitive pronouncements made in the near future on many of the now speculative issues covered by this book, a possibility that should compel anyone dealing with conservation transactions to consult qualified legal counsel.

PART I

Basic Principles

In part 1 we will take a look at the basic principles on which modern conservation transactions rely. This portion of the text will review various tools for voluntary land conservation, as well as fundamental principles of federal tax law that are a foundation for understanding the tax rules pertaining to conservation easements.

CHAPTER ONE:

An Overview of Voluntary Conservation Tools

To understand the operation of the tax law as it pertains to land conservation, a good place to start is by understanding the various types of tools that currently exist for undertaking voluntary land conservation. Following is a brief description of some of the most commonly used land conservation tools, not all of which will result in tax deductions.

I. Fee Interests

A *fee interest* (more technically an estate in "fee simple," or "fee simple absolute") at common law (the law created by judicial decisions, as opposed to statutory law created by legislative acts) primarily described an estate of inheritance—that is, one that could be passed on to one's heirs, as opposed to an estate limited to a specific term of years, for example. Fee ownership also refers to the ownership of all of the different interests that make up a parcel of real property. Real property is sometimes referred to as a "bundle of twigs." The twigs represent different kinds of interests that can be owned, either together or separately. For example, air rights, water rights, timber rights, mineral rights, and surface rights are all different aspects of the fee ownership. At common law the entire bundle of twigs is referred to as the *fee simple absolute*.

When one acquires a fee interest, one acquires the entire bundle of twigs that make up a given parcel of real property. However, typically, when one speaks of owning a fee interest in a nontechnical sense, one is merely referring to owning the right to possess and use the surface of a parcel of real property, regardless of whether rights such as mineral rights, water rights, or an access easement, for example, have been previously conveyed to others, all of which "off-conveyances" reduce the fee simple to something less than the complete bundle of twigs.

Traditional land conservation involved acquiring fee interests (in this case the term *fee* is used in its nontechnical sense). The federal government acquired land through conquest, purchase, and the power of eminent domain for national parks, forests, seashores, and so forth. Early private land conservation efforts also involved acquisition of fee interests.

Land conservation today still involves fee acquisition, although less extensively than in the past due to the inflated costs of real property and the additional costs of holding fee interests, including insurance, taxes, and maintenance. Some substantial conservation organizations such as The Nature Conservancy still depend extensively upon acquiring fee interests. Such efforts often involve the acquisition of the fee and then resale of the fee subject to a conservation easement reserved by the conservation organization to ensure that future use by the purchaser will be consistent with that organization's conservation goals. Such transactions are known as "conservation buyer transactions." Conservation buyer transactions are discussed in more detail in section VII of this chapter and in section II, B, 3 of chapter 4.

When a governmental agency or public charity (e.g., a land trust recognized as a public charity under section 501(c)(3) of the *Internal Revenue Code*) acquires a fee interest as a contribution, or for less than the fair market value of the fee, the grantor of the fee is entitled to a federal tax deduction.

II. Conservation Easements

Conservation easements are the primary tool of private land conservation today. According to the Land Trust Alliance's 2005 National Land Trust Census, in the past five years over 6.2 million acres of land have been protected by local and state land trusts through the use of conservation easements, compared to just over 2.5 million acres in 2000. Those 6.2 million acres of conservation easements contrast sharply with the increase in acquisition of fee interests by land trusts over the same period, which has been just over 480,000 acres.

Conservation easements, from a legal standpoint, are a mixture of different legal concepts. They have some of the attributes of contracts, some of the attributes of real property easements, and some of the attributes of charitable trusts. Much has been written about their origin and nature. Today, conservation easements are almost entirely creatures of state statutory law, typically based on, or copied from, the Uniform Conservation Easement Act first proposed in the 1980s by the National Conference of Commissioners of Uniform State Laws.

Because conservation easements were generally not enforceable under the common law, any conservation easement conveyed today must comply exactly with the state statutory law that authorizes conservation easements. Anything less than exact compliance may render the easement unenforceable and, therefore, under federal tax law nondeductible. Thus, any conservation easement *must* be written to conform to the requirements of the law of the state in which it is conveyed.

Conservation easements have the advantage of allowing the private ownership, use, and management of land to continue, subject to the restrictions on use imposed by the easement. Conservation easements leave land on local tax rolls for real property taxation, although typically at a reduced rate. Because a land trust that owns a conservation easement does not have responsibility for management of the land, or payment of taxes or insurance on the land, the financial burden of conserving land with an easement is less than preserving land by acquiring a fee interest. Finally, because the value of a conservation easement, which leaves ownership in private hands, is less than the value of the fee, purchasing conservation easements can be considerably less expensive than purchasing the fee.

Conservation easements are not without potential problems, however. First, as already mentioned, creating an enforceable conservation easement requires attention to statutory detail. Second, because ownership remains in private hands, land trusts face expenses for monitoring the use of land subject to easement and enforcing easements in case of violation. These are expenses that land trusts would not have if they owned the land in fee. Third, there are growing concerns that conservation easements, which are in most cases intended to be permanent, may be easily and improperly modified or terminated, thus eroding or eliminating the conservation benefits afforded by the easement and wasting the public's investment in the tax incentives that may have inspired the easement in the first place.

Again, the contribution or sale of a conservation easement for less than its fair market value to a public agency or land trust can generate federal tax benefits for the grantor of the easement. Where a conservation easement is contributed in compliance with the rules provided in section 170(h) of the *Internal Revenue Code*, the U.S. Treasury subsidizes the gift by granting both income and estate tax benefits to the donor of the easement.

III. Bargain Sales

A bargain sale is the sale of property (including a conservation easement) to a governmental agency or public charity, such as a land trust, for less than its fair market value. Sections 1011(b) and 170 of the *Internal Revenue Code* recognize that such a sale may, in part, constitute a charitable contribution and allow the seller to deduct from his income the difference between the sales price and the actual value of the property as determined by an independent appraisal.

In a bargain sale, the U.S. Treasury, in effect, subsidizes the purchase by providing tax benefits to the seller to help make up for the shortfall between what a land trust, for example, can afford to pay and what the property sold is really worth.

IV. Purchase of Development Rights

The purchase of development rights (sometimes referred to as PDRs) is really the purchase of a conservation easement on land. Because conservation easements typically reduce or eliminate the development potential of land by prohibiting future development, buying a conservation easement has come to be referred to as the purchase of development rights.

PDR programs are typically managed or subsidized by local or state governments and are often tied to the land-use planning of such entities. In some cases conservation easements are purchased that impose permanent restraints on future development. In other cases conservation easements may be purchased that only temporarily constrain development or allow the governmental entity that holds the PDRs to sell those rights to developers after infrastructure necessary to support development has been put in place. The use of PDRs for temporary land conservation is sometimes referred to as "land banking" or "development rights banking."

The purchase of a conservation easement in a PDR program for full value does not generate an income tax deduction, although there may be some estate tax savings from the restraint on future appreciation in land value resulting from the restrictions on development imposed by the conservation easement. However, if a PDR is bought for less than fair market value, the transaction may constitute a bargain sale, for which the seller may claim a charitable deduction.

A word of caution about PDRs: PDRs are typically structured by governmental agencies who may, or may not, have any concern about whether the grantor of the PDR receives a tax deduction for the transfer.

One should not assume that because the PDR is bargain-sold to a governmental entity, the transaction automatically meets the strict requirements of the federal tax code for deductibility. Unless the conservation easement involved meets all of the requirements of section 170(h) of the *Internal Revenue Code*, it will not be deductible.

V. Transfer of Development Rights

The transfer of development rights (TDR) is a complex land-use tool that allows landowners in an area designated by a locality as a "transfer zone" to sell development rights from their land to landowners in another area designated as a "receiving zone." Typically, transfer-zone land has been restricted to low density (often by "down-zoning," i.e., rezoning to reduce development potential), and the landowners there are "compensated" for the effect of these restrictions by being allowed to sell development potential they are no longer permitted to use to landowners in the receiving zones, where additional development is allowed. Receiving-zone landowners are allowed higher densities, but only if they acquire development rights to use those higher densities from landowners in transfer zones.

There is no rigid format for TDRs. However, in some cases localities require landowners in a transfer zone who sell TDRs to put conservation easements on their land to ensure that the elimination of development potential by the sale is permanent. In theory, conservation easements thus imposed supersede zoning. Thus, if some future local governing body decided to increase density on land from which development rights had been sold by rezoning that land, the rezoning would be ineffective. Of course, the success of such a scheme would depend on whether the holder of conservation easements on transfer-zone land would enforce those easements in the long run, and on whether there was any market demand for the TDRs.

Some extremely complex transactions grow out of the combination of TDRs, PDRs, and conservation easement contributions in states where all of these tools can be used together. Some states further complicate such transactions by allowing easement donors a tax *credit* against state income tax for the contribution of conservation easements, including the bargain sale of PDRs.

TDRs are typically sold to other private individuals and are not donated to governmental agencies or public charities, so charitable deductions are not involved.

7

VI. Cluster Development

Cluster development schemes are another planning tool used by localities. These schemes typically allow a landowner to concentrate all of the zoning potential of his property in one portion of that property by giving up the right to develop the balance of the property. This can be visualized by thinking of a checkerboard on which a player shoves all of his pieces into one corner, leaving the rest of the board empty. Depending on local zoning rules, the "open space" (the empty part of the checkerboard) resulting from moving development to one portion of a property may be preserved through the imposition of a conservation easement. Alternatives may include conveying the open space to a homeowners' association, or imposing restrictive covenants enforceable by adjoining residential development.

Where conveyance of a conservation easement to preserve the open space in a cluster development is mandated in exchange for increased density elsewhere, a charitable deduction is very unlikely (see chapter 4, section II, B, 1).

8

VII. Conservation Buyer Transactions

Conservation buyer transactions have been an increasingly important part of voluntary land conservation. They come in different forms and are described more fully in chapter 4, section II, B, 3. Briefly, these transactions depend on a conservation-minded buyer capable of using the federal income tax benefits associated with contributing a conservation easement (a "conservation buyer"). Land trusts try to match conservation-worthy land with conservation buyers. Once the conservation land has been conveyed to the conservation buyer, the buyer is expected to contribute a conservation easement to protect the land. Such a contribution can generate tax benefits that effectively reduce the buyer's cost of acquiring the property (the "acquisition cost"). The trick in conservation buyer transactions is figuring out how to ensure that the buyer conveys the easement, while, at the same time, preserving the buyer's tax deduction for the contribution.

Conservation buyer transactions work best if the buyer is bound to protect the land once he acquires it. For a number of years these types of programs worked quite successfully. Typically, when a land trust showed a prospective conservation buyer a property, it required the buyer to sign an agreement, or pledge, that if he acquired the property, a conservation easement would follow. However, in July of 2004, the IRS issued Notice 2004-41 critical of transactions in which a taxpayer claimed a tax deduction for the contribution of a conservation easement granted in connection with the purchase of property. The notice is vague, and IRS representatives have said (unofficially) that it was not directed at the kind of conservation buyer deal described here. Nevertheless, because the IRS has refused to clarify the notice, most attorneys have since been unwilling to advise their clients that binding conservation buyer agreements will result in deductible easement contributions.

An alternative to a conservation buyer transaction in which the prospective buyer pledges an easement if and when he acquires property is a transaction in which a land trust acquires a fee interest and resells the property but retains a conservation easement. Such deals work, although there is no deduction for the purchaser and the land trust loses the economic value of the easement in the transaction.

Another approach is for the buyer to "overpay" for property subject to an easement. For example, a buyer pays $2 million for land that, subject to easement, is worth $1 million. The land trust selling such land acknowledges that the buyer has overpaid by $1 million and acknowledges the overpayment as a charitable contribution. This structure is similar to other situations in which the IRS has allowed charitable deductions and has been (again, unofficially) acknowledged by the IRS as providing the basis for a deduction.

CHAPTER TWO:

Basic Tax Law Principles

I. The Importance of Tax Compliance

At a Senate Finance Committee hearing in 2005, an IRS official acknowledged that it had been ten years since the IRS had paid much attention to conservation easement contributions. In fact, of all of the approximately 115 reported court cases involving challenges to conservation easement deductions at that time, at most 5 related to compliance of the terms of the easement with the requirements of federal tax law. The rest were decided exclusively on appraisal and valuation issues. In the face of this history, it is not surprising that strict compliance with tax law requirements has not been taken seriously by many donors and land trusts.

With the *Washington Post* series alleging abusive conservation transactions by the nation's preeminent conservation organization in 2004, however, the picture changed dramatically. The series' criticism of The Nature Conservancy, whether or not well founded, ignited congressional investigations, draconian proposals for reform from the Congressional Joint Committee on Taxation, and much soul searching by the nation's land trusts. Ironically, the most important legislation enacted in the aftermath actually increased, rather than curtailed, tax benefits for easement contributions.

Nevertheless, the IRS has dramatically increased its scrutiny of conservation transactions. As of the date of this writing, the IRS has over 500 conservation easement deductions under audit; most of the land trusts in Colorado are under IRS scrutiny; two federal tax court decisions and a federal circuit court of appeals decision dealing with the *compliance* of conservation easements with requirements of the tax law, not just easement valuation, have been announced in the past two years; IRS agents in ease-ment audits are asking questions such as how much firewood for personal use the donor of an easement is allowed to remove from the property under easement, and what kind of pets the donor may keep on a conserved property. The days of benign neglect of conservation transactions by the government appear to be over.

Compliance with tax law has always been required; it is only that now it has become inescapably relevant to the survival of the tax benefits themselves and to the success of individual transactions. *No one should enter into a conservation easement transaction assuming that it will not be scrutinized.*

II. The *United States Code* and U.S. Treasury Regulations

The federal tax code is a statute: Title 26 of the *United States Code* ("U.S.C."). When reference is made in this book to "the Code," it is to Title 26, the tax code, unless otherwise stated. The Code is law as approved by Congress and signed by the president. Except for the United States Constitution, with which even the Code, Congress, and the presi-dent, must comply, the Code is *the* law.

Congress has also authorized the various departments of govern-ment to issue (to "promulgate") "regulations" that flesh out and imple-ment the U.S.C. In the case of Title 26 the Department of the Treasury promulgates the regulations. The Treasury Regulations (as they are offi-cially known) implementing the Code are found in section 26 of the *Code of Federal Regulations* (CFR). When reference is made in this book to "the Regulations" it is to section 26 of the CFR, the Treasury Regulations, unless otherwise stated.

Regulations are administrative guidelines, not the law—at least not in theory. It is possible for regulations to be inconsistent with the statutes they are supposed to implement. When this occurs, the federal courts have the authority to invalidate the regulations. Courts also have authority to invalidate statutes that violate the U.S. Constitution. That power is known as the power of judicial review. Judicial review leading to the invalidation of a regulation or statute is unusual. More important is that while the Treasury Regulations are not statutory law, they still carry the weight of law and must be given respect.

Congress has been criticized for passing "broad brush" laws and letting the unelected bureaucrats that run governmental departments provide the details through regulations. However, for better or worse, the

Regulations are the source of most of our knowledge about the federal tax law governing conservation easements and land trusts. The Regulations governing the deductibility of conservation easements are quite detailed and full of examples.

III. Tax Benefits: A Privilege Not a Right

The first thing to understand about a tax deduction is that it is not a right, unless the taxpayer has strictly complied with the rules. Tax deductions, like the entire tax code, are "creatures of statute," matters of "legislative privilege." Put simply, if a conservation easement fails to comply with *all* of the requirements of federal law, it is technically not deductible. It does not matter that the easement may have permanently restricted the donor's land; it does not matter that valuable conservation resulted. Ultimately, a federal tax deduction depends on *strict* compliance with tax law.

I once experienced the unforgivable nature of the Code personally. In writing a trust that was to be deductible from a decedent's estate, I inadvertently left one phrase out of the document. After the decedent died, the IRS audited his estate and sent me a polite letter asking about the missing phrase. There proceeded a series of meetings with different levels of IRS officials; at every one the agents were genuinely understanding of the mistake, acknowledged that the results that occurred were the results required by the Code, and sympathetic. However, in each meeting the agents' conclusion was that the deduction was a statutory privilege. The Code and Regulations spelled out *exactly* how this particular trust was to be written to qualify the estate for the deduction and, as I had failed to strictly comply with the requirements, no deduction was allowed. The result was that the estate paid an additional $100,000 in estate tax, and my malpractice insurer picked up the tab and raised my premium. *Strict compliance!*

There is no safety net. The only hope for a conservation easement that fails to strictly comply with the law is the chance that it will escape audit. The likelihood of an easement audit has historically been small, meaning that many errors may have gone unnoticed. However, the likelihood of an easement audit has increased, as noted. Neither easement donors nor land trusts should be willing to rely on chance when it comes to compliance.

Federal tax law governing the deductibility of conservation easements consists of the provisions of section 170(h) of the Code and the provisions of section 1.170A-14 of the Regulations. The provisions of the Code are brief, less than one page of text. The provisions of the

Regulations are over sixteen pages and 10,600 words. The Code and the Regulations, current as of the date of publication of this book, can be found in Appendices A and B, respectively, at the back of this book.

In addition to the Code and Regulations, the law governing the deductibility of conservation easements includes judicial decisions, such as those of the U.S. tax court and the U.S. court of claims, as well as other federal courts. Finally, there are IRS administrative materials, which include Private Letter Rulings (PLRs), Notices, and a host of other Treasury and IRS pronouncements.

Of all of these various types of tax law, the most important are the Regulations. The Regulations explain, in exhaustive detail, what the government expects a deductible conservation easement to look like. They also provide numerous examples of what is deductible and what is not. *No one who is unfamiliar with the Regulations should write a conservation easement that is intended to be deductible.* For that matter, no one who is unfamiliar with the Regulations should be involved in a transaction that depends on the deductibility of a conservation easement.

Author's note: What follows is the first of a great many examples in this book. Sometimes examples are drawn from actual cases, like the following one; sometimes they are purely hypothetical. Often I express an opinion as to how the IRS should treat the facts or express some other opinion about the outcome. The examples are intended to illustrate various points to help the reader understand sometimes highly oblique concepts; they are not formal legal opinions. They are based on made-up facts and often on unresolved legal issues. A formal legal opinion that can be relied upon must, necessarily, be based on the application of the law to actual facts.

Example One: The Great Northern Nekoosa Company contributed a conservation easement on 5,000 acres of land along the Penobscot River in Maine. In the easement the company reserved the right to remove gravel from the property for the purpose of maintaining roads on the property and building foundations for structures whose construction was reserved in the easement. The easement provided that neither gravel nor any other mineral on the property could be sold or used commercially.

The IRS challenged the deductibility of this easement on the grounds that the reserved right to remove gravel, even though restricted by the easement, constituted the right to "strip mine" the property. Strip mining is clearly prohibited by the Regulations. The company's $19 million tax deduction was disallowed by the IRS, and that position was upheld by the U.S. court of claims.

The fact that the easement permanently protected 5,000 acres of valuable wildlife habitat and scenery did not overcome the simple failure to comply with a very clear provision of the federal tax law. Many knowledgeable people think that the IRS and the court of claims got this decision wrong. However, it is strict compliance that will save a challenged easement, not the collective judgment of experts.

Example Two: The Browns donated a conservation easement on a farm in Virginia. The easement was contributed to one of the nation's most successful land trusts. The land trust agreed to prepare a "natural resources inventory" of the farm, as required by federal tax law. The easement went to record in December. The land trust produced the inventory many months later.

Fortunately for everyone, this easement transaction was not audited. Had the deduction been audited, the failure of the parties to produce and approve the inventory prior to the conveyance of the easement, as explicitly required by the Regulations, could have provided grounds for disallowance of the deduction, even though the easement did what the Regulations required.

This is an example of a deduction that survived by chance: the chance that there was no audit. The fact that the error was the result of reliance by the donor on the practices of a preeminent land trust would not have saved the deduction. Ignorance is no defense. It is possible that a court would have acknowledged the correctness of the IRS's position in challenging the deduction in this case but allowed the deduction anyway on grounds that the failure to comply was not substantive. However, the time and cost of challenging an audit alone are a high price to pay for sloppiness.

Whether the donor would have had a cause of action against the land trust had the deduction been disallowed is an open question.

IV. The Partial Interest Rule

The deduction allowed for conservation easements is an exception to the general tax rule that contributions of less than the donor's entire interest in a property ("partial interest gifts") are not deductible. Generally, the Code allows deductions only for the contribution of a donor's entire interest in the property given. The contribution of a conservation easement, being less than the donor's entire interest in the easement property, is a "partial interest" contribution. However, as mentioned in chapter 1, conservation easements—and several other types of partial interest gifts—are excepted from the prohibition against deductions of partial interest contributions.

The exceptions to the partial interest rule are for (1) the contribution of a remainder interest in the donor's personal residence or farm; (2) certain contributions made in trust; (3) the contribution of all of a donor's undivided partial interest in a property (e.g., if the donor owns a 50 percent interest in a farm, her contribution of that entire 50 percent interest is deductible); and (4) qualified conservation contributions. Qualified conservation contributions include conservation easements. The fact that a deduction for a conservation easement is an exception to the express prohibition against deductions for partial interests makes compliance with the requirements of the exception particularly important. See Regulations section 1.170A-7 for the prohibition and exceptions.

Example One: John Jones donated an apartment building to the XYZ Housing Foundation. He retained the right to use the penthouse apartment in the building for five years, rent free. The value of the gift was estimated at $10 million. The value of the retained right to use the penthouse was estimated at $1 million. John got no deduction. This contribution, while meaningful, was a partial interest gift and did not qualify under any of the exceptions to the partial interest rule.

Example Two: Bill Black contributed his family farm to a local land trust. Bill retained the right to reside on and use the farm for the remainder of his life. This contribution was deductible because it fit the exception to the partial interest rule for gifts of remainder interests in a personal residence or farm. The value of the contribution for deduction purposes was the value of the farm, discounted by Bill's life expectancy.

V. The Requirement for Donative Intent

In order to be deductible, the contribution of a conservation easement must have been made with "donative intent." Donative intent is the intention to make a charitable contribution. The courts have ruled that a contribution of property made out of a legal obligation is not a charitable contribution but the discharge of an obligation. The courts have also said that the discharge of a moral obligation negates charitable intent. However, there are no cases of which I am aware in which a charitable deduction has been disallowed purely because it was made due to a moral obligation. The existence of a moral obligation is also difficult to determine.

In addition, a contribution made in exchange for the receipt of something of value ("consideration") is not a charitable contribution unless structured as a qualified "bargain sale." Consideration may be a cash payment, or some other form of benefit such as a zoning approval. Donative intent is discussed in more detail in chapter 4, section II.

Example: Larry Brown asked the Harvard Land Trust (HLT) to help him find a buyer for his farm. Larry wanted HLT to find a buyer who would contribute a conservation easement on the farm after he bought it. HLT suggested that Larry grant HLT an option to purchase an easement from the buyer for $1,000. The option would give the HLT authority to ensure that the buyer would, in fact, convey the easement. Larry signed the option, and HLT put it to record. Several months later HLT found a buyer for the farm who agreed to pay the full, unrestricted price for the farm. The sale closed, and two weeks later HLT exercised the option. In compliance with the option, the purchaser contributed a conservation easement valued at $800,000 to HLT, for which HLT paid the option price of $1,000.

Unfortunately, the contribution was audited, and the IRS successfully disallowed the deduction. The reason is that, even though the purchaser received only $1,000 in exchange for the $800,000 easement, the contribution was made to discharge a legal obligation expressly binding the purchaser to convey the easement if the option was exercised. Compliance with this legal obligation did not constitute the donative intent necessary to make a charitable contribution.

The IRS had a second argument, as well: When the purchaser bought the farm, it was already encumbered by an option that restricted its value to its value with the easement in place, plus the $1,000 option price. In other words, the option itself restricted the value of the farm before the easement was contributed, so that there was little difference in the value of the farm before and after the easement was in place; therefore, the easement had little or no value. (Note that options do not always undermine deductions in this fashion if the person granting the option and conveying an interest pursuant to the option are the same. See chapter 4, section II, B.)

VI. Sham Transactions and the Step Transaction Doctrine

An important tool available to the IRS for examining the legitimacy of any tax deduction is known as the Step Transaction Doctrine. Under that doctrine the IRS may ignore the structure (or steps) of a transaction to determine whether the transaction has any substance other than tax avoidance. The IRS will eliminate ("collapse") any steps in a transaction that have no substantive purpose other than tax avoidance and evaluate the transaction without those steps. Only if the transaction without the collapsed steps has a substantive purpose other than tax avoidance will the tax benefits of the transaction be allowed.

The Step Transaction Doctrine has typically been applied to business-oriented "tax shelters." However, it has equal application to conservation transactions in which a party claims a charitable deduction. It doesn't matter if the transaction results in bona fide land conservation or if the conservation easement involved was in compliance with the Code and Regulations from a technical standpoint. The question is whether the steps of the transaction that led to the claim of a tax deduction by one or more parties had any purpose other than tax avoidance.

Example: A development company has just completed a major "conservation development" in which residential lots are surrounded by open space. The company wants to be able to assure lot purchasers that the open space is permanently protected. It also wants to provide a tax benefit to interested lot buyers. It conveys the open space land to a limited liability company (LLC) of which the development company is the sole member. The LLC then executes an enforceable pledge to a local land trust to convey a conservation easement, but only after two years have elapsed from the date of the option. During the first year the LLC conveys memberships in the LLC to the purchasers of the residential lots for $10,000 each. At the end of the year the company no longer holds an interest in the LLC, and there are ten new members. The land trust calls in the pledge as soon as the two-year time limit is passed, and a conservation easement is conveyed over the open space. Each of the owners claims a 10 percent share of the tax deduction as a result of membership in the LLC.

Let's look at the "steps" in this transaction:
1. Conveyance of open space land by developer to wholly owned LLC.

2. Grant of enforceable pledge by LLC to land trust.
3. Pledge conditioned on not being called for at least two years.
4. Sale of memberships in LLC to lot purchasers.
5. Call of pledge by land trust.
6. Deduction claimed by members of LLC.

If this transaction were audited by the IRS, the IRS would want to know the purpose of each of these steps other than tax avoidance. The IRS would very likely collapse this transaction because there was no substance to any of these steps in terms of the contribution of the conservation easement. The developer could have simply conveyed the easement and received the deduction; the steps were merely a means of shifting the benefits of the deduction from the developer to the purchasers—that is, tax avoidance.

19

VII. Quid Pro Quo Transactions

The Regulations provide that no deduction is allowed for a charitable contribution of a conservation easement when the easement is given in exchange for some bargained-for benefit. Such *quid pro quo* ("something for something") transactions come in number of varieties. Typical quid pro quo transactions include receipt of a governmental approval in exchange for a conservation easement, or an arrangement whereby two or more landowners agree to grant each other interdependent easements. Selling a conservation easement for less than its appraised value does not constitute a quid pro quo transaction. Such a sale, a bargain sale, is recognized by the Code and Regulations, if properly structured, as an exception to the quid pro quo rule.

Case law regarding quid pro quo transactions is a bit murky. Some cases have denied deductions for the grant of parkland or open space to a locality as part of a development approval, and other cases have allowed such deductions. The decisions appear to turn on the relative value of the approval versus the value of the contribution, as well as the degree of connectivity between the grant and the approval. To further complicate matters, the Regulations themselves suggest that, as long as what the easement donor received in exchange for the easement was less valuable than the easement, a deduction for the difference is allowable.

Example: Sol Blue owns a 300-acre farm. The zoning applicable to the farm allows it to be developed into ten 30-acre parcels, or 30 smaller parcels, provided that the smaller parcels are "clustered" on no more than 50 acres of the farm and that the remainder of the farm is permanently conserved by a conservation easement. Sol opted to develop using the "cluster" approach. The locality required Sol to grant it a conservation easement over the open space created by the cluster. After the subdivision plat and conservation easement went to record, Sol decided to claim a tax deduction for the easement. A local appraiser valued the easement at $250,000, which was the amount of the deduction sought by Sol. The IRS properly disallowed the deduction on the grounds that it was granted not with donative intent but to obtain approval of the cluster development and was therefore conveyed as part of a quid pro quo transaction. Note that had the easement been granted to a third-party land trust, rather than the locality, the transaction would still have been a quid pro quo because the purpose of granting the easement was to obtain approval of the cluster rather than to make a charitable contribution.

PART II

Regulatory Requirements for Deductible Conservation Easements

At the heart of the tax law governing conservation easement deductibility are the Regulations. The Regulations elaborate extensively on the provisions of Code section 170(h) and cover four major areas. The first area includes the requirements for a qualified conservation contribution and a description of the four elements of such a contribution: (1) a qualified real property interest, (2) conveyed to a qualified organization, (3) exclusively for a qualified conservation purpose, (4) in perpetuity.

The second area covered in the Regulations describes the requirement that a conservation easement be "exclusively for conservation purposes." The third area covers the requirement that a conservation easement protect conservation values permanently. This area deals with matters that may undermine that requirement: outstanding mortgages, "remote and future events," mineral rights and development, retention of use rights by the grantor, and extinguishment of an easement. The fourth area covered is the easement valuation process.

The Regulations are not structured quite as clearly as the preceding outline suggests, but this book will attempt to simplify the provisions by addressing them according to this structure.

CHAPTER THREE:

Qualified Conservation Contributions

This chapter covers the formal requirements of the Code and Regulations for the deductible contribution of a conservation easement.

I. Deductions Are Limited to Qualified Conservation Contributions: Regulations Section 1.170A-14(a)

The federal income tax deduction for the contribution of a conservation easement is, as already noted, purely a statutory creation. The Code and Regulations (particularly the Regulations) spell out in detail what it takes for the contribution of a conservation easement to qualify for a charitable income tax deduction, as well as for other tax benefits. Briefly stated, a conservation easement must be (1) a restriction on the use of land, (2) contributed to a qualified organization; (3) exclusively for "conservation purposes," (4) in perpetuity. When those four requirements are met, the contribution is deductible. How much of a deduction will be available, and how much of the available deduction can actually be enjoyed by the donor is covered in chapter 4.

These four primary requirements for deductible conservation easements are discussed in detail in section I, B through D of this chapter. However, first it is necessary to reemphasize several fundamentals.

A. The Partial Interest Rule Revisited

As noted in chapter 2, section IV, the partial interest rule precludes a federal income tax deduction for the contribution of less than all of a donor's interest in a property. For example, the gift of an automobile would not qualify as a charitable contribution if the donor reserved the right to use the car on Sundays. Nor would the contribution of a summer cottage if the donor reserved the right to use the property for five days out of the year. Such contributions are considered "partial interests" because they consist of less than all of the donor's interest in the property.

However, there are four exceptions to the partial interest rule. Three of these exceptions have relevance to land conservation. One is the exception for the contribution of a donor's entire interest in real property, even if that interest constitutes less than 100 percent of the property. For example, the contribution of all of a donor's interest in a two-week time share of a condominium in Honolulu would be deductible, even though the property contributed was less that 100 percent of the condominium, because the donor conveyed 100 percent of all the property interest he owned. For the same reason, if a donor owns only a 20 percent undivided interest in a ranch but contributes all of that interest, the contribution would be deductible according to the exception to the partial interest rule for contributions of 100 percent of a donor's partial interest in a property.

Another exception to the partial interest rule relevant to land conservation is for the contribution of a "remainder interest" in a personal residence or farm. A remainder interest is an interest in property granted by a landowner that takes effect upon his death. The contribution of such an interest, even though it is less than the donor's entire interest in the property, is deductible, provided that the remainder interest is in the donor's personal residence or farm. If the donor contributes a remainder interest in property held strictly for investment purposes, for example, the exception to the partial interest rule does not apply and the contribution is not deductible. Of course, the value of a remainder interest has less economic value than the value of a contribution of the property outright (the value of the "life estate," i.e., the value of the donor's right to use the property during his lifetime, must be subtracted), but that is a valuation issue, not a deductibility issue. Furthermore, the younger the donor, the less the deductible value of the contribution for the simple reason that the donee must wait longer (according to life expectancy or "mortality" tables) to enjoy the property than if the remainder interest is contributed by an older person.

The third exception relevant to land conservation is for qualified conservation contributions. A qualified conservation contribution must be of a "qualified real property interest."

The fourth exception to the partial interest rule is for the contribution of certain property interests in trust, which does not concern us here.

B. Qualified Real Property Interest:
Code Section 170(h)(2)(c)

A qualified conservation contribution is the contribution of a "qualified real property interest" according to the Regulations. Two types of interest in land are considered qualified real property interests. One is a conservation easement, referred to in federal tax law as a "perpetual conservation restriction." The other qualified real property interest, less often considered, is the owner's entire fee interest less a "qualified mineral interest." Both are statutory exceptions to the partial interest rule described in section I, A of this chapter.

1. Donor's Entire Interest Less a Qualified Mineral Interest:
Regulations Section 1.170A-14(b)(1)

The first type of qualified real property interest described by the tax law is the donor's entire interest in real property *except for* a "qualified mineral interest" in that property. In other words, the fee simple interest in the parcel less a qualified mineral interest. Such contributions are sometimes called "qualified mineral interest gifts," even though they are a gift of everything but the qualified mineral interest. Such contributions must be for conservation purposes.

A qualified mineral interest, according to Regulation section 1.170A-14(b)(1)(i), is the donor's "interest in subsurface oil, gas, or other minerals and the right of access to such minerals." When a landowner makes a contribution of his entire interest in property but retains an interest in such minerals, the contribution is deductible, even though it is less than the donor's entire interest in the property. Note that a qualified mineral interest is limited to subsurface minerals, not minerals recoverable by surface or "strip" mining. In other words, if the donor retains surface mining rights, the contribution is not deductible. However, the donor may retain the right to "access" subsurface minerals, which means the right to excavate or otherwise disturb the surface of the property as necessary to extract subsurface minerals.

2. A Perpetual Conservation Restriction:
Regulations Section 1.170A-14(b)(2)

The other form of qualified real property interest is a perpetual conservation restriction which includes conservation easements. Technically, a perpetual conservation restriction is "a restriction granted in perpetuity on the use which may be made of real property—including an easement or other interest in real property that under state law has attributes similar to an easement (e.g., a restrictive covenant or equitable servitude)" (Regulations section 1.170A-14(b)(2)). In other words, there are several types of legal means by which a restriction may qualify as a perpetual conservation restriction. In any event, the real property law that dictates whether a particular restriction is enforceable in perpetuity is controlled by the various laws of the 50 states, not federal law. Therefore, some understanding of the legal character of a conservation easement and the basics of state law is necessary.

a. The Legal Characteristics of Conservation Easements

The legal character of conservation easements is complex and not entirely clear—are they contracts, real property interests, or trusts? The Uniform Conservation Easement Act (UCEA), and the law of most states, classifies conservation easements as real property interests.

Among the important legal virtues of easements (easements in general, not just conservation easements) is that they bind not only the owner of the land who agreed to the easement, but future owners, as well (such easements are said to "run with the land"). The common law was very particular about how a landowner could bind the use of his land in the hands of future owners, because the common law has traditionally opposed restrictions on the future use of land (sometimes called "restraints on alienation"). The law was also concerned about how subsequent owners of easement land would know about the existence of easements over their land.

Generally speaking, an easement that failed to comply with the many common law requirements to run with the land would be treated as a "personal covenant" by the landowner granting the easement, making it binding upon him but not upon future owners.

b. Appurtenant Easements and Easements in Gross

There are two types of real property easements. The most common easements are those that specifically benefit another property—for example, a right-of-way easement across one parcel (called the "servient parcel") that provides access to another parcel (the "dominant parcel"). Such an easement conforms to the common law requirements to run with the land and is, therefore, enforceable against future owners. Easements involving dominant and servient parcels are known as "appurtenant" easements because the easement is appurtenant to the dominant parcel.

Another type of real property easement is known as an easement "in gross." An easement in gross benefits an individual, or the public, rather than any specific property. Because of this it does not comply with the common law requirement to run with the land, and, thus, while it may bind the grantor of the easement, it is possible that it will not bind future owners, depending on the state and the court being asked to enforce it. This isn't always the case, but it is a significant risk. One of the principal problems with the enforcement of easements in gross is knowing who should have the right (the "standing") to enforce them.

A conservation easement is an easement in gross because it does not benefit any specific parcel of land but runs to the benefit of the public. The "in gross" nature of conservation easements raised questions about their enforceability, at least in theory. To get around that, and because statutory law supersedes common law, statutes have been passed in all 50 states that specifically authorize conservation easements in gross, making them enforceable provided that the requirements of the statutes are met.

27

c. The Uniform Conservation Easement Act

The UCEA is merely a suggestion for state legislation recommended by the National Conference of Commissioners of Uniform State Laws. However, the UCEA provides the basis for a number of state statutes that authorize conservation easements. A copy of the UCEA is included as appendix C at the end of this book. In essence, what the UCEA does is to eliminate many of the common law requirements for easements to run with the land, requirements that made conservation easements, as easements in gross, potentially unenforceable.

The Code mentions restrictive covenants and equitable servitudes, in addition to conservation easements, as other forms of perpetual conservation restrictions, the contribution of which may qualify for a federal income tax deduction. However, those types of restrictions have not generally been used for land conservation.

d. The Necessity of Compliance with State Law

Because conservation easements are easements in gross and may be unenforceable in the absence of statutory authority, it is essential that all of the statutory requirements for conservation easements be met in drafting them. Failure to strictly comply with *state* laws dictating the form and content of conservation easements could result in a restriction on the use of land that does not comply with the federal requirement for a perpetual conservation restriction because the easement is not enforceable against future owners of the easement land. In such a case, a federal tax deduction could be denied, yet the restriction might still apply, at least to the landowner who granted the easement—not a happy outcome.

Example: Mary Evers contributed a conservation easement over her farm. The farm is located in a state that has enacted the UCEA. However, the state added two provisions to the act. One provision requires that in order to qualify to hold a conservation easement under the act, an organization must have done business within the state for at least five years. The other provision requires that all conservation easements be reviewed by the local planning commission for compliance with the local comprehensive plan.

Unfortunately, Mary contributed the easement to an organization that had been doing business in the state for only three years, and neither she nor the organization submitted the easement to the local planning commission for review. Even more unfortunately, her contribution was audited. The IRS pointed out that the easement was not a perpetual conservation restriction because it failed to comply with the statutory requirements. Mary's deduction was denied.

Even though the easement did not qualify as a perpetual conservation restriction because it failed to comply with state law, the easement could be enforceable against Mary as a personal covenant. If the land trust were to insist, it might be able to enforce such a personal covenant against Mary, even though the failure to comply with the state's version of the UCEA would preclude the trust from enforcing the easement against Mary's successors in title. Such a result would be the worst of all possible outcomes for Mary: no deduction and an enforceable restriction against her use.

While the land trust might be sympathetic and willing to release the restriction, that might constitute an "excess benefit transaction," or a violation of the trust's obligation to use its assets exclusively for public purposes, violating its charitable status. Thus, the trust might not be able to release the restriction. For more about the limitations on a land trust's authority, see the following section.

C. Qualified Organizations:
Regulations Section 1.170A-14(c)(1)

Conservation easements are peculiar subjects for a charitable deduction because they allow the donor, essentially, to have his cake and eat it, too. This, of course, makes the tax people suspicious. Letting someone get a tax deduction for donating a restriction on the use of land, but leaving that land in the hands of the donor, does open up the possibility of abuse. The principal safeguard built into the tax law to prevent abuse is the requirement that, to be deductible, a conservation easement must be held by a "qualified organization" that has the right to monitor use of the easement property for compliance with the easement and to enforce the terms of the easement.

The principle behind this requirement is that if an easement is held by the right type of organization, that organization will be an adequate and effective watchdog against violation of the restrictions imposed by the easement. The qualified organization requirement is critical, particularly because many properties subject to conservation easements change hands and may come to be owned by people who are either ignorant of or actively opposed to the restrictions imposed by the easement. In addition, the value of the development potential thwarted by conservation easements is inflating rapidly in many places, increasing the economic incentive for landowners, and others, to try to "break" conservation easements. Easement holders, in theory, provide the assurance that the substantial subsidy provided by the nation's taxpayers for voluntary land conservation is a good investment.

To ensure that the holders of deductible conservation easements enforce the easements they hold, Regulations section 1.170A-14(c)(1) limits potential holders to governmental agencies and public charities with the resources and commitment to protect the conservation purposes of the easement contribution. Specifically, the Regulations require the following:

- The organization must be one of the four types of organizations listed in the Regulations.
- The organization must have a commitment to protect the conservation purposes of the donation (this is typically found in the articles of incorporation or bylaws of a private organization).
- The organization must have the resources to enforce the restrictions imposed by the easement (Regulations section 1.170A-14(c)(1)).

Generally speaking, local, state, and federal governments and their agencies, and publicly supported charities, may all qualify (but none are automatically qualified) to hold deductible conservation easements. In addition, publicly supported charities may qualify to hold such easements.

Following is a more detailed description and discussion of the

29

types of organizations identified by the Regulations as potentially qualified to hold deductible conservation easements, and a discussion of some of the issues relating to these organizations where conservation easements are concerned. Types of organizations potentially qualified to hold deductible conservation easements are (1) governmental units; (2) organizations that receive a substantial amount of support from governmental agencies or directly or indirectly from the public and are not disqualified under Code section 501(c)(3); (3) public charities qualified under Code section 501(c)(3), one-third of whose support comes from the public, which includes most land trusts; and (4) organizations qualified under section 501(c)(3) that meet the requirements of section 509(a)(3) and are controlled by one of the three types of organizations described in (1) through (3).

1. Governmental Units: Regulations Section 1.170A-14(c)(1)(i)

States, U.S. possessions, and any political subdivision of any of the foregoing, as well as the United States itself and the District of Columbia (but in each case, only if the contribution or gift is made for exclusively public purposes), are all considered qualified organizations for holding deductible conservation easements. However, the fact that an organization is a governmental agency does not automatically satisfy all three criteria for being a qualified organization.

Not all governmental units meet the second and third provisos of the tax law—that is, not all governmental agencies have the necessary commitment and resources to enforce the conservation purposes of the easement in perpetuity. In the only reported case of an easement termination (*Hicks v. Dowd et al.*, 2007 WY 74 [2007]), a local government terminated a conservation easement on a 1,400-acre ranch in Wyoming because the landowner requested it; no conservation or financial offset (except for a release and indemnification agreement from the landowner to the locality) was obtained in exchange for the termination. While that case was decided on other grounds, it appears that the locality did not have the necessary commitment to protect the conservation purposes of the easement.

In addition, although a governmental unit may have authority (through taxation) to obtain the resources needed to enforce the restrictions of a conservation easement; it must actually appropriate the funds to do so. This isn't always done. I know of some easements held by localities that are almost never monitored because of the failure of the locality to appropriate the funds to do so. In other words, simply because an easement holder is a governmental unit is no assurance that it is a qualified organization.

Finally, the requirement imposed on public charities to file an information return (Form 990), which requires important disclosures about the holding and administration of conservation easements, is not imposed on governmental agencies. Thus, there is no good way to monitor whether governmental units are properly managing the easements they hold.

The foregoing aspects of governmental units suggest that when they hold deductible conservation easements, there should be an additional mechanism in place to ensure that they meet all three of the requirements to be a qualified organization, not just the first one.

The shortcomings of governmental units as easement holders should be kept in mind by the IRS and by landowners who sincerely seek to use conservation easements to ensure the permanent protection of their land.

2. Organizations Substantially Supported by Governmental Agencies or the Public: Regulations Section 1.170A-14(c)(1)(ii)

Organizations such as corporations; trusts; and community chests, funds, and foundations that receive a substantial amount of their support from a governmental unit or directly or indirectly (e.g., through other charities) from the public—provided they are not *disqualified* under Code section 501(c)(3) due to political activity—are qualified to hold deductible easements. Organizations qualified under this provision of the Regulations to hold deductible easements are not required to qualify under Code section 501(c)(3), provided they are not disqualified under that section due to political activities. Furthermore, such organizations are required to be organized and operated exclusively for charitable purposes, and no part of their net earnings may inure to the benefit of a private shareholder or individual, just as required of public charities exempt under section 501(c)(3). However, the public support requirement of such organizations is more generalized than for land trusts that are public charities and can be met based on all the facts and circumstances of their support.

3. Public Charities Exempt under Code Section 501(c)(3): Regulations Section 1.170A-14(c)(1)(iii)

The Regulations require that public charities, in order to hold deductible easements, must comply with several Code sections.

The first Code section is section 501(c)(3), which governs tax-exempt organizations and imposes the following requirements:

1. The organization may have *only* public charitable purposes.
2. The organization must be operated *exclusively* for charitable purposes.
3. *None* of the organization's assets may be used to benefit organization "insiders" (persons in a position to significantly influence the organization).
4. The organization may engage in no more than a very *limited* amount of legislative activity ("lobbying").
5. The organization may engage in *no* political activity (support of candidates for election).

A detailed discussion of how these requirements limit the authority of a land trust in its dealings with conservation easements and members of the public is contained in section I, E, 3 of this chapter. Suffice it to say here that significant penalties can be imposed on land trusts, land trust managers, and members of the public who violate these requirements by engaging in the improper management, modification, or termination of conservation easements. These requirements do much to ensure that a land trust honors its obligations to easement donors and the public in monitoring and enforcing the conservation easements it holds.

In addition to these requirements, a public charity, in order to qualify to hold deductible easements, must meet the "public support test" provided in Code section 509(a)(2), which requires that at least one-third of its support be from the general public (other than from "substantial contributors," i.e., contributors of more than $5,000, or 2 percent, whichever is higher, of the organization's annual support). This requirement is averaged over a five-year period. Note that this requirement is different from that imposed on government-affiliated organizations or organizations that are supported by other charities. Such organizations are required only to demonstrate that a "substantial amount" of their support comes either directly or indirectly (e.g., through other charities) from the general public or governmental entities. Note that "substantial amount" is not defined and depends on an examination of the facts and circumstances of the organization.

Failure of a public charity to meet the public support test may relegate the organization to "foundation" status, which limits the amount of charitable deduction a donor may claim and disqualifies the organiza-

---

The Value of Conservation Easement Contributions in Meeting the Public Support Test

Many land trusts report the value of conservation easements received as contributions on Form 990. But when easement values are high, treating conservation easements the same as cash contributions may jeopardize the land trust's ability to meet the public support test of Code section 509(a)(2). If easement values are included in overall public support calculations, one or two significant easements may constitute a disproportionate amount of a year's contributions and disqualify the contribution as being support from the general public. For example, if a land trust receives $200,000 in cash contributions and three conservation easements, each valued at $500,000, each conservation easement contribution would exceed the 2 percent threshold and be disqualified as public support. The land trust's public support would be only 11.8 percent ($200,000 / [$200,000 + $1,500,000] = 11.8%), far below the 30 percent required by the Code.

To avoid this problem, land trusts should consider the actual nature of conservation easements. They are not assets in any meaningful sense of the word. They cannot be sold because there is no market for them; they generally cost land trusts substantial sums to hold for stewardship and enforcement. They are, in fact, liabilities, not assets. Considered as such, it is my belief that they do not need to be reported as charitable contributions on Form 990. See also William T. Hutton, "Easements as Public Support: The 'Zero-Value' Approach," chapter 12 in the Conservation Easement Handbook, published by the Land Trust Alliance and the Trust for Public Land.

---

tion from holding deductible conservation easements (because it ceases to be a "public charity").

An alternative to complying with the one-third public support test may be for a land trust to seek to qualify under Regulations section 1.170A-14(c)(1)(2), under which it might be able to meet the more generalized "substantial amount" of the public support test.

4. Supporting Organizations: Regulations
Section 1.170A-14(c)(1)(iv)

Even if an organization does not meet the public support test, if that organization is created for the sole purpose of supporting (i) a governmental unit, (ii) an organization that receives a "substantial amount" of its support from the public, or (iii) a 501(c)(3) organization that receives at least one-third of its support from the public, it is qualified to hold deductible conservation easements. When such an organization is created to support a governmental unit (a so-called government-affiliated organization, such as a land trust set up and controlled by a local government), it is not required to file a Form 990 and, thus, is not subject to the same kind of scrutiny as are public charities.

5. Commitment to Protect the Conservation Purposes of the Easement: Regulations Section 1.170A-14(c)(1)

In addition to describing the types of organizations that are qualified to hold deductible easements, the Code requires that, regardless of type, an organization must have a commitment to protect the conservation purposes of the easement. The Regulations state that if an organization is "organized or operated primarily or substantially for one of the conservation purposes" (as described in section I, D of this chapter), it will be considered to have the necessary commitment. The Regulations require that an organization be organized *or* operated primarily for conservation purposes. This suggests that one or the other would be sufficient to establish the necessary commitment. However, it seems unlikely that an organization formally *organized* for conservation purposes but *operated* for other purposes would be considered to have the necessary commitment.

Typically, such a commitment is spelled out in the articles of incorporation (for organizations that are corporations) and bylaws of an organization. Such documents govern the authority of an organization. In theory, activities undertaken by an organization outside of the scope of the purposes for which it is organized, as described in the organizational documents, are ultra vires ("outside of") and voidable. Thus, if an easement holder is organized for conservation purposes, it would seem that it must also be operated for conservation purposes. However, most states have statutes that protect third parties dealing with organizations that undertake ultra vires actions from having such dealings invalidated to their detriment.

Example: The Gary Protection Society is a nonprofit organization the purposes of which, as spelled out in its articles of incorporation, are preservation of the scenic and historic character of Gary, South Carolina. For a number of years the society hosted speakers on historic preservation and promoted preservation in other ways, all within its corporate purposes. However, in 2003, John Doe proposed that the society become a partner with him in development of a historic farm on the outskirts of Gary. John's idea was that this partnership might overcome local opposition to the development. John had the society purchase the farm (with generous contributions from John, for which he claimed deductions).

The negotiations and purchase were conducted in some secrecy, and not all of the society's board members were involved. When the society announced to the public that the purchase had gone through, one of the board members who had been kept in the dark filed suit to have the purchase set aside on the grounds that it was ultra vires the society's corporate purposes. Ultimately, the local court ruled that the transaction was ultra vires the society's purposes, but it also found that the family that had sold the farm would be hurt if the sale was set aside; therefore, the court upheld the sale. What the IRS thought of, and did about, this transaction, is another, somewhat predictable, story.

Equally, if not more, important to its organizational purposes are an organization's actions. Although there is no record of the IRS having done so, the requirement that an organization have a commitment to conservation purposes would appear to provide solid ground for the IRS to refuse to recognize as qualified any organization that fails to diligently monitor and enforce the conservation easements that it holds, or that engages in improper easement modifications or terminations.

While the commitment requirement has not been tested, it imposes an objective standard on the holders of deductible conservation easements that provides a basis for the oversight and discipline of land trusts and governmental agencies alike. One of the questions raised by this obligation is whether it must be met with respect to each easement property, or can instead be met in a more general sense. In other words, can a land trust swap conservation on one property for better and more conservation on other properties and still meet the requirement?

The answer, technically, would seem to come directly from the Regulations. The Regulations state that to be qualified, an organization "must have a commitment to protect the conservation purposes of *the donation*" (emphasis added). Protection of the conservation purposes of the donation would seem limited to protecting the property that is subject to the donation, not some other property.

However, having made a clear statement, the Regulations go on to confuse the issue by stating in the next sentence, "A conservation group organized or operated *primarily or substantially* for one of the conservation purposes specified in section 170(h)(4)(A) will be considered to have the commitment required by the preceding sentence" (emphasis added). This makes it seem as though a general commitment to protect one or more conservation purposes, regardless of where those conservation purposes may be served, is sufficient, and that the commitment need not be met within the four corners of each easement property itself. The conservative response to this ambiguity would be that land trusts should always try to comply with the requirement *for each easement*.

Example: The Eider Land Trust holds 10 conservation easements amounting to 1,000 acres. The purpose of the easements is protection of a unique riparian and aquatic habitat. A wealthy developer convinced the land trust to allow one 5-acre building envelope on each easement, in exchange for which the developer agreed to make a payment to the land trust of $500,000 for each building envelope allowed. The trust agreed to the deal because it needed the $5 million to purchase additional habitat in the vicinity of the 10 easements, and it subsequently purchased conservation easements over an additional 2,000 acres with the $5 million. Two years later, the IRS, learning of the amendment of the original easements from the information reported by the land trust on Form 990, audited the trust. As a result of the audit, the IRS issued a letter to the trust, and published a notice, both to the effect that the Eider Land Trust had been determined not to be a "qualified organization" within the meaning of Code section 170(h) and that no easements contributed to it in the future would be eligible for federal tax benefits.

The IRS reasoning was that amending 10 easements to allow residential construction violated the conservation purposes of the easements because there were no locations on any of the easement parcels where construction could occur without significantly disrupting the important habitat on the parcel. Such a violation of the conservation purposes of the 10 conservation easements was conclusive evidence to the IRS that the Eider Land Trust lacked the commitment to protect the conservation values of its easements. The fact that the land trust used the money received from the amendments to protect more important habitat did not excuse it from its obligation to protect the conservation values of the easements it already held.

The IRS conclusion in this case was that the commitment to protect conservation values must be met within the confines of each easement property. There clearly is a solid counterargument, however, as suggested in the text preceding this example.

6. Necessary Resources: Regulations Section 1.170A-14(c)(1)

The Regulations require that to be a qualified organization, an organization must have the resources necessary to enforce restrictions imposed by the conservation easements it holds. However, the Regulations also expressly state that, in order to meet the resources requirement, an organization *does not* need to set aside a special fund.

37

The question of what resources a land trust *should* have in order to hold deductible easements is a somewhat controversial one. Small, unstaffed, community land trusts have had an important and positive impact on land conservation, particularly in the East. Such organizations truly represent grassroots land conservation. Nevertheless, it is unlikely that an organization that has neither staff nor funding available to monitor its easements on a regular basis, or to go to court to defend its easements, constitutes a qualified organization for purposes of holding deductible conservation easements.

This may seem a harsh assessment. However, when mere discovery in a lawsuit may consume several hundred thousand dollars, it is clear that more than several hundred dollars in the bank is necessary to defend a conservation easement. Furthermore, as development pressures continue to build, the temptation to break conservation easements to realize the possibly millions of dollars of development potential locked up in locally held conservation easements will inevitably lead to serious and well-funded legal challenges.

Furthermore, without regular, consistent, comprehensive monitoring of all the easements an organization holds, it is impossible to know whether the easement restrictions are being honored. That takes both funding and staffing.

In 2006 the IRS weighed in on the question of funding easement stewardship. Form 990 now requires that any public charity holding conservation easements (whether or not federal tax deductions were claimed with respect to such easements) must file a schedule describing its stewardship of the easements it held during the previous year. Among other things, the schedule must state the number of conservation easements physically monitored and how much money and staff time were expended in monitoring and enforcing easements held by the organization during the preceding year.

Example: The Greentree Land Trust was formed in 2006 by six very dedicated volunteers. One of the founders subsequently offered to contribute a conservation easement over a 300-acre farm that had been in her family for 250 years. In the easement the prospective donor wished to reserve the right for three home sites, to be located at the discretion of the land trust. The prospective donor planned to sell the farm to pay estate taxes once the easement was in place, and had already identified the purchaser, four families who had joined together to purchase the farm and develop the home sites.

At the time that Greentree accepted the conservation easement it had neither staff nor more than $2,000 in its bank account. Shortly after the contribution was complete and the four families purchased the farm, the families had a falling out and agreed to resolve their differences by allowing the fourth family to have its own home site. As construction on all four sites began, Greentree tried to raise funds to hire an attorney to enjoin the activity but raised only $1,000. Greentree's board was without alternatives, and the four houses were constructed. Greentree would not appear to be a qualified organization because it lacked the resources to enforce its conservation easements.

---

7. Accreditation

As a result of congressional concern over the qualifications of some existing land trusts to hold and enforce easements, the Land Trust Alliance (LTA) has established a voluntary accreditation program for land trusts and created an Accreditation Commission to oversee the program. Whether Congress will mandate such accreditation for all land trusts holding deductible easements is unknown at this time. Essentially, accreditation by the LTA requires adoption and implementation of its "Standards and Practices," as well as completion of an extensive, and somewhat grueling, questionnaire; submission of numerous documents; and an interview by the Accreditation Commission of land trust staff.

8. Transfers of Easements: Regulations
Section 1.170A-14(c)(2)

To ensure that deductible easements remain in the hands of qualified organizations, the Code also requires that every deductible conservation easement prohibit the transfer of the easement to any organization that is not a qualified organization. The Code further requires every deductible easement to provide that, in the event of transfer, the transferee must agree *in writing* to carry out the conservation purposes of the easement.

D. Qualified Conservation Purposes: Code Section 170(h)(4), Regulations Section 1.170A-14(d)

The Regulations devote a substantial amount of attention to describing the purposes of a conservation easement that will qualify the easement for a federal income tax deduction. These purposes are called conservation purposes. A great deal of detail and a number of examples of qualified conservation purposes are provided by the Regulations.

Until around 2006, compliance with the conservation purposes requirements of the Code and Regulations was not examined by the IRS. The primary focus of the IRS was on valuation of the easement. Out of over 115 reported cases in which a court reviewed an IRS challenge to a conservation easement deduction, only 5 dealt with the substance of the easement rather than its valuation, and none of those focused on whether the easement was for qualified conservation purposes. That neglect has now ended. In 2007 the U.S. tax court reviewed two IRS challenges to conservation easement deductions for failure to comply with the conservation purposes requirements (e.g., *Glass v. Commissioner*, 124 TC No. 16 [2005], *affirmed Glass v. C.I.R.*—F.3d—, 2006 WL 3740797 C.A.6 [2006], lost at trial and on appeal by the IRS; and *Turner v. Commissioner*, 126 TC No. 16 [2006], in which the IRS was successful). In addition, I am personally aware of several intensive audits in which the IRS focus was on compliance with the conservation purposes requirement, and I am certain that many such audits are being conducted.

While it would not seem that the actual language of an easement can alter the quality or characteristics of the land being protected by that easement, the IRS has made it clear that it expects the easement document to include a thorough description of the conservation purposes of the easement, as well as a description of how protection of the property advances those conservation purposes. This is best done in several ways.

First, the recitals ("whereas clauses") of the easement document

39

should contain an explicit reference to one or more of the conservation purposes as identified in the Regulations (preferably in the terms used by the Regulations, to avoid confusion). Second, the recitals should provide as much detail as reasonably practical, describing and elaborating upon the characteristics of the easement land that support the conservation purposes of the easement. Finally, the characteristics of the easement land should be detailed in the "natural resources inventory" required by the Regulations (see section III, A of this chapter), which should be incorporated into the recitals by reference.

There are four different categories of conservation purposes that qualify a conservation easement for federal tax benefits:

- preservation of land areas for outdoor recreation by, or education of, the general public
- protection of a significant, relatively natural habitat for fish, wildlife, or plants
- preservation of certain open space (including farmland and forestland) pursuant to a "clearly delineated" governmental conservation policy, or for scenic purposes, resulting in a significant public benefit
- preservation of a historically important land area or certified historic structure

Each of these purposes is discussed in some detail below.

1. Public Recreation or Education: Code Section 170(h)(4)(A)(i), Regulations Section 1.170A-14(d)(2)

The Regulations provide that the contribution of a "qualified real property interest" (see section I, B, of this chapter) for the purpose of preserving land for outdoor recreation by or education of the general public is a qualified conservation purpose. The Regulations (sections 1.170A-14(d)(2)(i) and (ii)) require that such a contribution must provide for (1) substantial and (2) regular use of the land by the public. Obviously, in order to qualify for this conservation purpose a conservation easement must provide for public access to the property.

Example One: The James family owns a private 80-acre lake. The family contributes a conservation easement over the lake and an access easement from the lake to a nearby public road. The stated purpose of the easement is to preserve the lake for public recreational use. The easement also grants the public the right to use the lake and access road on alternating weekends throughout the year. The remainder of the weekends the lake is closed to public use, but the easement does not allow any use of the lake by the owners that would diminish the quality of the lake for public outdoor recreation.

Such an easement should meet the requirements of the public recreation or education conservation purpose. The only potential issue is that the easement does not allow year-round, 365-day use of the lake by the public. The Regulations do not elaborate on the amount or extent of use required to qualify under this conservation purpose, other than to state that a contribution must allow for "substantial and regular use" by the public. Of course, full-time access would qualify. Whether use limited to alternating weekends qualifies is not certain. Presumably, access limited to one day per year would be insufficient, but see the following example.

Example Two: The Roths own land that is geothermally active. At the same time each year a spectacular geyser erupts. The rest of the year the geyser is dormant. The Roths put a conservation easement on the portion of their land where the geyser is located and grant an access easement from a local public road to allow public access to the site. The easement provides that the access and geyser area will be open on the one day each year when the geyser erupts. The easement further provides that the landowner will provide reasonable public notice of the event at least two weeks in advance and an interpretive lecture on the geyser and other geothermal features of the property on that day.

This easement should qualify as meeting the public recreational/educational conservation purpose, even though public access is severely restricted, because access is allowed on the one day of the year when something of public significance occurs on the property. Whether such an easement has any measurable economic value for deduction purposes is another question.

Conservation easements for public recreational or educational purposes are uncommon. If the property includes other conservation values, allowing extensive public use may be inconsistent with protection of those values and could undermine the deductibility of the easement (see the discussion of "inconsistent use" in section II of this chapter). If extensive public use is the landowner's goal, conveyance of property to a public agency in fee may be more practical.

2. Preservation of a Significant, Relatively Natural Habitat for Fish, Wildlife, or Plants: Code Section 170(h)(4)(a)(ii), Regulations Section 1.170A-14(d)(3)

Protection of wildlife habitat is an important part of many conservation easements. Habitat protection meeting the following criteria is a recognized conservation purpose:

- The habitat is significant.
- The habitat is *relatively* natural (i.e., some human alteration of the habitat will not necessarily preclude it from qualifying under this provision).
- The habitat is for fish, wildlife, or plants.

For this conservation purpose, the term *significant* includes the following:

- habitat for rare, endangered, or threatened species
- natural areas representing "high quality" examples of a terrestrial or aquatic community (e.g., islands with relatively intact coastal ecosystems)
- natural areas included in, or contributing to, the ecological viability of public parks or preserves

---

Example: The owners of a residentially zoned parcel of land fronting on Lake Michigan contributed a conservation easement over a portion of the parcel for purposes of protecting the habitat of an endangered species, the Lake Huron tansy, and a bald eagle roost. The easement covered a portion of the parcel 150 feet wide by 120 feet deep. A substantial part of the easement-protected land was in a very steep bluff. The easement allowed the landowner to construct a wooden footpath and observation stand on the protected portion. The IRS challenged the easement on the grounds that there was no significant conservation purpose for the easement and that the landowner had protected only a small portion of his property. The tax court and, on appeal, the U.S. Circuit Court of Appeals, both upheld the deductibility of the easement.

The foregoing example is drawn from the recent case of *Glass v. Commissioner*, 124 TC No. 16 (2005). The IRS lost the case in the tax court and appealed the decision to the U.S. Circuit Court of Appeals, *Glass v. C.I.R.*—F.3d—, 2006 WL 3740797 C.A.6 (2006), which affirmed the tax court's decision.

One question indirectly answered by the *Glass* case is how much land a conservation easement must protect to qualify for a federal deduction. Of course, the answer will vary, depending on the purpose of the easement. However, the tax court and the court of appeals both upheld the Glasses' deductions (there were two separate easement contributions in question), even though one of the easements protected an area of only 18,000 square feet, and the other easement covered an area of 31,200 square feet, the total being less than 7 percent of the donor's parcel. Each easement was upheld as an independently deductible contribution for the conservation purpose of protecting a "significant, relatively natural habitat."

Evidence showed that the Glass property was the location of a bald eagle roost (not nest), and that the Lake Huron tansy, an endangered species, grew on the property. The tax court and the court of appeals both ruled that each of the two conservation easements met the requirements of the habitat protection conservation purpose.

In addition, the two Glass easements covered less than 7 percent of the Glasses' 11-acre property (although several acres had earlier been protected by a conservation easement not involved in this suit), a fact that was raised by the IRS but did not defeat the deductibility of the two easements in question.

The case underscores the difference between the IRS's and the courts' views of the requirements for a deductible easement. The Glass case, in my opinion, represents a relatively generous (to the taxpayer) judicial view of the requirements of the Code and Regulations. However, it is important to keep in mind that while a landowner may ultimately win his case in court, the cost in time and money to go through the audit and appeal process to get judicial relief is substantial. Landowners may be better advised to err on the side of strict compliance instead of pushing the regulatory envelope with a marginal easement and relying on a judicial safety net for their deduction.

3. Open-Space Preservation: Code Section 170(h)(4)(A)(iii), Regulations Section 1.170A-14(d)(4)(i)

Probably the most widely used of the four conservation purposes is the open-space preservation purpose. However, compliance with that purpose is also the most challenging, at least if one takes seriously the Regulatory guidelines.

Easements protecting "open space" (and the Regulations expressly include farmland and forestland as eligible) qualify if they fit one of two categories:

- easements that preserve open space "for the scenic enjoyment of the general public" and
- easements that preserve open space pursuant to a "clearly delineated federal, state, or local governmental conservation policy"

Following is a detailed discussion of the requirements.

a. Scenic Easements: Code Section 170(h)(4)(A)(iii)(I), Regulations Section 1.170A-14(d)(4)(ii)(A)

A conservation easement that protects "the scenic character of the local rural or urban landscape" or "a scenic panorama that can be enjoyed from a park, nature preserve, road, water body, trail, or historic structure or land area" generally satisfies the requirements of the scenic enjoyment conservation purpose.

The Regulations (section 1.170A-14(d)(4)(ii)(A)) provide eight factors that, among others, may be considered in determining whether a view over any given property qualifies as scenic:

(1) The compatibility of the land use with other land in the vicinity;

(2) The degree of contrast and variety provided by the visual scene;

(3) The openness of the land (which would be a more sig-nificant factor in an urban or densely populated setting or in a heavily wooded area);

(4) Relief from urban closeness;

(5) The harmonious variety of shapes and textures;

(6) The degree to which the land use maintains the scale and character of the urban landscape to preserve open space, visual enjoyment, and sunlight for the surround-ing area;

(7) The consistency of the proposed scenic view with a methodical state scenic identification program, such as a state landscape inventory; and

(8) The consistency of the proposed scenic view with a regional or local landscape inventory made pursuant to a sufficiently rigorous review process, especially if the donation is endorsed by an appropriate state or local governmental agency.

However, the Regulations (section 1.170A-14(d)(4)(ii)(A)) also state, "'Scenic enjoyment' will be evaluated by considering all pertinent facts and circumstances germane to the contribution. Regional variations in topography, geology, biology, and cultural and economic conditions require flexibility in the application of this test, but do not lessen the burden on the taxpayer to demonstrate the scenic characteristics of a donation under this paragraph."

In other words, you will know a scenic view when you see it.

To qualify for the scenic conservation purpose, there needs to be visual (not necessarily physical) access to the property, or at least to a significant portion of the property, by the public (Regulations section 1.170A-14(d)(4)(ii)(B)).

The Regulations (section 1.170A-14(d)(4)(iv)(B)) provide the following examples of qualified scenic purposes:

1. preservation of a unique natural land formation for the enjoyment of the general public
2. preservation of woodland along a public highway pursuant to a government program to preserve the appearance of the area so as to maintain the scenic view from the highway (In this example, the significance of the view is enhanced by the government program.)
3. preservation of a stretch of undeveloped property located between a public highway and the ocean in order to maintain the scenic ocean view from the highway. (In this example, the land preserved is not the focus of the view; it merely provides an open foreground to the view.)

45

Example 3 illustrates the importance of understanding exactly what view is being protected. An open pasture may not, of itself, be a particularly scenic view, but it may provide the foreground for a scenic view that exists outside the boundaries of the easement property. Whether there remains a valid purpose for a conservation easement whose sole conservation purpose is protecting the foreground of a view that exists outside of the property if that view is destroyed is an interesting question. Such an eventuality might provide grounds for termination of the easement (see sections I, E, 3 and 4 of this chapter for a discussion of the grounds for easement termination). Does protection of such a scenic view constitute a qualified conservation purpose? In the regulatory example of protecting a fore-ground, the view itself was of the ocean, a view not likely to change over time. However, where the view is not on the protected property and is sus-ceptible to change, the example may no longer be relevant.

In the case of *Turner v. Commissioner*, 126 TC 299 (2006), the tax court ruled with respect to an easement whose purpose was protection of a historic property. The court found that the mere fact that the property adjoined a historic property did not make the easement property historic. By analogy, this could mean that unless a scenic easement protects property that is, in itself, scenic, it does not qualify as a scenic easement. However, this is pure speculation, as the courts have not yet addressed this question.

Another question is what kind of public access is necessary for a scenic easement. Must the public have access from adjoining property? What if the property is included within a broad vista seen from a moun-taintop located in a public park miles away? There is no guidance for answering these questions, except common sense (which, as Voltaire said, "is not so common").

Example One: James Joseph owns six acres along a heavily traveled public road. The six acres provide a view of a historic and very beautiful farmstead on a neighboring property owned by someone else. Joseph contributed a conservation easement over his six acres precluding the location of any structures on the property and imposing an affirmative obligation to main-tain the meadow that exists there. The IRS challenged Joseph's deduction on the grounds that the easement does not provide a "publicly significant benefit" (see the discussion of this requirement in section I, D, 3, c of this chapter) because the easement cannot guarantee that the historic barn located on the adjoining property will not be torn down in the future, elim-inating any significant public benefit from the easement. This is a convinc-ing argument; whether it would prevail is unknown.

Example Two: Assume the same facts as in the preceding example, except that, while Joseph's easement prohibited the location of any structures on the property, it did not require the owner to maintain the meadow, thus leaving open the possibility that a forest might grow up, blocking the view of the barn, protection of which view was the sole purpose of the easement. The IRS challenged the easement on the grounds that Joseph retained the right to a use that is "inconsistent" with the purposes of the easement (see the discussion of inconsistent use in subsection I, F of this chapter).

The inconsistency argument in this example is also a strong one for denying the deduction.

---

b. Easements Pursuant to a Clearly Delineated Governmental Conservation Policy: Code Section 170(h)(4)(A)(iii)(II), Regulations Section 1.170A-14(d)(4)(iii)

This is, perhaps, the most frequently used category of conservation purpose. There have been no cases reported involving challenges to conservation easements based on this category; however, if one reads the Regulations, it is clear that compliance is not a simple matter. Locally adopted zoning ordinances and comprehensive plans are often relied on as "clearly delineated governmental conservation policies" for purposes of compliance with this category. However, it is not at all certain that such generalized policies meet the requirement that the policy be "clearly delineated."

47

In order to qualify as an easement that preserves open space pursuant to a clearly delineated governmental conservation policy, the conservation policy must be more than a "general declaration of conservation goals by a single official or legislative body" (Regulations section 1.170A-14(d)(4)(iii)(A)). While the Regulations do not require a certification program for conservation easements under this category, they recommend that such contributions further "a specific, identified conservation project such as the preservation of land within a state or local landmark district that is locally recognized as being significant to that district; the preservation of a wild or scenic river; the preservation of farmland pursuant to a state program for flood prevention and control; or the protection of the scenic, ecological, or historic character of land that is contiguous to, or an integral part of, the surroundings of existing recreation or conservation sites."

The Regulations say that such programs need not be funded, but must, nevertheless, involve a "significant commitment by the government with respect to the conservation project" and provide the example of a preferential tax assessment or preferential zoning, for the purposes of protection of the property for conservation purposes.

Example One: Doris Farm is located in the A-2 agricultural zoning district of Quantum County. The A-2 zone allows agricultural uses, as well as single-family residential development on two-acre parcels. The zoning ordinance states that the purpose of the zone is to protect agricultural activity, while allowing flexibility for low-density residential use. The zone is also identified as implementing the local comprehensive plan's designation of the area around Doris Farm as one having traditionally been a farming area with high-quality agricultural soils that should be preserved for agricultural and low-density residential uses not requiring public utilities. The DEF Land Trust accepted a conservation easement on Doris Farm for the purpose of preserving its open space pursuant to a clearly delineated governmental policy. On audit, the IRS asked if there were more specific policies supporting the preservation of Doris Farm. Unfortunately, the answer was no.

In this case, the deduction would appear vulnerable because of the generalized nature of the governmental policies on which the easement relied.

48

Example Two: Assume the same facts as in the preceding example, except that in addition to the zoning and comprehensive plan designations, Quantum County provides a special reduced real property tax assessment for farmland to encourage farmers to keep their land in farming. Doris Farm enjoys this reduced assessment. The cost to local taxpayers for the special reduced assessment on Doris Farm is around $5,000 per year in lost tax revenue.

The combination of the planning policies, zoning, and preferential assessment probably collectively constitute a "clearly delineated governmental conservation policy." The Regulations call for a "significant commitment" by the governmental entity that has established the preservation policy to advance the policy, and the special assessment accorded Doris Farm is evidence of such a commitment, according to the Regulations (section 1.170A-14(d)(4)(iii)(A)).

Example Three: Again, assume the same facts. In addition, assume that Doris Farm is located within a state-established "agricultural district" that identifies the land within the district as playing an important role in the state's agricultural economy. The district designation requires a special review of any subdivision application filed with the local government to ensure that the division has minimal impact on the agricultural viability of land within the district. The district also requires a special agricultural impact assessment of any publicly funded project, such as new schools, roads, or utilities, proposed for land within the district.

The state-sponsored agricultural district in this example appears to be evidence of a clearly delineated governmental conservation policy "furthering a specific, identified conservation project" (Regulations section 1.170A-14(d)(4)(iii)(A)), strengthening substantially the case for deductibility. Note, however, that the restrictions imposed by the district, by reducing development potential on Doris Farm, may also reduce the amount of the deduction.

_____

_____

Example Four: Assume the same facts as in Example One. However, in addition to its A-2 zoning status, assume that Doris Farm hosts a colony of blue-footed ferrets, a recently discovered endangered species protected by the Endangered Species Act. The provisions of the conservation easement are tailored to ensure protection of the ferret habitat on the farm.

In this example preservation of the farm (in addition to preservation of a significant wildlife habitat) is pursuant to a clearly delineated federal governmental conservation policy in the form of the Endangered Species Act, making a strong case for the deduction.

49

_____

The foregoing examples attempt to illustrate a rather vague standard that seems to require something more than standard zoning classifications for support, but something less than a formal certification program. This is not an area where there have yet been any cases to provide guidance.

The Regulations do offer a form of "safe harbor" for easements whose purpose is advancing a clearly delineated governmental conservation policy. The safe harbor applies when a governmental unit adopts a resolution specifically endorsing a particular property as "worthy of protection for conservation purposes" (section 1.170A-14(d)(4)(iii)(A)). However, there are two problems in relying on this safe harbor: First, if a land trust asks for but doesn't receive the resolution, is pursuing the proposed easement pointless? Second, if a land trust does receive a supportive resolution for one project, must it then receive one for every easement intended to advance a clearly delineated governmental conservation policy?

Another possible safe harbor is provided for conservation easements accepted by a federal, state, or local government agency. The Regulations say that such acceptance "tends to establish the requisite clearly delineated governmental policy." However, they also state that "such acceptance, without more, is not sufficient. The more rigorous the review process by the governmental agency, the more the acceptance of the easement tends to establish the requisite clearly delineated governmental policy" (Regulations section 1.170A-14(d)(4)(iii)(B)).

c. Open Space Easements Must Also Yield a Significant Public Benefit: Code Section 170(h)(4)(A)(iii), Regulations Section 1.170A-14(d)(4)(iv)

Conservation easements that rely on the "open-space" category, whether they are scenic easements or easements pursuant to clearly delineated governmental conservation policies, must also "yield a significant public benefit." The Regulations (section 1.170A-14(d)(4)(iv)(A)) list eleven criteria for the evaluation of public significance:

(1) The uniqueness of the property to the area;
(2) The intensity of land development in the vicinity of the property (both existing development and foreseeable trends of development);
(3) The consistency of the proposed open-space use with public programs (whether federal, state or local) for conservation in the region, including programs for outdoor recreation, irrigation or water supply protection, water quality maintenance or enhancement, flood prevention and control, erosion control, shoreline protection, and protection of land areas included in, or related to, a government approved master plan or land management area;
(4) The consistency of the proposed open-space use with existing private conservation programs in the area, as evidenced by other land, protected by easement or fee ownership by organizations referred to in section 1.170A-14(c)(1), in close proximity to the property;
(5) The likelihood that development of the property would lead to or contribute to degradation of the scenic, natural, or historic character of the area;
(6) The opportunity for the general public to use the property or to appreciate its scenic values;
(7) The importance of the property in preserving a local or regional landscape or resource that attracts tourism or commerce to the area;
(8) The likelihood that the donee will acquire equally desir-

able and valuable substitute property or property rights;

(9) The cost to the donee of enforcing the terms of the conservation restriction;

(10) The population density in the area of the property; and

(11) The consistency of the proposed open-space use with a legislatively mandated program identifying particular parcels of land for future protection."

Example One: John contributes a conservation easement "pursuant to a clearly delineated governmental conservation policy" on his farm. The local government passes a special resolution identifying preservation of John's farm as a priority. However, the farm is located in a largely vacant region of a Plains state, is surrounded by other farmland, and is more than 20 miles from any population center.

The IRS audits the easement. It concedes that the local government's resolution satisfies the requirement that protection of the farm be pursuant to a clearly delineated governmental conservation policy. However, the IRS takes the position that the easement does not yield a significant public benefit for the following reasons: The farm is not unique. There is neither existing nor foreseeable development in the area, and there are unlikely to be any public or private conservation programs in the area with which preservation of the farm is consistent. While development of the farm could lead to degradation of the area, such development is highly unlikely. The remoteness of the farm makes it unlikely that there would be significant public enjoyment of its scenic value; there is virtually no tourism, so preserving the land is unlikely to attract tourism or commerce. The cost of enforcement is likely to be marginal (and it is hard to tell whether this is a positive or negative factor under the Regulations). Local population density is low. There are unlikely to be any legislatively mandated protection programs including the farm.

While one could argue that the local government's resolution supporting preservation of the farm qualifies as a "public conservation program," with which protection of the farm is consistent, on the whole it would appear that the deduction in this example is quite vulnerable.

51

Example Two: Edith Small recently purchased a 10-acre parcel adjoining her 50-acre estate outside of Sun Valley, Idaho. The property consists of a small, rolling meadow with 200 feet of frontage on a frequently traveled public highway. Edith paid $5 million for the parcel, and, taking enhancement to her estate from protecting this property into account, a qualified appraiser has informed her that a conservation easement eliminating all development potential on the parcel would be worth $4 million.

Edith could use the entire deduction and would enjoy federal tax savings from the contribution of $1.4 million. The local land trust, which Edith has asked to take the easement, is trying to decide whether to do so.

Essentially, the benefit to the public is protection of a 200-foot strip of scenic highway. However, the land trust learns that the highway is already protected by a long-standing scenic highway district regulation that prohibits any development within 500 feet. That regulation effectively precludes Edith from building anything on the 10-acre parcel that would be publicly visible. While the easement does remove valuable development rights, the only purpose is scenic, and the existing highway district regulations already preclude development that would interfere with the view. In addition to the regulations, topography makes development of the frontage of the parcel quite difficult and there are clearly better home sites on the 10 acres than those that would be prevented by the easement. Finally, the land trust considered that the easement contribution would, essentially, be asking the public to pay $1.4 million for protection of the 200-foot frontage.

In the final analysis, the land trust decided not to accept the easement because in view of the $1.4 million "cost" of the easement, the additional protection afforded the public by the easement over existing regulations was not considered "publicly significant."

Whether it is necessary (or even appropriate) for a land trust to judge the qualifications of a conservation easement for federal income tax benefits is a matter of considerable debate today. The foregoing example puts the land trust in the position of anticipating arguments that might be made in an audit by the IRS and judging the proposed conservation easement on the basis of how well the easement would stand up in such an audit. The point of the example is to show how such an approach might work, not to advocate the approach. Of course, without considering whether the proposed easement yielded a significant public benefit, the land trust could legitimately reject the easement because it believed that the cost of monitoring and enforcing the easement in perpetuity far outweighed any public benefit that would be provided.

d. Prevention of Intrusion or Future Development: Regulations Section 1.170-14(d)(4)(v)

One area of increasing concern among land trust professionals, and the IRS, involves conservation easements in which the donor retains development potential that is not consistent with the preservation of open space. While there is a general rule that reserving uses inconsistent with the conservation purposes of a conservation easement may preclude a deduction (see section II of this chapter), if the easement is contributed with the conservation purpose of protecting open space, there is an *additional* requirement that the easement may not permit "a degree of intrusion or future development that would interfere with the essential scenic quality of the land or with the governmental conservation policy" that otherwise qualifies it as preserving open space (Regulations section 1.170A-14(d)(4)(v)).

Many landowners believe that deductibility depends solely on obtaining an appraisal of the easement showing that it has reduced the value of the easement property. For example, "My appraiser says that this easement has reduced the value of my property by $1 million; therefore, I am entitled to a deduction." This is wrong. The Code and Regulations focus first on whether a conservation easement confers a significant public benefit. Only if such a benefit is conferred is the financial value of the easement relevant. Eliminating development potential sufficient to reduce the value of the easement property, but retaining development rights that interfere with the open-space purposes of the easement, does not qualify for a federal tax deduction, because the Regulations require an open-space conservation easement to eliminate *any use* of the property that may interfere with its open-space purposes.

53

Example One: Joe Doaks recently purchased Lost Pine Farm, which consists of 200 acres of highly scenic pasture and woodland along a heavily traveled state road. Doaks put a conservation easement on the farm that reduced development potential from the 50 residential lots permitted under local zoning, to 5 residential lots. However, the easement reserves Joe's right to locate the 5 lots squarely within the public's view of the property.

A deduction in this example would likely be denied, because the reserved development permits "a degree of intrusion that would interfere" with the scenic quality of the property.

Note that the degree of intrusion is not qualified; that is, the Regulations do not provide that the degree of intrusion must be significant or substantial—it is sufficient merely that it "interfere." A conservative view of the Regulations' failure to condition this requirement would be that any intrusion opens the donor to disallowance of a deduction.

Example Two: Assume the same facts as in the preceding example, except that Doaks reserved 15 residential lots in the easement but restricted their location, and all other improvements on the property, to a portion of the property that is screened from the public view by the woodland and a hill. The easement prohibits removal of the woodland, or recontouring or removal of the hill, and requires replanting of trees that die.

A deduction should be allowed in this example, assuming that the reserved uses don't impair other "significant conservation interests" (see section II, A, 1 of this chapter).

Example Three: Assume that the Doaks easement reserved only one residential lot, the location of which is to be determined by Doaks, at his sole discretion, in the future.

A deduction is unlikely in this example because Doaks could choose to locate the home site squarely in the middle of the view-shed. Unfettered discretion reserved by a landowner to locate improvements in most easements, regardless of purpose, is likely to jeopardize the possibility of a deduction because of the potential to locate improvements in a manner that is inconsistent with the purposes of the easement.

Example Four: Assume that the Doaks easement reserved 10 residential lots, the locations of which are to be determined in the future but subject to the prior approval of the land trust to which the easement has been granted.

This example appears to comply with the Regulations because the land trust's control over the future location of the sites ensures that the future sites will not be located so as to interfere with the view or other significant conservation interests. Even though the easement does not impose limits on the land trust's discretion in approving the future location of the lots, it can be presumed that, because the land trust is a qualified organization, it will approve only locations that are consistent with the conservation purposes of the easement. Nevertheless, it would help if the easement provided criteria for the land trust to consider in approving future lot locations, or provided, generally, that the land trust could not grant approval for any uses of the property that would be inconsistent with the conservation purposes of the easement.

---

e. Public Access: Regulations
Sections 1.170A-14(d)(4)(iii)(C) and (D)

Easements intended to preserve open space pursuant to a governmental conservation policy are not required to provide public access in order to be deductible, and the land subject to such an easement need not be publicly visible. However, land with an easement whose purpose is scenic preservation must be at least visually accessible to the public. What is "public" is an open question. However, it is doubtful that it means "neighbor" or even "neighborhood." To be safe, the "general public"—that is, anyone and everyone—must have at least visual access to scenic property. If access is limited to members of a club, or residents in a neighborhood, for example, even if the club or neighborhood is extensive, the requirement is probably not satisfied because not all members of the public have access.

4. Historic Preservation: Code Section 170(h)(4)(A)(iv), Regulations Section 1.170A-14(d)(5)

The Code recognizes two types of historic conservation purposes for federal tax benefits: preservation of a "historically important land area" and preservation of a "certified historic structure." The Code provisions governing historic preservation easements have recently been revised to address abuses, and an entire new set of rules has been added to the Code to govern preservation of structures in designated historic districts. In addition, the Code governing preservation of historic structures has been revised. Note that the Regulations have not yet been revised to reflect these changes in the Code. Finally, a recent U.S. Tax Court decision has provided some additional insight into the meaning of the tax law governing the preservation of historic land areas.

a. Historic Land Areas: Code Section 170(h)(4)(A)(iv), Regulations Section 1.170A-14(d)(5)(ii)

A historically important land area includes the following:

> (A) An independently significant land area including any related historic resources (for example, an archaeolog-

ical site or a Civil War battlefield with related monuments, bridges, cannons, or houses) that meets the
National Register Criteria for Evaluation in 36 CFR
60.4 (P.L. 89-665, 80 Stat. 915);

(B) Any land area within a registered historic district
including any buildings on the land area that can reasonably be considered as contributing to the significance of the district; and

(C) Any land area (including related historic resources)
adjacent to a property listed individually in the
National Register of Historic Places (but not within a
registered historic district) in a case where the physical
or environmental features of the land area contribute
to the historic or cultural integrity of the property."
(Regulations sections 1.170-14(d)(5)(ii)(A)–(C))

Example: The following facts are drawn from the case of *Turner v. Commissioner*, 126 TC 299 (2006). The Turners purchased a parcel of land containing a little over 29 acres in Fairfax County, Virginia. About 15 acres were located in a designated floodplain, and all of the land was located in a historic overlay district designated by the county. The parcel was located in the vicinity of George Washington's home, Mount Vernon, and adjoined Washington's Grist Mill. The Turners contributed a conservation easement on this parcel with the dual conservation purposes of protecting open space and protecting a historic land area. This example will focus on that part of the tax court's decision dealing with the historic purpose.

The Turners argued that limiting development on their par-
cel would help protect the adjoining Grist Mill. However, the tax court (citing Senate Committee Report 961007, at p. 12; 1980-2 C.B. at 605, which provided legislative history explaining the intent of the tax provisions in question here) ruled that federal tax law provides that a "histori-
cally important land area" includes only "independently significant land areas (for example, a Civil War battlefield) and historic sites and related land areas, *the physical or environmental features of which contribute to the historic or cultural importance and continuing integrity of certified historic structures* such as Mount Vernon, or historic districts such as Waterford, Virginia, or Harper's Ferry, West Virginia" (Turner v. Commissioner, p. 306; emphasis added by the tax court).

The tax court found that the Turner conservation easement did not meet the requirements of protecting a historically important land area or structure because (1) nothing of historic significance occurred on the protected property; (2) there were no historic structures on that property; (3) merely being close to a historic land area or structure did not make the Turners' property historic; and (4) there was nothing about the physical or environmental features of the Turner property that contributed to the historic character of the Grist Mill.

---

b. Certified Historic Structures: Code Sections 170(h)(4)(A)(iv) and (B), Regulations Section 1.170A-14(d)(5)(iii)

The second category of recognized historic conservation purpose is preservation of a certified historic structure. Two types of structures qualify: (1) structures listed on the National Register of Historic Places; and (2) structures located within registered historic districts, which structures have been certified by the secretary of the interior as being "of historic significance to the district." A certified historic structure includes both depreciable property (i.e., commercial property) and a personal residence.

In 2006, as part of the Pension Protection Act, Congress amended Code section 170(h) to substantially tighten the requirements for conservation easements that protect certified historic structures (as previously noted, the new laws are not yet reflected in the Regulations). While some of the provisions of the 2006 act pertaining to conservation easements have expired, the provisions governing historic preservation easements are permanent. Paragraph (B), quoted below, is entirely new law; paragraph (C) of the Code has been revised to narrow the category of property whose preservation qualifies for federal tax benefits. Paragraph (C) now limits that category to buildings within a registered historic district, *but only if* such buildings are certified by the secretary of the interior as being of historic significance to the district. The new law excludes the protection of land areas within such districts as a qualified historic purpose.

New paragraph (B) addresses two areas of abuse. First, it requires that, in order to qualify for a deduction, a conservation easement whose purpose is protection of a historically significant structure *must* protect the *entire exterior* of the structure—not just a portion as permitted by prior law—and it must allow no changes in the exterior of the structure inconsistent with its historic character. This provision eliminates the "facade easement," which preserves only the front of a building while allowing significant change to other portions of the exterior.

Second, the donor of the easement and the holder of the easement must enter into an agreement certifying, "under penalties of perjury," that the holder is a qualified organization within the meaning of section 170(h) of the Code and also has the "the resources to manage and enforce the restriction and a commitment to do so" (Regulations section 1.170A-14(c)(1)). The intent of this provision is to weed out sham land trusts that were marketing the tax benefits of contributing marginal facade easements. This provision adds perjury penalties to the existing law governing qualified organizations, and it makes both the easement holder and the easement donor liable for those penalties.

In addition, the new law requires that the full appraisal of any easement protecting the exterior of a structure be filed with the return on which the deduction is claimed, regardless of the amount of deduction claimed (the law pertaining to other conservation easements requires that the appraisal accompany the return only if the deduction claimed exceeds $500,000).

Here is the new paragraph (B) in its entirety:

> (B) Special rules with respect to buildings in registered historic districts.—In the case of any contribution of a qualified real property interest which is a restriction with respect to the exterior of a building described in subparagraph (C)(ii), such contribution shall not be considered to be exclusively for conservation purposes unless—
>
> (i) such interest—
>> (I) includes a restriction which preserves the entire exterior of the building (including the front, sides, rear, and height of the building), and
>> (II) prohibits any change in the exterior of the building which is inconsistent with the historical character of such exterior,
>
> (ii) the donor and donee enter into a written agreement certifying, under penalty of perjury, that the donee—
>> (I) is a qualified organization (as defined in paragraph (3)) with a purpose of environmental

protection, land conservation, open space preservation, or historic preservation, and
(II) has the resources to manage and enforce the restriction and a commitment to do so, and

(iii) in the case of any contribution made in a taxable year beginning after the date of the enactment of this subparagraph, the taxpayer includes with the taxpayer's return for the taxable year of the contribution—
(I) a qualified appraisal (within the meaning of subsection (f)(11)(E) [of section 170 of the Code]) of the qualified property interest,
(II) photographs of the entire exterior of the building, and
(III) a description of all restrictions on the development of the building. (Code section 170(h)(4)(B))

In addition, Congress added a requirement for the payment of $500 with the filing of any tax return claiming a deduction in excess of $10,000 for conservation easements contributed to protect historically significant structures, as provided in Code section 170(h)(4)(B). This requirement is included in Code section 170(f)(13).

Example One: Alex Gray owns a famous hotel, Greensleeves, which is listed on the National Register of Historic Places. After he had a very good year with the hotel, his accountant recommended that he put a conservation easement on the property to generate a tax deduction to shelter some of his income. Alex saw an ad in the local paper for the Cash for History Preservation Trust promising "painless tax benefits for historic preservation." He called Cash and was informed that all he needed to do was protect the front of his hotel with a conservation easement and he could then collect hundreds of thousands in tax savings, provided he pay 30 percent of his tax savings to Cash to cover its expenses of holding the easement.

Alex and Cash drafted a conservation easement that protected the front of the building but allowed expansion of the structure, including the front, provided that the existing facade was not altered. Alex claimed a deduction of $500,000, generating a tax savings of $175,000, of which he paid $52,500 to Cash. Shortly thereafter, he embarked on a major expansion plan in which the current facade became an "architectural element" of the new front of the building.

Alex's return, however, was audited, and his entire deduction was disallowed because the easement didn't protect the entire building, and because Alex and Cash failed to execute the required agreement.

Example Two: Assume the same facts as above, except that Alex's easement does, in fact, protect the entire hotel and allows no modifications to any part of the exterior that would be inconsistent with the historic character of the building. In addition, Alex and Cash execute an agreement to the effect that Cash is a qualified organization that has the resources and commitment to monitor and enforce the terms of the conservation easement.

However, on audit, the IRS determines that Cash is a wholly owned subsidiary of Tax Shelters-R-Us, and that all of the revenues paid to Cash go directly to its parent corporation, so that Cash actually has no resources to monitor or enforce its fifty different historic easements. Alex knew nothing of Cash's lack of assets. While the easement deduction is allowed, Cash's CEO is indicted for perjury.

Note that the new law does not require that the statements in the required agreement be true, only that they be made. Thus, it appears that the penalty for providing false information in the agreement is liability for perjury, not disallowance of the deduction. In addition, Cash, in the preceding example, loses its public charity status because it has not been operated "exclusively" for charitable purposes (see the discussion of this requirement in section I, E, 3, c of this chapter).

Alex's deduction in the preceding example could have been disallowed had the IRS taken the position that Cash was not a qualified organization (which it wasn't). A contribution of a conservation easement to an entity that is not a qualified organization is not a "qualified conservation contribution."

c. Public Access: Regulations Section 1.170A-14(d)(5)(iv)

For a historic preservation easement to be deductible, the public must have at least visual access to the historic area or structure.

E. The Conservation Purposes of the Contribution Must Be Protected in Perpetuity: Code Section 170(h)(5)(A), Regulations Section 1.170A-14(a)

To be eligible for an income tax deduction, the conservation purposes advanced by the easement must be protected in perpetuity. Practically speaking, this means that the grantor of a conservation easement must permanently relinquish the right to terminate or modify the easement without the consent of the holder of the easement. It also means that the easement must be binding upon all future owners.

This requirement can cause considerable consternation in a prospective easement donor and often, in landowner advisors. The perpetuity requirement can be put in some perspective by recalling that every real estate contract requires a landowner to give up the right to unilaterally change the terms of the contract, and that subdivisions dictate future land use every bit as effectively as a conservation easement.

61

Many people wonder if they can provide for their easement to terminate if the tax benefits are denied for some reason or turn out to be less than anticipated. Of course, the answer is no, because such a provision violates the requirement that the easement be granted in perpetuity. Virtually any provision included in a conservation easement that could cause the easement or any portion thereof, or rights relinquished therein, to revert to the owner violates the requirement of perpetuity. This does not mean that the landowner may not retain rights in the easement to use property that is subject to the easement, or retain rights that are conditioned on approval by the holder of the easement, provided that such retained rights are consistent with the conservation purposes of the easement. Provided that the right is reserved in the easement initially, its exercise does not constitute the reversion of relinquished rights in violation of the perpetuity requirement.

Example One: James contributes a conservation easement to the Z Land Trust. In the easement he reserves the right to continue use of the existing residential compound and, in the event that he has children (he is unmarried at the time of the contribution), to one additional residential compound for each child he may have in the future, provided he is still the landowner, up to a total of three additional compounds. The Z Land Trust has the right to review and approve location of the children's compounds to ensure that their location is consistent with the conservation purposes of the easement.

James's contribution should be deductible, even though he has reserved the rights to create additional residential compounds in the future. These are reserved rights within the context of a perpetual easement. While the reserved rights may reduce the value of the contribution, they do not violate the requirement that the easement be granted in perpetuity, and they are not inconsistent with the conservation purposes. Had the easement not made the additional residential compounds subject to the prior review and approval of the land trust, the reserved rights would have been considered inconsistent with the conservation purposes of the easement and disqualified the easement for a deduction. (See section II, A of this chapter regarding inconsistent uses.)

Example Two: Instead of reserving the rights to designate future residential compounds for his children, James reserves the right, should he have children in the future, to terminate the easement over 10 (specifically designated) acres of the 250 acres he placed under easement with the Z Land Trust, provided that he pays Z the fair market value of that portion of the easement.

This provision probably (again there is no case law or administrative ruling on this) disqualifies the easement for any deduction because it violates the requirement that the easement be perpetual. Because there is only one easement over the 250 acres, termination of a portion of the easement would likely be construed as termination of the entire easement. James might have a counterargument in this case, that only that portion of the deduction pertaining to the 10 acres be denied. Certainly, if James had reserved the right to terminate the entire easement, there would be no deduction. How James would fare in the example given is less clear. However, had James received proper legal counsel, he would have left the 10 acres over which he reserved the termination right entirely out of the easement.

---

1. Exception for Remote and Future Events: Regulations Section 1.170A-14(g)(3)

The Regulations provide an exception from the perpetuity requirement for events that may cause termination of a conservation easement, provided that such events are "remote" and "future" and "so remote as to be negligible." The example given in the Regulations is the termination of a conservation easement by operation of what is known as a "marketability of title" statute. Such statutes require that nonpossessory interests in land (interests that do not involve physical possession, "inchoate interests") must be rerecorded periodically to remain in force. Failure to rerecord such an interest causes it to terminate. A conservation easement constitutes such an inchoate interest and may automatically terminate in the event that the easement is not rerecorded within the specified period of time.

Unfortunately, the example given in the Regulations does not do a very good job of reflecting the requirement that circumstances triggering termination be "so remote as to be negligible." This is because termination under a marketability statute is not so remote as to be negligible but is instead a completely predictable event that will occur at a specific time if the land trust does not rerecord the easement prior to that time.

Perhaps the most important lesson from this example is to alert land trusts that there are statutes in a number of states that can cause termination of conservation easements if the land trust does not rerecord its easements within the statutory period.

2. Perpetual Conservation Easements and the Rule against Perpetuities

Many states have either statutory or constitutional requirements regarding the "vesting" of property held in trust for others. *Vesting* refers to the transfer of ownership of property held in trust to the beneficiaries of the trust, outright and free of trust. Such vesting requirements are typically referred to as the "rule against perpetuities." The rule, which comes from the common law, typically requires that any property held in trust vest outright in a beneficiary, free of trust, within a stipulated period of time. Occasionally, it is argued that the requirement that a conservation easement be perpetual violates the rule. However, because a conservation easement vests immediately in the holder of the easement once the easement is conveyed, the rule does not apply.

However, the rule does raise a more fundamental question, which is whether it is appropriate for an easement donor to dictate to future generations how her land is to be used. This is a big and important question that is beyond the scope of this book. Suffice it to say here that such a question goes to the heart of our system of private property, in which many land-use decisions with long-lasting effects—for example, the development of subdivisions, shopping malls, and amusement parks—are granted to individual owners. The perpetual nature of conservation easements should be considered in that context.

3. Amending Perpetual Conservation Easements

In spite of the requirement that a conservation easement be perpetual to be deductible, easements are inherently contracts and, like any contract, can be amended if all of the parties to the contract agree. However, there are very substantial limitations imposed by current law on a land trust's ability to amend (and terminate) conservation easements.

a. The Charitable Trust Doctrine

The argument has been made that conservation easements are, or at least should be, governed by the "charitable trust" doctrine, which would substantially limit the powers of the parties to amend them. See Nancy A. McLaughlin (an advocate of application of the doctrine), "Rethinking the Perpetual Nature of Conservation Easements," *Harvard Environmental Law Review* 29 (2005), 422, 424; and C. Timothy Lindstrom (who questions application of the doctrine), "*Hicks v. Dowd*: The End of Perpetuity?" 8 Wyo. L. Rev. 25 (2008). Whether or not application of the charitable trust doctrine to conservation easements is appropriate is the subject of some limited, but intense, debate as of the date of publication of this book.

The Land Trust Alliance's publication *Amending Conservation Easements: Evolving Practices and Legal Principles*, published in September 2007, carefully discusses this sensitive issue, pointing out that compliance with the doctrine "may" be required in some states under some circumstances, and that the "most conservative" approach to easement amendment would be to assume that the doctrine applies. In addition, the comments to the Uniform Conservation Easement Act were amended in February of 2007 to incorporate a recommendation that the doctrine be followed in the amendment and termination of conservation easements.

However, the charitable trust doctrine has not been generally applied to date (as the LTA's publication described in the preceding paragraph is careful to note). If applied in its fullest form to conservation easements, the charitable trust doctrine would have significant, and not necessarily positive, implications for the daily operations of many land trusts.

In fact, the Uniform Conservation Easement Act, and most state easement statutes, continue to provide that "a conservation easement may be created, conveyed, recorded, assigned, released, modified, terminated, or otherwise altered or affected in the same manner as other easements" (UCEA, section 2).

b. Excess Benefit Transactions

In any event, and regardless of the application of the charitable trust doctrine, the fact that easements are contracts does not mean that they can be freely terminated, or even amended, by land trusts. This is because the Regulations (section 1.170A-14(c)(1)) require that, in order to be an "eligible donee" to hold conservation easements (see section I, C of this chapter), a land trust must ensure that it is operated exclusively for charitable purposes and must not allow any of its assets to inure to the benefit of any land trust "insider." Violation of these very clear rules by improperly amending or terminating a conservation easement could result in the imposition of substantial economic penalties on the parties (including land trust personnel) and the loss of charitable status.

Code sections 501(c)(3) and 4958(c)(1) impose substantial limitations on the actions of land trusts; in particular, land trusts are prohibited by tax law from participating in "excess benefit" transactions (as described in Code section 4958(c)(1). An excess benefit transaction is one in which a public charity, or other tax-exempt organization, directly or indirectly provides an economic benefit to any "disqualified person" in excess of the value provided by that person in exchange for the benefit.

A disqualified person is any person who is, or for a period of five years *preceding* the transaction was, in a position to exercise substantial influence over the exempt organization, including family members of the disqualified person. Excess benefit transactions violate the requirement that "no part of the net earnings of [a public charity] inures to the benefit of any private shareholder or individual" (Code sections 4958(a) and (c)). The Code imposes an excise tax in the amount of 25 percent of the value of any excess benefit received and requires repayment of the benefit, as well. In addition, the Code imposes fines upon land trust managers engaging in excess benefit transactions (Code section 4958(a)(1), Regulations section 53.4958-7).

Example One: X Land Trust pays its executive director $500,000 per year. The position is part-time, and the Land Trust holds only six conservation easements.

This is an excess benefit transaction because the amount paid for the executive director's services is far in excess of the value of those services to the Land Trust. Overpayment for services is a typical type of excess benefit transaction.

Example Two: Mary is the widow of John, who was a member of the Y Land Trust board when he died four years earlier. The Y Land Trust agrees to an amendment of the conservation easement on John and Mary's farm to allow construction of a small cottage for a full-time nurse for Mary.

This also is an excess benefit transaction, assuming that Mary pays nothing to the land trust for the amendment. Even though Mary was not on the land trust board, and even though John died four years earlier, Mary is still within the definition of "disqualified person." However, if Mary pays the land trust fair value for the amendment, it is no longer an excess benefit transaction, although the amendment may constitute a violation of the land trust's obligation to protect the conservation purposes of its easements in perpetuity.

66

Disqualified persons include "substantial contributors" to the organization. A substantial contributor is someone who has given, or bequeathed, more than $5,000 to the organization, or 2 percent of its annual receipts, whichever is greater, in any given year (Code section 507(d)(2)(A)). It is an open question whether the contribution of a conservation easement, and nothing more, makes the donor a substantial contributor. However, because the real question is whether the contribution is one that gives the donor substantial influence over the organization, it is quite possible that the donor of a highly valuable conservation easement is a substantial contributor and, therefore, a disqualified person. This is an important question because if an easement donor is a disqualified person, amending that donor's conservation easement may be an excess benefit transaction.

c. The Exclusivity Requirement

An additional limitation on the ability of land trusts to amend or terminate conservation easements comes from the requirement that public charities be "organized and operated exclusively" for charitable purposes. Organizations are allowed tax-exempt status only if they engage "primarily" in activities that accomplish one or more exempt purposes—that is, if no more than an "insubstantial part of [an exempt organization's] activities [are] not in furtherance of an exempt purpose" (Regulations section 1.501(c)(3)-1(c)). Note that the prohibition against excess benefit transactions (private inurement) and the requirement that an exempt organization be operated exclusively for exempt purposes are different requirements. (See *United Cancer Council, Inc. v. C.I.R.* 165 F.3d 1173 (7th Cir., 1999) for a judicial delineation of the two limitations.)

As noted in the preceding subsection, violation of the prohibition against excess benefit transactions can result in the imposition of stiff fines; however, excise taxes do not apply to violation of the requirement that public charities be operated exclusively for their exempt purposes. In either case, the IRS has the authority to revoke the offending land trust's exempt status.

The threat of these substantial sanctions represents an important constraint on a land trust's ability to amend or terminate an easement. Furthermore, Form 990, which is the information return all public charities, including land trusts, are required to file annually with the IRS, now requires that land trusts disclose and explain any conservation easement amendments made during the preceding year. Therefore, it is likely that IRS scrutiny of easement amendments will increase.

d. Commitment to Protect the Conservation Purposes

One final constraint on the ability of a land trust to amend, or terminate, a conservation easement is the requirement that to hold a deductible conservation easement a land trust must "have the commitment to protect the conservation purposes of the donation." An organization that allows easement terminations or amendments in a manner that is inconsistent with the conservation purposes of the easement fails to qualify as an "eligible donee" because it demonstrably lacks "the commitment to protect the conservation purposes of the donation" as required by Regulations section 1.170A-14(c).

Example: Mrs. McCreedy donated a conservation easement on her farm in 1995. At that time she reserved three home sites, one for herself, and one for each of her two grandchildren. In 2000 her daughter had a third child. Mrs. McCreedy now wants to amend her easement to allow a fourth home site so that each of her grandchildren can have a house. From a contract law standpoint, if Mrs. McCreedy and the land trust agree to amend the easement to allow the fourth home site, they can do it. However, such an amendment would violate the requirement that the land trust be operated "exclusively" for charitable purposes.

Mrs. McCreedy points out that she owns another farm about five miles down the road that consists of several hundred acres and is not protected. She asks whether the land trust could agree to amend the existing easement to allow the fourth home site if she puts that farm under easement. She also owns 50 acres of prime timber that is a nesting ground for a bald eagle,which is not protected and adjoins the original easement.

For the land trust to avoid an "excess benefit transaction" in responding to Mrs. McCreedy's request, the net financial results to Mrs. McCreedy of any amendment must be, at a minimum, neutral. To ensure that, the land trust must arrange for an appraisal of the effects of the requested amendment, and any net financial benefit to Mrs. McCreedy would have to be offset, in the form of protection of either the farm down the road or the adjoining 50-acre timber parcel, or both. The land trust should arrange for the appraisal and should be reimbursed by Mrs. McCreedy for the cost, and for any other costs incurred in undertaking the amendment. This leaves the question of whether an amendment should be granted in any case, and if it should be, what the proper offset might be from a conservation standpoint. From a tax law standpoint it is clear that the results of the amendment must be financially neutral, or negative, for Mrs. McCreedy. However, if there is no conservation offset, would that affect the status of the land trust as a qualified organization because it lacks the required "commitment to protect the conservation purposes of the donation," as required by Regulations section 1.170A-14(c)? It might.

Amending an existing conservation easement to include additional property is more properly done by a new conveyance, not an amendment. A conservation easement is an interest in real property, and in order to convey such an interest, a formal deed of conveyance is more likely to be effective than an amendment of a previous conveyance. A fresh conveyance also does a better job of putting people on notice of the new easement.

---

4. Judicial Modification or Termination:
Regulations Section 1.170A-14(g)(5)(ii)

The Regulations recognize that a conservation easement may be terminated by a court in the event that, "due to changed circumstances," the use of the property for conservation purposes has become "impractical or impossible."

Courts typically have the authority to terminate, or modify ("reform"), trusts where the original intent of the grantor of the trust can no longer be accomplished with the trust property. (See, for example, George Gleason Bogert, *The Law of Trusts and Trustees*, 3rd ed., chapter 22, section 433.) This authority is necessary because trusts may last long after they were originally established, and many changes not contemplated when the trust was created may occur that defeat the purpose of the trust. Conservation easements are similar to trusts in this respect, and the authority of courts to terminate and reform trusts is believed to extend to easements. This authority comes from the charitable trust doctrine, which is described in section III, E of this chapter.

The power of a court to terminate or modify a conservation easement on the grounds that it can no longer achieve its original purpose is an exception to the tax rule that conservation easements must be perpetual.

Example One: Mr. Jax contributed a conservation easement on 25 acres on the outskirts of Tucson in 1980. At the time of the contribution the acreage was the site of a magnificent group of saguaro cacti, each believed to be over 200 years old. In 1995 a freak windstorm obliterated the stand of saguaros. At that time the land was owned by Mr. Jax's son, who went to court and sought to have the easement modified to allow public use of the property as a park, so that he could sell the parcel to the City of Tucson. The action was brought because the holder of the conservation easement did not believe it could allow the amendment, as termination would confer a substantial financial benefit on the landowner in violation of the holder's charitable status (i.e., the amendment might constitute an excess benefit transaction).

Whether the land trust's position was right or not, the court, considering all of the facts, agreed that the original purpose of the easement could no longer be accomplished and permitted the easement to be modified to allow use of the property as a public park. The court felt that use of the property as a public park at least advanced the original donor's intent to provide a public benefit with the land. A portion of the sale's proceeds was required to be paid to the easement holder (see the discussion of payment of proceeds resulting from easement extinguishment in section III, E of this chapter).

Example Two: Assume the same facts as in the first example, except that the property is now surrounded by intense commercial and industrial development. The landowner petitioned the court to terminate the easement on the grounds that there is no longer any public purpose that could be served by preservation of the 25 acres. The court considered requiring that the land be used for a public park, but recognized that it was too remote from residential development and that the surrounding uses made it highly unlikely that anyone would choose to use such a park. The court

69

agreed to termination of the easement on the grounds that there was no longer any public purpose to be achieved by keeping the land open. The owner then sold the land to the adjoining textile mill, which promptly turned it into a much needed parking lot. The owner received $3 million for the land. Under a provision of the easement required by the Regulations (the extinguishment provision noted in the preceding example), the owner was required to share the payment with the land trust.

If it had applied the charitable trust doctrine, the court could also have required that the proceeds of the sale be used for some public purpose. How that would intersect with the Regulations requirement that the proceeds of the sale be shared with the land trust is unknown.

---

5. Subordination of Mortgages: Regulations Section 1.170A-14(g)(2)

The priority of conflicting rights to real property is determined by who recorded his interest in the property first. Generally speaking, the law provides that anyone taking title to property takes that title subject to all matters actually known to the person taking title, as well as all matters of public record. Being of public record means that a document describing the matter is recorded in the office designated by law for the recordation of deeds in the locality where the property is located (typically a county clerk's office or register of deeds office). Everyone is charged with knowledge of matters put to record, whether or not they actually know of them. This is very important in terms of the enforceability of conservation easements, because a conservation easement will not be enforceable against anyone whose interest in the easement property precedes (typically by prior recordation) recordation of the easement.

For this reason, existing mortgages must be subordinated to a conservation easement in order for the easement to be enforceable in perpetuity, and therefore, deductible. Failure to subordinate an outstanding mortgage puts the holder of the mortgage in a position to foreclose on the property and sell it free from the restrictions of the easement in the event of a default in payment of the mortgage.

Although it might seem unlikely that any mortgage holder would subordinate its position to the kind of restrictions on development typically imposed by a conservation easement (normally resulting in a reduction in property value), mortgage holders frequently agree to such subordinations. Most mortgage holders will subordinate their interest to a conservation easement provided that the easement property retains enough value after the easement is conveyed ("equity") to comfortably cover the outstanding balance on the mortgage. In some cases a mortgage holder may refuse to subordinate or may require the prospective easement donor to put up additional security.

The Regulations do not specify when subordination must occur. The best and safest practice is for the mortgage holder to join in the easement deed. In any event, it seems likely that subordination must be completed by the date of filing the tax return on which the easement contribution is first deducted.

It could be a grave mistake to record a conservation easement without the commitment of the mortgage holder to subordinate, because if the mortgage holder fails to subordinate, the donor may find his land permanently restricted by an easement that isn't deductible.

Keep in mind that although the Regulations speak only of subordination to mortgages, there are a number of different interests like mortgages that may also take priority over a conservation easement and cause the property to be conveyed free of the restrictions of the easement. Examples include deeds of trust, liens imposed by law for failure to pay for labor and materials ("mechanic's liens"), and recorded options or contracts of sale. It is likely that the IRS would consider failure to subordinate any of these kinds of interests to a conservation easement to be grounds for disallowing an easement deduction.

71

II. Uses Inconsistent with Conservation Values Must Be Prohibited: Regulations Section 1.170A-14(e)(2)

The "inconsistent use" provisions of the Regulations constitute an important limit on the rights a donor may retain in a conservation easement and still qualify for a deduction. The IRS is closely examining easements for evidence that donors have reserved uses that are inconsistent with the conservation purposes of their easements. In a recent audit in which I was involved, IRS agents raised issues such as "The easement reserves the donor's right to cut firewood for use in his personal residence on the property: How is the residence heated? How much wood does this provision allow the landowner to cut?" And "The easement reserves the donor's right to have domestic pets on the property: How many pets? What kind of pets? Must the pets be kept inside or can they roam free?" Fortunately, the answers to the questions appeared to satisfy the agents.

The Regulations state that the prohibition against inconsistent uses is not intended to prohibit uses of easement property just because they may be intensive, provided that such uses do not impair significant conservation interests. Uses such as selective timber harvesting and farming fall within this category.

A. The Inconsistent Use Prohibition Is Extensive: Regulations Section 1.170A-14(e)(2)

The Regulations require conservation easements to contain a comprehensive prohibition against all uses that may be inconsistent with any of the conservation purposes of the easement.

1. "Other Significant Conservation Interests" Must Be Protected

In addition to the prohibition against uses of easement property that are inconsistent with the conservation purposes identified in the easement, a deduction will be denied if an easement donor has retained any rights to the use of the easement land that would permit the destruction of significant conservation interests, *even if protection of those interests is not a specific conservation purpose of the easement*: "A deduction will not be allowed if the contribution would accomplish one of the enumerated conservation purposes but would permit destruction of other significant conservation interests" (Regulations section 1.170A-14(e)(2)).

The Regulations give an example of an easement whose purpose was to support a government flood control program. However, the easement permitted the unrestricted use of pesticides that could destroy a naturally occurring ecosystem on the easement land. According to the Regulations, the reserved right to use pesticides made possible the destruction of "other significant conservation interests," disqualifying the easement for tax benefits.

The fact that the Regulations expressly require conservation easements to protect other significant conservation interests comes as a surprise to many people. Furthermore, it is hard to know what may be included within the phrase "other significant conservation interests." It is clear from the example in the preceding paragraph that the requirement goes beyond the specific conservation interests identified for protection in the easement.

It makes sense that "other significant conservation interests" would be limited to those interests whose protection is identified in the Regulations as a qualified conservation purpose. In other words, other significant conservation interests are likely to be limited to preservation of habitat, open space preservation (both scenic and pursuant to a clearly delineated governmental conservation policy), and historic values. Protection of public recreational or educational uses would appear to be outside the scope of "conservation interests" in this context.

It is understandable that a landowner would be reluctant to include in a conservation easement a provision that no one can explain; however, ignoring expressly stated provisions of the tax law risks losing a deduction. Most landowners and their advisors, in my experience, are willing to include the prohibition against use of easement property that would result in the destruction of other significant conservation interests, just to be on the safe side.

Example: Jake owns a 1,000-acre ranch. A small creek that is spawning ground for cutthroat trout, an important and threatened game species, flows through the ranch. Jake grants an easement pursuant to a clearly delineated governmental conservation policy intended to preserve the historic ranches in Jake's region. Jake's easement has been individually endorsed by the locality. The easement allows no development of the property but does allow continued ranching on the property. The right to ranch reserved in the easement is very general, and the easement says nothing about protection of the creek or the trout.

The deductibility of this easement is questionable, even though the easement has effectively kept development from 1,000 acres of historic agricultural land and is valued at over $40 million. The deduction is questionable because the easement allows ranching in a manner that is inconsistent with maintaining the quality of the creek and the trout spawning ground, neither of which was identified as a conservation purpose of the easement, but which are likely to be considered "other significant conservation interests."

---

2. Exception to the requirement to Protect Other Significant Conservation Interests: Regulations Section 1.170A-14(e)(3)

The law provides an exception for uses inconsistent with significant conservation interests, provided that such uses are necessary to support the specific conservation purposes of the easement. This exception makes it possible for a landowner to retain rights essential to uses of the easement property that are central to advancing the conservation purposes of the easement.

Example: The Santa Costa Ranch in California is a historic vineyard dating back to the days of the Spanish conquistadores. It is listed on the National Register of Historic Places. The family that owns the ranch contributed a conservation easement on the ranch for the purpose of preserving its historic characteristics and structures. However, successful operation of the vineyard requires the intensive use of fertilizers, pesticides, and herbicides. The conservation easement reserves the right to use agricultural chemicals "as necessary to maintain the current level of vineyard production."

This reserved right is likely to harm the riparian and aquatic habitat located on the southern edge of the ranch, although the easement requires that a one-hundred-foot natural buffer be maintained along the stream that runs through that area. On audit, the IRS challenged the reserved right to use agricultural chemicals on the ground that it constitutes a use inconsistent with the riparian and aquatic habitat ("other significant conservation interests"), even though the sole conservation purpose of the easement is historic preservation.

The landowner countered the IRS argument by demonstrating that use of the reserved agricultural chemicals is "necessary" to continue production levels on the ranch. The case went to tax court, and the court ruled in favor of the landowner because the evidence supported the landowner's claim that use of agricultural chemicals is necessary to keep the vineyard in operation, which, in turn, is necessary to achieve the conservation purpose of preserving the historic vineyard operation. The court ruled that this reserved inconsistent use falls within the exception to the prohibition against reserved uses inconsistent with other significant conservation values.

B. Inconsistent Use Rules for Open-Space Easements: Regulations Section 1.170A-14(d)(4)(v)

As noted in section I, D, 3, c of this chapter, a deduction for an easement whose purpose is the preservation of open space (scenic open space, or open space pursuant to a clearly delineated governmental conservation policy) will be denied if the landowner retains rights to use land that would "permit a degree of intrusion or future development that would interfere with the essential scenic quality of the land or with the governmental conservation policy that is being furthered by the donation" (Regulations section 1.170A-14(d)(4)(v)).

The relationship of this rule and the more general one applying to all conservation purposes, and whether the exception noted in the preceding section applies to the rule directed solely at open-space easements, is not clear. The standards contained in this regulation are limited to open-space conservation easements (scenic easements and easements furthering a clearly delineated governmental conservation policy) and do not apply to other types of easements. However, the rule requiring the prohibition of uses inconsistent with other significant conservation interests would appear to apply in all cases. While the terminology of the regulation limited to open-space easements is different from the more general prohibition against inconsistent uses, it is hard to find any real basis for distinguishing the two rules. It would seem that if an open-space easement meets the more general prohibition against inconsistent uses, it complies with the prohibition specifically directed to open-space easements. However, based on the rule of statutory construction (interpretation) that the "specific governs the general," it is likely that for open-space conservation easements the provisions of Regulations section 1.170A-14(d)(4)(v) take precedence over the more general inconsistent use provisions.

Example: Mr. Green bought 600 acres along a heavily traveled public road in a small western resort town known for its spectacular scenery. He reserved the right to construct two houses on the property, one for himself and one for his guests. The houses are required to be set back from the road by nearly a third of a mile. However, because the property consists exclusively of open pastureland, the houses, which are likely to be substantial, would be visible from the road. Also, any screening established around the houses would be out of keeping with the rest of the property, which is completely open. The purpose of the easement is protection of the scenic view across the property.

This example raises the question of whether an easement has to be "perfect" to be deductible. Without the easement, the property could have been, and likely would have been, developed into 40 large-lot home sites. With the easement in place, the development of the property is limited to 2 home sites. Nevertheless, the easement allows a use that would interrupt the current unsullied view across the expansive pasture.

The reserved rights to residential development are "inconsistent" with the conservation purpose of the easement to protect the scenic view over the pasture. However, should the easement be deductible? Yes. There is no question that limiting the use of the property to 2, rather than 40, home sites goes a long way toward protecting the view and provides a significant public benefit. Could the IRS argue that reserving 2 home sites violates the requirements of the Regulations? Yes. Would it win the case in court? It is doubtful, but not certain, that a court would apply so restrictive a standard.

C. Dealing with Inconsistent Uses

In some cases a landowner will insist on reserving a use that is potentially inconsistent with the conservation purposes of his easement, or other significant conservation interests. In such cases it may be necessary for a land trust to work with the landowner or forgo the opportunity for a conservation easement. One possible solution is to leave land areas that may be subject to potentially inconsistent uses out of the easement.

The tax law judges a conservation easement not by what has been "left out" of the easement but by what is included, provided that the easement complies with the tax law requirements. In the *Glass* case (see section I, D, 2 of this chapter) one of the two easements challenged by the IRS protected only 18,000 square feet out of a total of 11 acres owned by the donor (less than 4 percent of the total acreage of the property), and the other easement protected 31,200 square feet of the 11 acres. One of the arguments made by the IRS in the *Glass* case was that the easements didn't accomplish a publicly significant conservation purpose because the donors protected only a very small portion of their property. The Sixth Circuit Court of Appeals rejected this argument in *Glass v. C.I.R.*—F.3d—, 2006 WL 3740797 C.A.6 (2006), p. 13.

Given the language, ruling, and circumstances of the *Glass* case, and the complete lack of any provision dictating that a deductible easement cover all of a donor's property, excluding from the easement that land on which the donor may undertake inconsistent uses appears to be a reasonable strategy.

D. No Deduction Is Allowed Where Surface Mining Rights Are Retained: Regulations Section 1.170A-14(g)(4)

Further related to the prohibition against inconsistent uses are the provisions prohibiting surface mining, and strictly limiting other forms of mineral extraction, on easement property. Generally speaking, retention of mineral rights in a conservation easement, or lack of control over mineral rights when

> ## A Caution about the Federal Gift Tax: Code Section 2503
>
> Some landowners who choose to exclude a portion of their land from a conservation easement for purposes of undertaking uses inconsistent with the easement may still want to see the excluded area protected in some fashion, or a land trust may agree to carving out an inconsistent use area on condition that the area is protected. Protection of an inconsistent use area carved out of a conservation easement may be accomplished through the conveyance of a separate conservation easement for which no deduction will be claimed. This protects the inconsistent use area but does not taint the deductible easement with the inconsistent use.
>
> It is important in granting such a nondeductible easement to ensure that the easement is a qualified conservation contribution, even though no deduction is sought. This is because federal tax law taxes partial interest gifts that are not qualified as charitable contributions. Code section 2522(d) allows a gift tax deduction for a qualified conservation contribution even though the contribution does not have a qualified conservation purpose (see chapter 8, section III, C, for discussion of this peculiar exception to the rule requiring a qualified conservation purpose).

granting a conservation easement, jeopardizes the deductibility of the easement. The Code distinguishes between minerals recoverable by "surface mining methods" and minerals recoverable only by other means.

1. Surface Mining: Code Section 170(h)(5)(B), Regulations Section 1.170A-14(g)(4)(i)

The provisions of this section of the Code are premised on the assumption that surface mining is inherently inconsistent with all conservation values—a safe assumption. However, these provisions pose significant challenges to otherwise important and meaningful conservation, particularly in the West, where the federal government holds the mineral rights on vast stretches of land.

a. Split Estate Issues

The problem of the "split estate"—that is, one where mineral rights and surface rights are separately owned—is a major one in the western states, where mineral rights were typically retained by the U.S. government when the land was homesteaded. Where minerals have been retained by the government, or otherwise separated from the ownership of the surface, a conservation easement cannot control how they are removed from the property unless the owner of the minerals joins in the easement, or unless the easement preceded separation of the minerals from the ownership of the surface. See the discussion of priority of interests in title (section II, E, 5 of this chapter).

Recently, these issues have extended beyond the matter of deductibility into eligibility for the purchase of conservation easements with federal funds under the Farm and Ranch Protection Program (FRPP) administered by the U.S. Natural Resources Conservation Service. Grants under that program, which is one of the only remaining federal programs providing grant funding for the purchase of conservation easements, have been restricted to the purchase of easements on land where minerals are intact or where the probability of mining is "so remote as to be negligible" (see section II, D, 1, c of this chapter for a discussion of this exception).

b. The Surface Mining Prohibition: Code Section 170(h)(5)(B)(i), Regulations Section 1.170A-14(g)(4)(i)

A conservation easement that reserves the right to recover minerals ("a qualified mineral interest") by any surface mining method is not deductible. A qualified mineral interest is "the owner's interest in subsurface oil, gas, or other minerals and the right of access to such minerals" (Regulations section 1.170A-14(b)(1)(i)). Therefore, every conservation easement for which the donor intends to seek a charitable contribution deduction *must* include a prohibition against surface mining. The prohibition must be comprehensive and apply to every type of activity that could be construed as surface mining, including gravel extraction for any purpose (see the discussion of the *Nekoosa* case in the following paragraph).

One of the few cases to disallow a charitable deduction for the contribution of a conservation easement because of failure to comply with the regulations involved an easement in which the grantor had reserved the right to excavate gravel for purposes of maintaining roads on the easement property and constructing foundations for structures, the right to which was reserved on the property. This reservation resulted in the denial of a $19 million tax deduction because the IRS successfully argued that it constituted a right to surface mining. See *Great Northern Nekoosa Corp. v. U.S.*, 38 Fed.Cl. 645 (1997). This case underscores the importance of strict compliance with the Regulations, particularly when they provide a clear prohibition, such as the prohibition against surface mining.

c. Exception from the Prohibition: Code Section 170(h)(5)(B)(ii), Regulations Section 1.170A-14(g)(4)(ii)

The law provides an exception from the prohibition against surface mining where the mineral rights and surface rights have been separated and the probability of surface mining on such property "is so remote as to be negligible." In order to qualify for this exception the law requires several things. First, minerals must have been separated from surface rights prior to June 13, 1976. Second, the owner of the surface rights and the owner of the mineral rights may not be related to one another or in business with one another.

A letter from a qualified geologist stating that the probability of surface mining is so remote as to be negligible provides evidence (not necessarily conclusive) that property proposed for a conservation easement is qualified for this exception. The Regulations provide that in considering remoteness "geological, geophysical or economic data showing the absence of mineral reserves on the property, or the lack of commercial feasibility" should be considered (Regulations section 1.170A-14(g)(4)(iii)). A qualified geologist typically provides a "remoteness letter" based upon her evaluation of such matters.

The geologist's report is not conclusive; it is one expert's opinion regarding the state of the minerals on the property and can be refuted by the IRS. Anyone intending to obtain a tax deduction for the contribution of a conservation easement over land where mineral rights have been separated should obtain the evaluation of a qualified geologist as to the probability of surface mining. Note that such a report is not a legal requirement, but "remoteness" is. The report simply provides information regarding remoteness on which a prospective donor can base a decision about proceeding with a contribution. Therefore, such a report should be obtained prior to the contribution to preserve the prospective donor's alternative not to restrict his land if surface mining potential exists that could thwart a deduction.

The law also provides that if minerals were separated from surface rights *after* June 13, 1976, the conservation easement must prohibit all surface mining (Regulation section 1.170A-14(g)(4)(B)). This suggests that for land where minerals were separated prior to June 13, 1976, no such prohibition is necessary. However, to be on the safe side, it would be prudent to include such a prohibition in any conservation easement, regardless of when, or whether, minerals were ever separated from the surface rights.

d. What Minerals Are Affected by the Suface Mining Prohibition?

When one considers surface mining, one typically thinks of coal strip mines. However, the law's prohibition against surface mining may apply to other substances that, on occasion, are defined as minerals, including gravel, sand, and clay. As noted above, the IRS successfully challenged a $19 million tax deduction when the easement donor retained the right to extract gravel from the property (*Great Northern Nekoosa Corp. v. U.S.*, 38 Fed.Cl. 645 [1997] described in section II, D, 1, b of this chapter).

The Code does not define the word *mineral* for purposes of the prohibition against surface mining. Because the word is used in a federal statute, the federal courts have the authority to define it as they see fit. Even though there is a presumption that state law should be incorporated in filling gaps in federal law, it is not an absolute presumption. To ensure fair and equal application of the definition for all taxpayers, it is likely that the federal courts would seek one definition that applied throughout the United States. For a comprehensive discussion of the legal meaning of *mineral* throughout the 50 states and as applied federally, see 95 A.L.R. 2d 843 (originally published in 1964).

To be on the safe side, the term *mineral* should be assumed to include substances typically considered minerals—such as coal, oil, and gas—as well as substances such as sand, clay, gravel (and possibly even peat), the removal of which would result in extensive disruption of the surface of land. It is clearly the intent of the Code to preclude deductions in which extensive surface disturbance would occur for any reason.

Example: Susan Jones wants to protect her ranch. For over a century Susan's family has taken gravel from a several-acre area on the ranch to maintain roads on the ranch. Susan insists to the local land trust that the conservation easement must reserve her right to continue that use. However, the land trust fears, correctly, that such a reservation would preclude Susan's tax deduction.

The land trust, therefore, suggests that the conservation easement exclude the area of the gravel deposit entirely, thus preserving both the right to extract gravel and the deduction. However, concerned that under some future circumstances, the unprotected gravel deposit might be converted to some other use, the land trust insists that Susan place a restriction on the gravel deposit as well, without claiming a deduction for that restriction. Susan does so, making sure that the gravel deposit restriction also qualifies as a qualified conservation contribution, so that, even though she will not be claiming a deduction for that restriction, it will be exempt from the federal gift tax. See the discussion of "Dealing with Inconsistent Uses" and the cautionary note in section II, C of this chapter.

---

2. Other Minerals: Code Sections 170(h)(5)(B)(i) and (6), Regulations Section 1.170A-14(g)(4)(i)

In addition to the outright prohibition against any form of surface mining, the Regulations provide that no deduction will be allowed for any easement that reserves the right to recover any qualified mineral interest by any method that is inconsistent with the conservation purposes of the easement. This may seem a superfluous provision, given the general prohibition against reservation of inconsistent uses already described, but the Regulations provide additional direction as to how the right to extract minerals, other than by surface mining methods, may be reserved and still be consistent with the conservation purposes of the easement. A deduction will not be denied if the easement retains the right to engage in a form of mining (*but not surface mining*) that meets the following three criteria:

1. The mining will have only a limited impact on the property;
2. the mining will have only a localized impact on the property; *and*
3. the mining will not be irremediably destructive of significant conservation interests (Regulations section 1.170A-14(g)(4)(i)).

As already noted, the principal problem with mineral interests is the potential donor's lack of control over such rights. When mineral rights have been separated from the surface, assuming that commercially recoverable mineral deposits exist on the property, the requirements of the tax law cannot be met by merely inserting controls over extraction in the easement. Such provisions will not bind anyone who obtained (or retained) title to the minerals prior to the conveyance of the conservation easement. To be bound by the terms of a conservation easement the owner of any minerals whose claim to the minerals predates the easement must subordinate his interest in the minerals to the easement.

The Regulations provide two examples of easements in which the reservation of the right to extract minerals did not preclude a deduction; those examples are not particularly helpful, however. The following examples are more specific but have not been tested.

Example One: Sam Murdo operates a ranch on 2,000 acres that was homesteaded by his grandfather in 1880. Sam's grandfather was a shrewd man and made sure that he obtained the mineral rights with the property.

Sam approaches the local land trust about contributing a conservation easement. He is willing to prohibit surface mining on the ranch, but he wants to retain the right to explore for and extract the subsurface oil and gas reserves that are there. He agrees to an easement that does the following things:

1. limits mineral extraction to no more than one well per 160 acres;
2. limits the amount of land that can be disturbed for each well (exclusive of roads and pipelines) to no more than 5 acres;
3. requires the location of the drilling pads to be reviewed by the land trust to ensure that no significant habitat or scenic view is disrupted;
4. limits the roads accessing the drilling pads to locations and designs agreeable to the land trust;
5. requires that all pipelines leading from the wells be located underground and requires prior review and approval of all pipeline locations by the land trust;
6. requires reclamation of any disturbed land to the condition of the surrounding undisturbed land when all extraction activities at a well are completed, or in any event in any case where a well has been operated for less than 30 days during any five-year period; and
7. requires complete reclamation of the property at the completion of all mineral extraction activities within a period of one year after production or when there has been no well operating for more than 30 days during a five-year period.

Sam also agrees to pay a "reclamation fee" of one-half of 1 percent of the gross sales of all oil and gas produced on the property to the land trust, to be placed in a segregated fund and used to reclaim the property in the event of failure of the owner to reclaim the property within the period stipulated in the easement, and after reasonable notice from the land trust. If such reclamation has been completed to the land trust's reasonable satisfaction within the stipulated time period by the landowner, the amount of all escrowed reclamation fees will be returned to the landowner.

These provisions in Sam's conservation easement should satisfy the requirements that the impact of mineral extraction have no more than a limited, localized impact not irremediably destructive of conservation values.

Example Two: Assume the same facts as in the preceding example, except that Sam's grandfather made a gift of the mineral rights on the ranch to his brother. Sam's cousins, Bill and Larry, now own the minerals on the ranch. Sam obtains a report on the minerals on the ranch from a qualified geologist. The report indicates that there are no surface minerals having any commercial value on the ranch; however, there are valuable and recoverable subsurface oil and gas reserves.

Sam approaches his cousins with his proposal to contribute a conservation easement on the ranch. He shows them the language described in Example One that he plans to insert in the easement regarding mineral extraction. They agree to subordinate their mineral interests to the terms of the easement, provided that Sam pays them one-half of any tax benefits that he receives as a result of the contribution of the easement. Sam agrees. The agreement of Sam's cousins to subordinate to this provision binds them and anyone taking an interest in the minerals from them to the terms of the easement and should satisfy the Regulations.

III. Other Requirements

The Code and Regulations contain a number of requirements that govern the administration and enforcement of conservation easements. They are described below.

A. Natural Resource Inventory: Regulations Section 1.170A-14(g)(5)(i)

At the heart of a land trust's ability to monitor and enforce a conservation easement is a detailed record of the condition of the easement property at the time the easement was conveyed. Without such a record it would be extremely difficult to identify and document violations. The record is also important for the landowner, because it is his defense against an erroneous claim by a land trust that he has created a condition that did not exist when the easement was conveyed and that constitutes a violation of the easement.

Regardless of the practical need by both parties for a record of the condition of easement property at the time of its conveyance, the Regulations require such a record if the donor retains in the easement any rights to the future use of the easement property. This "natural resource inventory" must be prepared and made available to the donor and the prospective holder of the easement *prior to the conveyance of the easement.*

While the requirement that the inventory be available prior to easement conveyance seems a mere technicality, it is an express part of the requirements for deductibility and should be taken seriously. The point of the timing of this requirement is that, to ensure easement compliance, the holder of an easement must know what the property is like from the moment it takes possession of the easement.

The Regulations (sections 1.170A-14(g)(5)(i)(A)–(D)) provide a list of *suggested* matters to be covered in the inventory:

(A) The appropriate survey maps from the United States Geological Survey, showing the property line and other contiguous or nearby protected areas;

(B) A map of the area drawn to scale showing all existing man-made improvements or incursions (such as roads, buildings, fences, or gravel pits), vegetation and identification of flora and fauna (including, for example, rare species locations, animal breeding and roosting areas, and migration routes), land use history (including present uses and recent past disturbances), and distinct natural features (such as large trees and aquatic areas);

(C) An aerial photograph of the property at an appropriate scale taken as close as possible to the date the donation is made; and

(D) On-site photographs taken at appropriate locations on the property. If the terms of the donation contain restrictions with regard to a particular natural resource to be protected, such as water quality or air quality, the condition of the resource at or near the time of the gift must be established.

Equally important to obtaining the inventory is being able to locate the inventory when it is needed. Some land trusts record the inventory with the easement; others prefer to treat it as confidential and keep it in the land trust's files. In any case, the inventory must be kept safe and available and should be used as an integral part of the regular monitoring of use of any easement property.

The inventory is evidence of the condition of easement property on the date the inventory was compiled (not on the date of the conveyance). It is not, however, conclusive evidence and, unless the parties so agree in the easement, it does not preclude either party from providing additional evidence of the condition of the easement property at any given time. Note that the Regulations require substantially the following statement to be included with the inventory and signed by the parties: "This natural resources inventory is an accurate representation of [the protected property] at the time of the transfer" (Regulations section 1.170A-14(g)(5)(1)(D)).

B. Notice Requirements: Regulations
Section 1.170A-14(g)(5)(ii)

One of the regulatory provisions that is sometimes overlooked in easement drafting is the requirement that the owner of easement property notify the holder of the conservation easement prior to exercising any rights reserved in the easement, *if such exercise might impair the conservation interests protected by the easement*. This requirement is occasionally objected to by easement donors, who feel it is intrusive. However, one ignores explicit requirements of the Regulations at one's peril. To be prudent, a conservation easement should expressly provide something along the following lines: "The Grantor shall notify the Grantee prior to undertaking any use of the property that may impair the conservation interests protected by this easement."

Here is the text from the Regulations (section 1.170A-14(g)(5)(ii)): "*Donee's right to inspection and legal remedies.* In the case of any donation referred to in paragraph (g)(5)(i) of this section [i.e., any contribution in which the easement donor reserves rights to the future use of the easement property], the donor must agree to notify the donee, in writing, before *exercising any reserved right, e.g. the right to extract certain minerals, which may have an adverse impact on the conservation interests associated with the qualified real property interest*" (Emphasis added).

C. Monitoring Requirements: Regulations
Section 1.170A-14(g)(5)(ii)

To be deductible, conservation easements must grant to the easement holder the right to enter the easement property at reasonable times to inspect the property for compliance with the terms of the easement. Easements often, as a courtesy to landowners, provide for notice of some form to the landowner prior to entry by a land trust for monitoring. This is a reasonable provision, *provided* that prior notice to a landowner is *not* a requirement for entry in all cases. Where an emergency threatening the conservation purposes of the easement is reasonably believed by a land trust to exist, the land trust must have immediate access to the property for monitoring and enforcement, regardless of prior notice provisions. Lack of such authority undermines the perpetual nature of the easement and the ability of the easement holder to enforce its terms.

Here is an example of an emergency access provision: "No notice shall be required in the event that the Grantee reasonably believes that activities ongoing, or threatened, on the property would significantly impair the conservation values protected by this easement; provided that, as soon as practical, the Grantee shall provide written notice to the Grantor describing the actions taken and the need therefor; and further provided that the Grantee shall limit its remedial actions pursuant to this provision to those necessary to prevent damage to such conservation values."

D. Enforcement and Restoration: Regulations
Section 1.170A-14(g)(5)(ii)

The requirements provided by the law for enforcement and restoration should be considered *the minimum* enforcement provisions for an effective conservation easement, not the *only* provisions.

1. Restoration

The Regulations require that deductible conservation easements must provide for enforcement by legal means, specifically including restoration of the easement property in the event of a violation. Most easements require restoration, but only to the condition that existed prior to the violation. This makes sense. However, the Regulations actually provide that restoration must be to the condition of the easement that existed *on the date of the conveyance of the easement*. This appears a bit unreasonable. Given my avowed policy of strict compliance, even with questionable requirements, I suggest including this restoration provision as written in the Regulation. However, I believe that the provision can provide an exception for changes that have been made to the easement property that are consistent with the terms of the conservation easement.

Example: Sol Green donates a conservation easement over 200 acres, one-third of which is forested. The easement reserves the right to timber the forested portion of the property, subject to a plan for timber management that has been approved by the land trust. Sol timbers about 20 acres of the property consistent with the approved plan. The following year he sends in a bull-dozer to clear debris. That clearing is in violation of the easement, because the timber management plan required leaving debris to provide habitat.

The Regulations would require restoration of the improperly cleared area to the condition on the date of conveyance of the easement—in this case, fully forested with mature trees. Obviously, that is not possible, and removal of the trees was not a violation of the easement because it was done according to the approved plan. A provision requiring restoration to the condition existing on the date of the easement conveyance "except for changes made that are consistent with the terms of the easement" would allow the property to remain in its timbered state, while requiring replacement of the removed debris or the addition of comparable cover for wildlife.

---

2. Other Remedies, Damages, and Attorney's Fees

Other legal remedies, while not mandated, are typically provided in conservation easements. Among those remedies are provisions for obtaining an injunction against actions threatened, or ongoing, that are inconsistent with the conservation purposes, as well as damages and recovery of costs.

I think it is fair for enforcement provisions and damages to be made available to landowners, as well as land trusts, because land trusts as well as landowners may violate easement terms. For example, the failure of a land trust to respond to reasonable requests within periods specified in the easement or overzealous monitoring that becomes harassment constitutes an easement violation. In such cases, the easement should provide remedies to the landowner.

In addition, easements typically provide that the holder of a conservation easement may obtain reimbursement from a landowner for attorney's fees, expenses, and court costs incurred in enforcement actions. These provisions are typically triggered only if such actions are successful. I believe

that, where an easement holder has acted in "deliberate and willful" violation of the terms of a conservation easement, the landowner should be entitled to recover attorney's fees, expenses, and court costs, as well.

However, a purely reciprocal attorney's fee provision can seriously
undermine a land trust's willingness (and therefore ability) to properly
enforce the terms of a conservation easement. This is because the threat
that failure to succeed in an enforcement action will result in liability, not
only for the land trust's own legal fees, but the landowner's as well, could
easily discourage land trusts from seeking judicial enforcement of easement
violations if they are less than certain of success. Very few enforcement
actions, no matter how justified, are guaranteed of success.

3. Replacement Cost Damages

An important enforcement issue that is sure to become more important as
the economic value of the development potential captured by easements
increases is the proper measure of damages for an easement violation. The
threat of damages to cover replacement of damaged resources may do little
to discourage the landowner's violation of an easement in a very high-end
real estate market. For example, if a landowner wants to clear a "view cor-
ridor" to a spectacular view in violation of the terms of a conservation easement but resulting in an increase in the value of the easement property by
$1 million, how likely is it that the threat of damages equal to the costs of
replanting removed vegetation will be sufficient to deter the violation?

One suggestion is to provide in the easement itself that in the
event of an easement violation that destroys conservation values in a
manner that cannot be restored (e.g., clear-cutting an old-growth forest),
damages shall be due in an amount equal to the cost of purchasing an easement protecting comparable conservation values in the vicinity of the
easement that has been violated. The Regulations do not require such a
provision, and many landowners may object. However, landowners who
are giving up valuable rights to their property in order to ensure its permanent protection may be amenable to such provisions because they can be
very effective at discouraging future owners from violating the easement.

E. Extinguishment of an Easement: Regulations Section 1.170A-14(g)(5)(ii)

Easements can be extinguished (terminated). There may be serious negative consequences for the parties to a conservation easement termination,
but, legally speaking, there is nothing to prevent the holder of an ease-

ment and the owner of the easement land from agreeing to terminate a conservation easement at any time.

The Wyoming Supreme Court recently ruled in the first reported case of a voluntary easement termination between the holder of an easement and the landowner. In *Hicks v. Dowd* (see section I, C, 1 of this chapter), the Wyoming Supreme Court let the termination of a conservation easement by a local government stand, even though there was no meaningful compensation for the termination. Although the trial court invited the Wyoming attorney general to intervene in the case, he declined (although, as of the date of this writing, there is some indication that he may reverse his position and accept the Wyoming Supreme Court's invitation to him to reconsider intervention), and the plaintiff who sought to enforce the easement was ruled not to have "standing" (the right) to sue. For more information about the *Hicks* case see C. Timothy Lindstrom, "*Hicks v. Dowd*: The End of Perpetuity?" 8 Wyo. L. Rev. 25 (2008).

The Regulations make no provision for the "improper" termination of a conservation easement, such as occurred in the *Hicks* case, although it clearly violates the perpetuity requirement. However, the Regulations do anticipate the possibility that an easement may be extinguished by a court according to common law principles known as the doctrine of cy *pres*.

The doctrine of cy pres, sometimes referred to as the "charitable trust doctrine," permits a court to modify or terminate a trust established for public charitable purposes when the original purposes for which the trust was established can no longer be accomplished for some reason. While conservation easements are not "trusts" in the normal sense of the word, they have some of the attributes of charitable trusts in that they are often charitable contributions whose purpose is to benefit the public.

Concerns about improper easement termination are growing, although improper easement terminations remain rare. Nevertheless, the concern has started a debate nationally about whether application of the doctrine of cy pres to conservation easements is needed or appropriate. Essentially, application of the doctrine would require judicial oversight of almost all easement terminations *and* modifications. To date the doctrine has not been applied generally to conservation easements, and some questions have been raised about the appropriateness of applying it at all. For an extensive discussion of the need and appropriateness of applying the doctrine of cy pres to conservation easements, see Nancy A. McLaughlin, "Rethinking the Perpetual Nature of Conservation

Easements," *Harvard Environmental Law Review* 29 (2005), 422, 424; and C. Timothy Lindstrom, "*Hicks v. Dowd*: The End of Perpetuity?" 8 Wyo. L. Rev. 25 (2008).

Nevertheless, the Regulations (section 1.170A-14(g)(6)) provide for termination of an easement according to the principles of cy pres, as follows:

- if the termination was by court order;
- if the termination was due to changed circumstances, making continued use of the property for the conservation purposes impractical or impossible; *and*
- if the holder of the easement is required to use its share of any proceeds resulting from the termination of an easement in a manner consistent with the conservation purposes of the easement (see section III, F of this chapter regarding how the holder's share of proceeds is determined).

The most typical form of easement termination is through governmental exercise of the power of eminent domain (condemnation), for, in most cases, conservation easements are private property and are subject to that power. Most condemnation proceedings never go to court but are settled by the parties outside of court. Such settlements are called "payment in lieu of condemnation."

As a practical matter, there is little that a private land trust can do when confronted by a threat of condemnation by a governmental agency except negotiate price. The real threat is that the governmental agency will refuse to pay anything for the condemnation of a conservation easement on the grounds that it has no value. However, the Regulations require that all deductible easements provide for payment to the easement holder of a portion of the proceeds of any "sale, exchange, or involuntary conversion" resulting from the termination of a conservation easement. This means that, even if the condemning authority does not recognize any value in a conservation easement for which compensation is required, the owner of the condemned easement property will be required to pay a percentage of the compensation that she has received to the easement holder.

The Regulations do not expressly allow for settlements in lieu of condemnation (because the easement termination in such a case was not by "court order,") implying that easement holders should force governmental agencies to go to court, so that the easement over the portion of the property that the government seeks to take is judicially terminated. However, settlements in lieu of condemnation make sense, provided that the easement holder obtains its pro rata share of a fair payment for the condemned property. It seems unlikely that the IRS would challenge a reasonable settlement in lieu of condemnation, even though the Regulations do not expressly recognize such settlements as appropriate means of terminating a conservation easement.

F. Division of Sales Proceeds in the Event of Extinguishment: Regulations Section 1.170A-14(g)(6)(ii)

Termination of conservation easements is discussed in section I, E, 3 of this chapter. As noted there, in addition to allowing for judicial termination of conservation easements, the Regulations require that an easement must provide for a division of sales proceeds between the owner of easement property and the holder of the easement in the event of a sale of the property after the termination of an easement in whole or in part.

The Regulations (section 1.170A-14(g)(6)) require that deductible conservation easements contain the following provisions:

- the easement holder's interest in the easement is a vested property interest;
- the fair market value of the easement holder's interest is at least equal to the proportionate value that the easement, at the time of the contribution, bears to the value of the unrestricted property as a whole at the time of the contribution;
- the proportionate value of the easement will remain constant; and
- in the event that the easement is terminated, the proceeds of any subsequent sale, exchange, or involuntary conversion of the easement property shall be divided between the owner of the easement property and the easement holder based on that proportionate value.

Example: If River Ranch is worth $1 million in its unrestricted state and $300,000 as restricted by an easement, the easement is worth $700,000 ($1,000,000 – $300,000), 70 percent ($1,000,000 / $700,000) of the unrestricted value of the property, which is the proportionate value of the unrestricted property represented by the easement. If the ranch is subsequently condemned for public use as the site of a new school, for example, and the proceeds of the condemnation are $2 million, the proceeds must be divided and distributed by the owner of the ranch: $1,400,000 (.70 × $2,000,000) to the easement holder and $600,000 (.30 × $2,000,000) to the owner of the ranch. Note that these values do not include improvements because it is assumed, in this example, that improvements are not restricted by the easement and are not, therefore, included in its value.

The Regulations do not state how the value of the easement as of the date of contribution is to be determined. However, the value is clearly the same value as that claimed on the donor's tax return for charitable contribution purposes (the Form 8283 value; Form 8283 is the summary of the easement appraisal required to be filed with the easement donor's tax return, see chapter 6, section II, A) *as accepted for the final determination of tax due*. It is always possible that the value shown on Form 8283 will *not* be the value accepted for determining the donor's amount of tax due. The IRS may challenge the Form 8283 value, and the parties may settle on a different number; or the parties may not agree to settle, a different value may be determined through a judicial review of the IRS disallowance, and there may be appeals of that decision right up to the U.S. Supreme Court. Therefore, it is in the interests of the easement donor (but not necessarily the holder, as the deduction claimed on Form 8283 is almost always likely to be the highest valuation for the easement) to rely on the value as finally determined for federal tax purposes, not the Form 8283 value.

The following language is suggested:

> This Easement constitutes a real property interest immediately vested in the Grantee with a fair market value that is at least equal to the proportionate value that this Easement, as of the date of conveyance, bears to the value of the Property as a whole at that time. This proportionate value shall remain constant. The values applicable for purposes of the calculations required by this subparagraph shall be the values *finally used to determine the value of this Easement for purposes of any federal income tax deduction allowed with respect to the conveyance of this Easement.*

PART III
Income Tax Benefits

There are significant income tax benefits associated with the charitable contribution of conservation easements, provided that the easement document complies with all the requirements of Code section 170(h) and the accompanying Regulations, as discussed in part 2. Income tax benefits provided to conservation easement donors are a significant incentive for voluntary land conservation. However, like most tax incentives, they work best for those with high incomes.

The deduction for the contribution of a conservation easement is relatively simple in concept. However, the various statutory limitations, and the somewhat less than clear conceptual limitations (most prominently the requirement for "donative intent"), significantly complicate the deduction and limit the number of circumstances in which it may be available, even though the easement document meets all of the requirements described in part 2.

CHAPTER FOUR

Tax Benefits

I. Calculation of the Tax Benefit

Calculation of potential income tax benefits from the contribution of a conservation easement is complex, although estimating the theoretical *maximum* benefit is not. Here again, the calculation of tax benefits should not be undertaken without the assistance of a tax expert knowledgeable about conservation easement deductions and familiar with a prospective donor's tax circumstances.

Soliciting contributions based on projected tax savings can get a land trust into trouble very fast. This is because, in some cases, such solicitation may be considered the marketing of a tax shelter; the unauthorized practice of law; or, where projections and actual benefits are significantly different, fraud or misrepresentation. So, why read this section at all? Because understanding the tax mechanics for land trust personnel is essential to a realistic approach to the promotion of voluntary conservation. Furthermore, if you are a tax professional, you are in a position to provide projections and advice regarding potential tax benefits.

A. The Value of the Easement Is Deductible: Code Sections 170(a) and (h), Regulations Section 1.170A-14(h)(3)(ii)

The value of a conservation easement that complies with the requirements of Code section 170(h) may be deducted from the donor's income for purposes of calculating the donor's federal income tax. Remember that a deduction represents a reduction in the amount of income against which tax is imposed, not a direct dollar-for-dollar offset against income tax as is the case with an income tax credit. Therefore, the actual tax benefit is only a percentage of the amount of the deduction.

The value of a conservation easement for purposes of the deduction is typically the difference in the value of property before the easement contribution and after the easement contribution (see chapter 5 for a discussion of easement valuation).

Example: Mr. Jones contributes an easement on land that is valued at $1 million before the contribution. After the contribution the land is valued at $300,000. The value of the easement is $700,000 ($1,000,000 – $300,000): the difference in the value of the land before and after the easement is in place.

B. Calculating the Maximum Tax Benefit

The *maximum* possible federal income tax benefit (i.e., the tax savings resulting from an easement deduction) that may be enjoyed from the charitable contribution of a conservation easement is calculated by multiplying the appraised value of the easement by the top federal tax rate. Many states with an income tax provide a deduction for easement contributions as well. In such cases, adding the applicable top federal and state tax rates together, and multiplying the value of the easement by those combined rates, provides the maximum possible combined federal and state income tax benefit from any easement contribution. However, it is important to note that very few donors will enjoy the maximum benefit due to a number of restrictions imposed by tax law on how the deduction is used. These restrictions are described in the following sections.

As of January 2007, the top federal income tax rate for individuals was 35 percent (ranging from 10 percent). The top federal income tax rate for "C" corporations (corporations taxed as separate entities) was 39 percent (starting at 15 percent but not increasing incrementally). "S" corporations, and other entities, such as limited liability companies and partnerships, pass income and deductions through to their owners, and they are then figured into the individual's personal tax return (see the discussion of various entities in section V of this chapter).

Example: If Mr. Jones resides in a state with a 6 percent income tax that allows a deduction for the contribution of a conservation easement, he would enjoy an additional state income tax benefit of $42,000 (.06 × $700,000).

Another way to calculate the total maximum benefit for Mr. Jones would be simply to add the top federal and state rates together and multiply the value of the easement contribution by that combined rate (41 percent).

The federal tax system is a graduated system, in which lower income is taxed at lower rates. As a result, all taxpayers pay less than the top rate of tax on some portion of their income, so the overall rate of tax paid is always less than the "marginal rate" imposed on their income (i.e., the highest rate of tax imposed on their income). Some taxpayer's income is insufficient for any of it to be taxed at the top rate. For example, the 2007 federal tax rates for married persons filing jointly are 10 percent on income up to $15,650; 15 percent on income from $15,651 to $63,700; 25 percent on income from $63,701 to $128,500; 28 percent on income from $128,501 to $195,850; 33 percent on income from $195,850 to $349,700; and 35 percent on all income over $349,700. Rates for single filers and married persons filing separately are different. If a married couple's income is no higher than $200,000, their marginal rate will be only 33 percent, and the tax benefits they would receive from any charitable deduction will likely be less than the benefits enjoyed by a couple with a 35 percent marginal rate.

Because of the graduated tax system, an accurate computation of the tax benefits that will result from a conservation easement deduction for any given individual must take into account all of the different rates at which the income sheltered by the deduction would have been taxed.

Example: In 2007 Sharon and Sol Green contributed a conservation easement valued at $200,000; that is the amount they are entitled to deduct from their income for federal tax purposes. The Greens' income in 2007 was $400,000. The conservation easement was their only charitable contribution in 2007. The effect of that contribution was to reduce the Greens' taxable income to $200,000 (ignoring for a moment the 3 percent phase-out in certain itemized deductions, discussed in section I, I of this chapter).

According to the tax rate schedules for a married couple for the year 2007, the first $15,651 of the Greens' income would be taxed at 10 percent (.10 × $15,651 = $1,565.10); the next $48,049 would be taxed at 15 percent (.15 × $48,049 = $7,209.35); the next $64,800 at 25 percent (.25 × $64,800 = $16,200); the next $67,350 at 28 percent (.28 × $67,350 = $18,858); the next $153,850 at 33 percent

(.33 × $153,850 = $50,770.50); and the balance of $50,300 at 35 percent (.35 × $50,300 = $17,605).

Disregarding the reductions in income allowed the Greens (personal exemptions, standard or itemized deductions, etc.), the total tax due on the Greens' income would be $112,207.95, just over 28 percent of their income. The income tax on the $200,000 sheltered by the conservation easement deduction would have been $67,006 ([.35 × $50,300 = $17,605] + [.33 × $149,700 = $49,401] = $67,006). This tax is 33.5 percent of the $200,000 sheltered by the easement deduction. Thus, the actual tax benefit received by the Greens was not 35 percent but 33.5 percent of the $200,000 easement ($67,006 / $200,000).

As the preceding example demonstrates, calculating the *actual*, not theoretical, tax benefit from an easement contribution is not simple. Other deductions, filing status, and the number of personal exemptions will affect the donor's income, thereby affecting applicable tax rates, just as the total amount and kind of income will affect applicable rates. Without factoring all of these variables together, which can best be done by actually filling out a tax return for the donor that includes all of these variables, an accurate estimate of the tax benefits of an easement contribution for any given individual or couple cannot be made.

Some states, in addition to allowing a charitable deduction for the contribution of a conservation easement, allow a credit against state tax due for easement contributions. Discussion of state tax credits, and other state tax benefits, is beyond the scope of this text (there is a short discussion of the federal tax treatment of state tax credits in section VI of this chapter). However, tax credits are powerful incentives because they *directly offset tax due* on a dollar-for-dollar basis, rather than merely reducing the amount of income subject to tax, as is the case with an income tax deduction. Of course, state tax rates are considerably lower than federal tax rates. In addition, some states allow easement donors to sell their credits to other taxpayers in the state. The ability to sell a credit makes the credit valuable to easement donors whether or not they have significant tax liability.

C. The Amount of the Federal Deduction Is Subject to an Annual Limitation: Code Section 170(b), Regulations Section 1.170A-8(a)

The Code does not allow taxpayers to deduct more than a fixed percentage of their annual income for charitable contributions, no matter how large that contribution may have been. More than any other feature of federal tax law, this limitation disadvantages low-income donors. This is particularly significant when it comes to conservation easement deductions, because while some of the nation's most valuable land, from a natural resource standpoint, is farm and ranch land, few family farmers and ranchers have substantial incomes. Therefore, the tax incentive for them to protect their land is significantly reduced compared to the incentive for wealthier individuals.

In 2006 Congress, as part of the Pension Protection Act, amended the provisions of the Code that limit the percentage of income against which a person making a qualified conservation contribution may claim a deduction. By increasing the percentage of income against which a conservation easement deduction may be taken, Congress made the tax incentives for easement contribution much more meaningful for landowners with smaller incomes, and particularly for landowners whose income comes mostly from the business of farming or ranching.

Unfortunately, the 2006 law expired at the end of 2007; however, Congress continues to consider making it permanent. *Note that the following discussion of annual limitations is divided into "2006 law" and "current law" to reflect this 2006 revision. However, because the 2006 law will apply only to easements donated in 2006 and 2007,* readers need to know both laws, recognizing that the current law applies to all conservation easements contributed before 2006 and after 2007, unless Congress renews the 2006 provisions.

1. The Current Law: Code Section 170(b)(1)(C)(i), Regulations Section 1.170A-8(d)(1)

Again, the current law is the law applicable to all conservation easements except those contributed in 2006 and 2007.

a. Individuals

Under the current law, when an individual makes a contribution of "certain capital gain property" (i.e., property held for more than one year, which would include a conservation easement on land owned by the donor for more than one year), the federal income tax deduction for that contribution is limited to 30 percent of the donor's "contribution base" (Regulations section 1.170A-8(e)). *Contribution base* is adjusted gross income (the amount shown on line 38 of Form 1040) without regard to the amount of the contribution or any "net operating loss carry-back" (if you have it, you will know what it is!) (Code section 170(b)(1)(G)).

Example: Mr. Jones's easement is worth $700,000. He has owned the property that is subject to his easement contribution for five years. Therefore, the easement is considered the contribution of long-term capital gain property, limiting his deduction to 30 percent of his contribution base. Mr. Jones's income is $250,000 annually (and he has no net operating loss carry-back, thank heavens); therefore, he may deduct only $75,000 (.30 × $250,000) for his easement contribution each year, even though the value of the easement is $700,000.

Under both the current law *and* the 2006 law, if the easement contribution is made in the first year the donor owns the easement property, the deduction is allowed up to 50 percent of the donor's contribution base. This is because the contribution is not considered to be a contribution of capital gain property but of ordinary income property (for our purposes, property held for one year or less) (Regulations section 1.170A-8(b), Code section 170(b)(1)(A)). However, under both the current law and the 2006 law, a deduction for ordinary income property cannot exceed the donor's basis in the easement (Code section 170(e)(1)). Note that "basis in the easement" is *not* basis in the easement property, but basis in the easement itself. The basis limitation is discussed in section I, H of this chapter.

Example: Mr. Jones contributed his easement six months after he purchased the easement property. Therefore, the property was treated as "ordinary income property," and the deduction may be used up to 50 percent of Mr. Jones's contribution base. In this case he may deduct $125,000 (.50 × $250,000) of the value of the easement and carry the unused balance of the contribution forward. However, his deduction cannot exceed his basis in the easement.

After the first year of ownership, an individual donor may *elect* to limit the amount of the deduction to her basis in the easement gift and thereby qualify for the 50 percent limitation rather than the 30 percent limitation. (See Regulations section 1.170A-8(d)(2).) *However*, for easements contributed in 2006 and 2007, which are subject to the 2006 law, that election is not needed because, as will be described below, the 50 percent limitation applies regardless of the donor's "holding period." That election is once again relevant under the current law. If the donor makes this election, however, the amount of his deduction will be limited to his basis in the easement, just as it would be for the contribution of property owned for one year or less.

In any event, the aggregate amount of *all* of a donor's charitable deductions (e.g., easement contributions and other contribution such as cash and securities) made during a tax year is limited to 50 percent of the donor's contribution base (including conservation easement deductions that are limited to 30 percent of the donor's contribution base). Thus, if the donor has made contributions for which charitable deductions are available in addition to the conservation easement gift, the value of the other contributions may reduce the amount of the deduction that may be taken for the easement contribution.

Example: If Mr. Jones made other charitable gifts amounting to $100,000 during the year in which he donates his conservation easement he may, in effect, deduct only $25,000 of his easement gift because his total deduction for charitable gifts is limited to 50 percent of his contribution base ([.50 × $250,000] – $100,000 = $25,000). However, as described below, Mr. Jones may "carry forward" the unused portion of his conservation easement deduction to future tax years.

---

b. C Corporations

"C" corporations (corporations whose income is taxed at the corporate level, rather than at the shareholder level, as is the case with "S" corporations) may deduct no more than 10 percent of their "taxable income" for charitable contributions, regardless of the length of time the contributed property has been owned by the corporation (Code section 170(b)(2)). "Taxable income" is a smaller figure than "adjusted gross income" because it is income reduced by all deductions. *This rule is not changed by the 2006 law unless more than 50 percent of the corporation's income is from "the business of farming" and the stock of the corporation is not publicly traded* (see section I, C, 2, b of this chapter regarding treatment of C corporations under the 2006 law). (Section V of this chapter discusses the differences between individuals, corporations, and partnerships, etc., in terms of conservation easement contributions.)

2. 2006 Law: Code Section 170(b)(1)(E)(i)

As noted above, Congress *temporarily* changed the percentage limitations for qualified conservation contributions in 2006 and 2007. (The

Regulations had not, as of the date of this writing, been changed to reflect the 2006 law.) The 2006 *law* increased the percentage of contribution base against which a donor may claim a deduction for a qualified conservation contribution from 30 percent to 50 percent, regardless of the length of time the easement property had been owned by the donor. In other words, the 30 percent limitation does not apply to easements contributed on land owned for more than one year if the easements were contributed in 2006 or 2007. Although the 2006 provisions have now expired, because they may be reinstated permanently (and because they continue to apply to easements contributed in 2006 and 2007), a discussion of those provisions is provided here.

The 2006 law applies to "qualified conservation contributions." As described in chapter three, qualified conservation contributions include two types of contributions: (1) all of the owner's interest in property except for a qualified mineral interest, and (2) a conservation easement. In other words, the expanded tax benefit applies to both types of contributions.

Example One: Mr. Jones's easement is worth $700,000. He has owned the property that is subject to his easement contribution for five years. Although this is considered a contribution of capital gain property, subjecting him to the 30 percent limitation under the old law, under the 2006 law the limitation was increased to 50 percent. Mr. Jones's income is $250,000 annually. Thus he may deduct $125,000 of his easement contribution (.50 × 250,000), which means he may deduct the entire value of the easement within a five-year period.

Example Two: Mr. Blue contributed his entire ownership interest in a West Virginia farm valued at $1 million, but reserved a "qualified mineral interest." This makes his contribution a qualified conservation contribution. His contribution base is $500,000 per year. Mr. Blue may use the $1 million against 50 percent of his contribution base annually, allowing him to deduct $250,000 annually, using up the deduction in four years.

Example Three: Instead of reserving the minerals in his West Virginia farm, Mr. Blue was more generous and contributed the entire fee interest without reservation. The value of the gift, because it includes some valuable minerals, is $2 million. However, because Mr. Blue did not reserve a qualified mineral interest, his contribution is not considered a qualified conservation contribution, and the new law does not apply. Mr. Blue has owned the farm for over a year, so his annual deduction is limited to 30 percent of his contribution base. Therefore, he may deduct only $150,000 per year for the contribution. Furthermore, he has only five years to carry forward any unused portion of the contribution (see section I, D of this chapter) and thus is unable to use $1.1 million of his contribution.

This inequitable result (at least when compared to the treatment Mr. Blue would have received had he reserved the mineral rights in his gift of the farm) is due to the failure of the 2006 law to distinguish between conservation easements and gifts of all of an owner's interest except for a qualified mineral interest.

---

a. Special Rule for Farmers and Ranchers: Code Section 170(b)(1)(E)(iv)

Under the 2006 law if a qualified conservation contribution was made by a "qualified farmer or rancher" in 2006 or 2007, the deduction could be taken against 100 percent of the donor's contribution base. A qualified farmer or rancher is someone (including a corporation whose stock is not "readily tradable on an established securities market") who derived more than 50 percent of her income from the "business of farming" in the year of the contribution.

Code section 170(b)(1)(E)(v) provides that the definition of *farming* under the 2006 law is the definition currently found in Code section 2032A(e)(5), which is as follows:

(A) cultivating the soil or raising or harvesting any agricultural or horticultural commodity (including the raising, shearing, feeding, caring for, training, and management of animals) on a farm;

(B) handling, drying, packing, grading, or storing on a farm any agricultural or horticultural commodity in its unmanufactured state, but only if the owner, tenant, or operator of the farm regularly produces more than one-half of the commodity so treated; and

(C) the planting, cultivating, caring for, cutting of trees, or the preparation (other than milling) of trees for market.

The definition of *farm* for purposes of the foregoing is found in Code section 2032A(e)(4): "The term 'farm' includes stock, dairy, poultry, fruit, furbearing animals, and truck farms, plantations, ranches, nurseries, ranges, greenhouses or other similar structures used primarily for the raising of agricultural or horticultural commodities, and orchards and woodlands."

In order for the 100 percent limit to apply, the conservation easement must ensure that the easement land remains "available" for agriculture. This is *not* a requirement that the easement mandate farming or ranching, but only that the easement provide that the land remain available for agricultural use. The requirement that agricultural use be allowed does not apply to 50 percent limit deductions.

Under the *2006 law*, if the requirement that more than 50 percent of the donor's income come from the business of farming is met in the year of the easement contribution, it does not appear to matter what source the donor's income is from in the carry-forward years; the 100 percent limit will continue to apply.

Example One: Sam's income from farming was $75,000 in 2006 when he contributed an easement on his farm. His total income was $100,000 due to some investments. Therefore, Sam qualified to use his deduction up to 100 percent of his $100,000 income. In the year after he made his contribution, he sold some shares of stock. As a result, his income from farming, which remained $75,000, represented only 40 percent of his income. He may continue to take the unused portion of his easement deduction against 100 percent of his income.

Example Two: Sara sold a conservation easement on her farm for $300,000, which is half of its appraised value of $600,000. The sale was treated as a bargain sale, and Sara was entitled to a $300,000 deduction. Her income from farming is $200,000, which is her total income. However, in the year of the bargain sale, her income from farming was less than 50 percent of her total income because of the proceeds from the sale of the conservation easement. Because those proceeds were not "income from the business of farming," she was not entitled to the 100 percent limit but had to work with the 50 percent limit.

Regardless of what Sara's income may be in the years during which she carries forward this deduction, she is still subject to the 50 percent limit because she failed to meet the requirement for the 100 percent limit in the year of the contribution. The same result would occur had she sold a portion of her farm outright, again because the proceeds from such a sale are not income from the business of farming.

---

b. Treatment of Limited Liability Companies and Corporations

Because the Code treats most limited liability companies as partnerships for purposes of taxation, it is likely that the requirement under the 2006 law that more than 50 percent of income be from the business of farming applies at the membership level, not the entity level. In other words, the fact that the limited liability company itself derives more than 50 percent of its income from the business of farming does not allow its members to write off the deduction for an easement contributed by the limited liability company against 100 percent of their income unless they, individually, derive more than 50 percent of their income from the business of farming. There is no guidance on this point as of this writing.

Example One: Sam Evans is a rancher. He has a large ranch that he runs with his family through a family-owned corporation, the Lazy J LLC. Lazy J is a limited liability company (taxed like a partnership, not as a separate entity) and, under the 2006 law, is allowed to enjoy the 2006 law's tax benefits for a conservation easement contributed by the LLC in 2007. Lazy J's adjusted gross income in 2007 was $1 million, which it passed through to its members in proportion to their ownership in the company. Of that income $550,000 was from the business of farming, and the rest was from investments. Sam Evans owns 80 percent of the company and, therefore, was entitled to $800,000 of the Lazy J's income, which came to him as 55 percent farm income and 45 percent investment income, the same as the percentage of income to the LLC. That constituted Sam's sole source of income.

The Lazy J's conservation easement was valued at $10 million. As a limited liability company, it passed the entire amount of the deduction through to its members. Therefore, Sam is entitled to an $8 million charitable contribution deduction (.8 × $10,000,000). Because more than 50 percent of his income was from the business of farming, he is allowed under the 2006 law to take this deduction against his entire $800,000 income, eliminating any taxable income. Sam can take this deduction annually until it is used up. Under the 2006 law he may spread this deduction over a total of 16 years. In this case he would use up the deduction in 10 years ($800,000 × 10 = $8,000,000), assuming his income does not change.

Example Two: Sam has a brother named Frank, who owns the other 20 percent of the Lazy J Ranch. Frank is a lawyer, and his income for 2007 was $250,000 from his practice. He received $200,000 as his share of the income from the Lazy J. He is entitled to a portion of the deduction for the easement contribution equal to 20 percent of the value of the easement, or $2,000,000 (.2 × $10,000,000). However, he cannot take this deduction against more than 50 percent of his contribution base, because less than 51 percent of his income was from the business of farming, even though the Lazy J's income was entirely from the business of farming. Thus, his deduction will be limited to $225,000 ([$200,000 + $250,000] × .5) in the year of the contribution and in the carry-forward years, assuming his income does not change.

The 2006 law also applies to C corporations that contributed conservation easements in 2006 or 2007, if more than 50 percent of their income comes from the business of farming, *provided* that the stock of the corporation is not publicly traded (generally, is not listed on any stock exchange). The restriction against corporations with publicly traded stock appears to represent an effort to distinguish between family-owned corporations and business corporations that engage in agriculture. Recall that a C corporation's income is taxed at the corporate level, not the shareholder level.

Example: XYZ Corporation is a C corporation. Its stock is not publicly traded and is wholly owned by a small group of farmers who have used the corporation to acquire and hold certain real property for hay production for their individual farming operations. All of XYZ's income is from the sale of its agricultural products. XYZ contributed a conservation easement that preserves the real property it owns for agricultural use and as scenic open space. The easement is valued at $1 million. XYZ's taxable income is $50,000 per year. Under the current law XYZ would be limited in using the easement deduction to only 10 percent of its taxable income. However, because the easement was contributed in 2007, it is governed by the 2006 law and may use the deduction up to 100 percent of its taxable income. As noted below, XYZ will be able to carry the unused portion of the deduction forward for fifteen years. Assuming that its income remains the same, XYZ will be able to use $800,000 (16 × $50,000) of the deduction, assuming that its income does not change in future years.

D. Unused Portions of a Deduction May Be Used in Future Years: Code Sections 170(b)(1)(C)(ii) and (D)(i), Regulations Section 170A-10(c)(1)(ii)

If the donor of a conservation easement (or any other form of charitable contribution) does not have enough income in the year of the contribution to use up all of the deduction generated by the contribution, the Code allows the donor to "carry forward" the unused portion of the deduction to future years. Generally, an unused deduction may be carried forward for no more than 5 years. However, in 2006 Congress changed the carry-forward limit for qualified conservation contributions to 15 years. As with the other provisions described immediately above, these provisions of the 2006 law have also expired and apply only to easements contributed in 2006 and 2007. Together with the increase in the amount of income against which an easement donor may take his deduction, this provision represented another significant step in making conservation easement deductions beneficial to landowners with lower annual incomes; hopefully, it, along with other 2006 provisions, will be renewed.

The discussion of the carry-forward provisions will also be divided according to the current law and the 2006 law.

1. Current Law: Code Sections 170(b)(1)(C)(ii) and (D)(i), Regulations Section 170a-10(c)(1)(ii)

Under the current law any unused portion of an easement deduction can be carried forward for five years after the year of the contribution (a maximum of six years within which the deduction may be used) or until the amount of the deduction has been used up, whichever comes first.

Example: Joan's 2005 conservation easement contribution is valued at $300,000. Her annual income was $100,000. Under the current law (which also applies to easements contributed in 2005), Joan is allowed to deduct up to 30 percent of her contribution base for the contribution. That means she can deduct $30,000 per year (.3 × $100,000), assuming her income remains the same. With the five-year carry-forward period,

Joan can deduct a total of $180,000 of the $300,000 contribution value (6 × $30,000), assuming her income does not change, forcing her to lose $120,000 ($300,000 − $180,000) of the deduction's value.

---

2. 2006 Law: Code Section 170(b)(1)(E)(ii)

The 2006 law increased the carry-forward period from 5 years to 15 years, or until the amount of the deduction is used up, whichever comes first.

Example: Assume that John Wells donated a conservation easement valued at $900,000 in 2007. Assume also that his annual contribution base is $140,000. That would allow Wells to use up to $70,000 per year of the $900,000 deduction ($140,000 × .50). Over the 6-year period during which he could use the easement deduction under the current law, he could deduct only $420,000 (6 × $70,000). However, because his contribution occurred in 2007, it is governed by the 2006 law, and, assuming no change in his contribution base, Wells can deduct the entire amount of the $900,000 contribution because he has 15 years to carry the deduction forward and needs only 13 ($900,000 / $70,000).

Because the 2006 law applies to all qualified conservation contributions made in 2006 and 2007, not just conservation easements, and because such a contribution is considered a qualified conservation contribution, the contribution of a fee interest reserving a qualified mineral interest also qualifies for the 15-year carry-forward period. The contribution of a fee interest that includes mineral rights will not qualify. As noted earlier, this unusual outcome is due to the reliance of the 2006 law on the definition of *qualified conservation contribution* in Code section 170(h)(1).

E. Prioritizing Deductions: Code Section 170(b)(1)(E)

Under the current law (Code section 170(b)(1)(C)(i)) contributions of easements on property the donor owned for more than one year are to be taken into account only after all other contributions have been deducted. Remember that such contributions, because they are contributions of property held for more than one year, are limited to 30 percent of the donor's contribution base. If the conservation easement was on property held for one year or less, the deduction is allowed up to 50 percent of the donor's contribution base, as previously noted, and there is no priority imposed on which of such contributions is deducted first.

The now expired 2006 law (Code section 170(b)(1)(E)) regarding qualified conservation contributions allowed deductions for easements contributed in 2006 and 2007, regardless of the length of time the property subject to the easement was owned by the donor, "to the extent the aggregate of such contributions does not exceed the excess of 50 percent of the taxpayer's contribution base over the amount of all other charitable contributions allowable under this paragraph." Thus, under both the current law and the 2006 law, the calculation of the amount of a deduction for the contribution of a conservation easement, regardless of the length of time the donor has owned the easement property, can be made only after calculating the amount of other charitable deductions allowed for a particular tax year.

Example: In 2005 John contributed a conservation easement valued at $500,000. His annual income was $250,000. During 2005 he also made a contribution of one acre to his church for use as a parking lot. The one acre is valued at $100,000 for purposes of John's charitable deduction. This contribution, because it is a contribution of capital gain property, is subject to an annual limitation of 30 percent of John's contribution base. Therefore, John is entitled to deduct $75,000 ($250,000 × .30) for this contribution, carrying forward the remaining $25,000 to the following year. However, he is also entitled to deduct the excess of 50 percent of his contribution base over the amount of the one-acre gift for the conservation easement. This excess amounts to $50,000 ([$250,000 × .5] − $75,000). This $50,000 will be fully used by a portion of the conservation easement deduction.

The following year John's income remained at $250,000, and he had, in addition to the balance of his one-acre and easement contributions, a cash gift deduction of $50,000 (which is subject to an annual limitation of 50 percent of his contribution base under both the 2006 law and the current law). Therefore, he may deduct $25,000 (the balance of his one-acre contribution) and $50,000 for his cash contribution. This leaves $50,000 of his contribution base ([$250,000 × .5 − $75,000] remaining, against which he may use another $50,000 of his conservation easement deduction. That leaves $400,000 of John's easement contribution remaining to deduct over the next 14 years ($500,000 − $100,000).

Because the 2006 law limits easement deductions to the difference between 50 percent of the donor's contribution base and the donor's other charitable contributions, the easement deduction gets used only after all other deductions are used, up to the 50 percent limit. This is actually beneficial to a donor contributing an easement in 2006 or 2007 because the 2006 law provided more time to use up a conservation easement deduction than it allowed for other types of contributions. But for the prioritization rule, donors during 2006 or 2007 might mistakenly choose to deduct their easement before deducting other contributions for which the carry-forward period is shorter, running the risk of losing the benefit of a portion of the easement deduction.

F. Tax Benefits Expire at Donor's Death

In the event that the donor of a conservation easement dies before he has used up a conservation easement deduction (or any other deduction, for that matter), the deduction expires with the donor. In other words, the deduction cannot be carried beyond the final return filed for whatever portion of the last tax year the decedent lived. If the contribution was made jointly by a husband and wife on jointly owned property (i.e., tenancy by the entireties or joint tenancy with right of survivorship), the surviving spouse may continue to claim the balance of any deduction remaining after the death of the first spouse.

Example: John and Mary contributed a conservation easement on land that they owned as joint tenants with right of survivorship. They claimed a deduction of $1 million for the contribution. Three years later John died, leaving $500,000 remaining of the deduction. Mary lived for another two years, during which she was able to use an additional $150,000 of the easement deduction. She lived for 50 days into the tax year, and her executor was required to file a final return for that 50-day period. Mary's income for that period was $30,000; thus, the executor may claim $15,000 of the remainder of the deduction on Mary's final return. However, the unused balance of the deduction, of $335,000 ($1,000,000 − $500,000 − $150,000 − $15,000) was lost with Mary's death.

G. Phasing Easement Contributions to Extend Income Tax Benefits

The failure of Congress to renew the provisions of the 2006 law that provided for the increase in the annual limitation for deductions of conservation easements from 30 percent to 50 percent has renewed the importance of a technique used prior to the 2006 law. That technique is the "phasing" of easement contributions. Even if Congress renews the 2006 provisions, phasing may be useful for easement contributions that are very large in relation to the donor's income.

Phasing simply means contributing several smaller easements in succession, rather than one big easement. By dividing one conservation easement into several, and phasing her contribution over time, the donor gets the benefit of several successive carry-forward periods in which to use the deduction, rather than just one.

Example: (Note that the following example assumes an easement contribution made in 2007, therefore governed by the 2006 law. However, this example illustrates the technique, which will be even more effective for contributions governed by the current law.) Mrs. Blue donated a conservation easement over her 1,000-acre ranch in 2007. The value of the easement is $6 million. Mrs. Blue's average annual income is $500,000. The maximum deduction that she can realize, assuming she is subject to the 50 percent annual limitation and that her income does not change, is $4 million (.50 × $500,000 × 16).

However, Mrs. Blue could increase the amount of the deduction she can use by protecting her ranch in two phases, using two separate easements donated at different times. For example, the first easement could cover 500 acres of her ranch. Assume that the value of that easement is $2,500,000 (taking into account the increase in the value of the unrestricted portion of the ranch due to the conservation easement; see chapter 5 for a discussion of "enhancement"). Over a 10-year period Mrs. Blue would be able to fully deduct that gift (.50 × $500,000 × 10 = $2,500,000). Once that gift was fully deducted, assume that Mrs. Blue donated a second easement, worth $5 million (considering appreciation), over the remaining 500 acres of the ranch. By the time of that gift, assume that her average annual income had increased to $700,000. Over the 15 years beginning with the second easement contribution, she would have been able to fully deduct the $5 million gift (.50 × $700,000 × 15 = $5,250,000). Of course, if Congress does not renew the 2006 law, Mrs. Blue's second contribution would be subject to the 5-year carry-forward period provided under the current law, necessitating perhaps a third phase in her ranch protection plan, to allow full use of the deduction.

Mrs. Blue could have phased her easement gifts differently by first donating an easement over the entire ranch that eliminated half the development potential that she ultimately intended to remove from the ranch. A second easement would eliminate the balance of the development potential. However, unless carefully done, the reservation of development potential in the first easement could provide the IRS with grounds to argue that the reserved development rights constitute inconsistent uses (see chapter 3, section II for a discussion of inconsistent use).

Whether a landowner phases easements by putting a series of them over physically distinct parts of her property, or by reducing development potential on the entire property in steps with different easements, *each* easement must *independently* meet the standards of Code section 170(h), including, in the case of open-space easements, the requirement that each easement must generate a publicly significant benefit. The law will not allow easement donors who phase their easements to point to the cumulative effect of a series of easements as making those easements compliant with the law; compliance must be accomplished with each separate easement.

In a phased conservation plan such as Mrs. Blue's, the donor should include a provision in her will directing her executor to contribute an additional conservation easement that completes protection of the property. A full draft of the intended easement should be incorporated into the will to avoid uncertainty. Such a conveyance will not qualify for any income tax benefits but will qualify for full estate tax benefits, which could be significant. The will provision also ensures that the phased protection project is completed.

H. Some Easement Deductions Are Limited to Basis: Code Section 170(e)(1), Regulations Section 1.170A-4(a)(1)

"Basis" is an important concept in tax law. Essentially, it is what a property owner has paid for a particular property, plus the value of improvements made to that property. Basis becomes important when the property owner sells the property because the tax on the sale of the property is imposed on the difference between the seller's basis in the property and what the seller receives for the property. The difference is known as "taxable gain."

Example: Susan paid $2,000 per acre for her 100-acre farm in 1995. She built several new barns and renovated the old farmhouse. Altogether she put $75,000 into the improvements. Therefore, her basis ("adjusted basis" in this case because the improvements she paid for require her original basis to be adjusted upward) in the farm is $275,000 ([$2,000 × 100] + $75,000). Susan sold the farm in 1998 for $500,000 (the farm was not a personal residence but an investment property, so was not eligible for the personal residence tax exclusion). Her gain on the sale, therefore, was $225,000 ($500,000 – $275,000), which was subject to capital gains tax.

Basis is also an important concept when it comes to the tax deduction for a conservation easement if the donor of the easement has owned the easement property for less than one year at the time of the contribution. According to the tax law, if an easement donor contributes an easement on land that he has held for less than one year, the easement contribution is treated as the contribution of "ordinary income property" (as opposed to capital gain property).

Under both the current law and the 2006 law, as noted earlier, the contribution of a conservation easement on property owned by the donor for one year or less could be deducted up to 50 percent of the donor's contribution base. However, the donor cannot deduct more than his basis in the easement under either the current law or the 2006 law. It is important to note that the limitation is to the donor's basis *in the easement*, not the easement property, which is quite different.

A taxpayer's basis in a conservation easement is a function of two factors: (1) the amount that the donor actually paid for the easement property (his basis in the property); and (2) the percentage of the value of the unrestricted easement property represented by the easement, as determined in the appraisal of the easement. To determine the donor's basis in the easement, you multiply factor 1 by factor 2.

Example: Assume that Mr. Blue's basis in his property is $250,000 (the purchase price). He donated a conservation easement on the property six months after purchasing the property. The appraiser determined that the property before the easement was in place was actually worth $500,000, and that the restricted value of the property after the easement was in place is $250,000. Thus, the easement was worth 50 percent of the appraised value of the property unrestricted by the easement ($250,000 / $500,000). Although the value of the easement as determined by the appraisal is $250,000 ($500,000 – $250,000), Mr. Blue's basis in the easement is only $125,000 (.50 × $250,000); therefore, his deduction is limited to $125,000. Had Mr. Blue waited for 366 days or more after his purchase of the property to contribute the easement, he would have been entitled to claim the entire $250,000 as a deduction (although the IRS is skeptical of dramatic increases in the value of easement property occurring in a relatively short period of time). This result would be the case under both the current law and the 2006 law.

Generally speaking, when the appraised value of easement property prior to the easement is the same as, less than, or only slightly more than the donor's basis in that property, the limitation-to-basis rule will not make a significant difference in the amount of the deduction. However, when the appraiser determines that the "before-easement" value of the property is substantially more than what the donor paid for that property, the limitation to basis can make a significant difference in the amount of the deduction.

In effect, the limitation-to-basis rule is an automatic penalty for landowners who take aggressive positions with respect to conservation easement deductions claimed for recently purchased easement property.

I. Limitation on Itemized Deductions: Code Section 68

The Code imposes a further limitation on certain types of itemized deductions, including charitable deductions. This limitation is known as the "overall limitation on itemized deductions." It applies to the itemized deductions of taxpayers reporting more than a certain level of income.

For individuals whose adjusted gross income in 2007 exceeded the "threshold" level of $156,400 ($78,200 for married taxpayers filing separately), the amount of any charitable deduction, including those for conservation easement donations, must be reduced. The reduction required is 3 percent of the amount by which the taxpayer's income exceeds the threshold, or 80 percent of the total amount of itemized deductions, whichever is less.

This limitation is being phased out over the next several years. For tax years 2006 and 2007 the limitation amount is two-thirds of the original 3 percent (i.e., 2 percent) reduction otherwise applicable; for tax years 2008 and 2009 the limitation amount is one-third of the original 3 percent (i.e., 1 percent). The limitation will be eliminated after 2009. See Code section 68(f). Note that the threshold level of income over which the limitation applies is adjusted annually for inflation.

Example: Mr. and Mrs. Gray earn $500,000 annually, which they report on a joint income tax return. The Grays contributed a conservation easement valued at $2 million in 2006. They are allowed a deduction for their ease-ment contribution in the amount of $250,000 due to the 50 percent limi-tation ($500,000 × .50). The phase-out rule requires the Grays to reduce the amount of the deduction by the lesser of 3 percent of their income over the threshold amount ($150,500 in 2006, for individuals filing joint returns) or 80 percent of the total of their itemized deductions. Three per-cent of their income over $150,500 amounts to $10,485 ([$500,000 − $150,500] × .03). Assuming that they have itemized deductions (including the deduction for the easement) totaling $200,000, 80 percent of their total itemized deductions would amount to $160,000 ($200,000 × .80). Therefore, the Grays must reduce the total of their itemized deductions by $10,485, which is the lesser of the two alternatives. Because the easement gift generated 75 percent of their total of itemized deductions, it could be said that 75 percent of the phase-out of $10,485, or $7,863.75 ($10,485 × .75), applies to the easement deduction, reducing it from $250,000 to $242,136.25. However, under the phase-out of this limitation, the limita-tion is only two-thirds of $10,485, or $6,989 (.66 × $10,485).

J. The Alternative Minimum Tax

The alternative minimum tax (AMT) is intended to ensure that all people pay their fair share of tax. Because Congress believed that certain wealthy individuals were getting an inordinate benefit from certain types of item-ized deductions, the AMT requires those individuals to figure their tax without the benefit of those deductions. Those deductions are known as "tax preference items" and originally included the deduction for charitable contributions of appreciated property (deductions based on the appreciated value of the donor's property regardless of what the donor paid for that property). Prior to 1993, contributions of conservation easements were tax preference items. (See Code section 57(a)(5)(C)(iv).) However, the Code provision treating gifts of appreciated property as tax preference items was repealed, effective December 31, 1992, by P.L. 103-66 (1993).

In other words, the AMT does *not* apply to conservation ease-ment contributions. Charitable contributions of conservation easements are no longer considered tax preference items.

II. Donative Intent Is Required

Donative intent is the intention to make a charitable contribution. Without donative intent there is no charitable contribution and no deduction. There is nothing in the Code or Regulations pertaining to conservation easements that spells out the requirements of donative intent; those requirements come primarily from case law. However, the IRS has made it clear that donative intent is a pre-condition to receiving a charitable deduction for the grant of a conservation easement.

In most conservation easement contributions, donative intent is not an issue, even when the primary motivation of the donor is to obtain tax benefits. The IRS once challenged an easement deduction, in part on the ground that the donor was primarily motivated by the desire to obtain a tax deduction, not by donative intent, and therefore should not be entitled to a deduction. However, the court reviewing the IRS position said that the desire to obtain a tax deduction did not preclude donative intent and recognized the intent of Congress to provide incentives for charitable behavior through the tax code. See *McLennan v. U.S.*, 994 F.2d 839 (1993).

Donative intent becomes critical, however, in more complex transactions—particularly conservation buyer transactions and transactions involving the grant of zoning, or other regulatory benefits in connection with the grant of a conservation easement.

A. Dual Purpose Contributions

The Supreme Court has said that in order for a grant of property (I am being careful here not to prejudge the nature of the conveyance by calling it a contribution) to be a charitable contribution, the person making the grant cannot receive value for the grant that is equivalent to or in excess of the value of the grant (*U.S. v. American Bar Endowment*, 477 U.S. 105, 106 S.Ct. 2426 (1986)).

The *American Bar Endowment* case is important because it dealt with payments by taxpayers that included both a payment for services and a charitable contribution. The Supreme Court held in that case that a taxpayer who makes a payment to a charity in excess of the value of any benefit received in exchange has made a charitable contribution to the extent of the excess payment. The Court called this a "dual character" payment: part payment for services and part charitable contribution. However, as the Court noted, the essence of a charitable contribution is the payment in excess of the value of benefits received.

In its reasoning in *American Bar Endowment* the Supreme Court appeared to evaluate the taxpayer's actions based on the objective measure of the difference between the value of the contribution and the value of benefits received in exchange, not on the subjective measure of his intention. This suggests that the *intention* of an easement donor is not as important as whether he receives equivalent or greater value in exchange for the easement.

In a previous case that did not involve a charitable deduction but revolved around whether an individual had made a gift to another individual, the Supreme Court said that a grant made out of either a *moral* or a *legal* obligation was not a gift. See *Commissioner v. Duberstein*, 363 U.S. 278, 80 S.Ct. 1190 (1960). The ruling in this case, that a discharge of a moral obligation is not a gift, has never been rejected by the courts and should be respected. However, it has never been applied to a charitable contribution and, as a justiciable matter, would be extremely difficult to evaluate. In my opinion, the more important question is the quantitative one of whether the donor receives value equivalent to or greater than the value of his contribution.

The Regulations regarding conservation easement contributions also follow the quantitative approach:

> If, as a result of the donation of a perpetual conservation restriction, the donor or a related person receives, or can reasonably expect to receive, financial or economic benefits that are greater than those that will inure to the general public from the transfer, no deduction is allowable under this section. However, if the donor or a related person receives, or can reasonably expect to receive, *a financial or economic benefit that is substantial, but it is clearly shown that the benefit is less than the amount of the transfer*, then a deduction under this section is allowable for the excess of the amount transferred over the amount of the financial or economic benefit received or reasonably expected to be received by the donor or the related person. (Regulations section 1.170A-14(h)(3)(i); emphasis added)

Example One: The classic example of the dual purpose contribution is the purchase of a ticket to a charity ball. Say the price of the ticket is $250, and the value of the dinner, band, and so forth is estimated at $100 by the charity sponsoring the event. The charity provides each ticket purchaser with a statement that the value of benefits received for the $250 payment is $100, and that the balance is accepted as a charitable contribution. The IRS has stated (see Rev. Rule 67-246) that the ticket purchaser is entitled to claim a $150 charitable contribution in such a case.

Example Two: The Blue Lake Land Trust has a 100-acre parcel of land for sale. The land trust has said it will retain a conservation easement on the land that allows only camping and other noncommercial recreational activities. The trust paid $500,000 for the land and is seeking to recover its entire purchase price, so it is offering the land, subject to easement, for $500,000. However, it has an appraisal indicating that, with the easement in place, the land is worth only $100,000. George Jones agrees to purchase the land for $500,000, provided that the land trust will provide him with a letter like the "charity ball" letter from the preceding example. The letter states that George paid $500,000 for property valued at $100,000 and that the difference is accepted as a charitable contribution. The IRS has, off the record, stated that the overpayment is deductible as a charitable contribution. It should be deductible as a "dual purpose contribution" and based on Regulations section 1.170A-14(h)(3)(i).

B. Quid pro Quo Transactions

In addition to donative intent issues relating to dual purpose contributions, there are other donative intent issues when a landowner grants a conservation easement in exchange for some form of regulatory approval, or as part of some other agreement requiring the contribution of the easement. These types of transactions are sometimes referred to as quid pro quo ("something for something") transactions. While the dual purpose contributions described in the preceding section appear to fall within the category of quid pro quo, they are eligible for some level of deduction because of the excess of the value of the contribution over the benefit received, and the objective evidence (in the form of the written acknowledgment) that the excess was considered by the parties as a charitable contribution.

However, a conservation easement conveyed as part of a quid pro quo transaction in which the donor is obligated to make a contribution is typically not deductible. This is because easements granted in such transactions are pursuant to some contractual or regulatory obligation, and neither the grantor of the easement nor the recipient of the easement enters into the transaction with charitable intent. The conveyance of a conservation easement, even if made for less than the value of the easement, if made pursuant to a contractual or regulatory obligation, precludes donative intent because the grant is mandatory, not voluntary. It is possible, but unusual, for a landowner and a governmental body conferring some regulatory approval to the landowner in exchange for the landowner's conveyance of a conservation easement to intentionally structure the transaction as a charitable one. Properly structured, and where the easement's value, based on a qualified appraisal, exceeds the value of the approval, the landowner might be able to successfully claim a charitable deduction.

Nevertheless, as a general proposition, any time the conveyance of a conservation easement is *required*, either by contract or by regulation, it will not be deductible. There is one exception: if the contractual obligation is to make a contribution. The most common example is a payment or conveyance pursuant to an enforceable charitable pledge or option made either to a public charity or a governmental entity. Performance, *by the original maker*, of a pledge or option to make a charitable contribution (including a qualified bargain sale) is deductible, at least to the extent that the value given exceeds any value received, because the original commitment (e.g., the pledge or option) was voluntarily made as a charitable act. Note the emphasized language in the preceding sentence. If the pledge or option is ultimately performed by someone other than the person making the pledge or granting the option, it is likely that performance will be considered the discharge of an obligation of another, which is not a charitable contribution.

Following are various situations in which contractual or regulatory obligations are likely to preclude a deduction for the grant of a conservation easement:

1. Cluster Development Projects

A growing number of localities allow a landowner to increase residential density, or simply to cluster permitted residential density, in exchange for the grant of a conservation easement on that portion of the property from which the clustered density has been derived. Because the grant of the easement is a requirement of local regulation, there is no donative intent and, therefore, no deduction. See Technical Advice Memorandum (TAM) 9239002 (1992); see also *Stubbs v. U.S.*, 428 F.2d 885 (1970).

Example One: Elmer Fuddie owns 50 acres in Cracker County. Cracker County allows Elmer up to 1 house for every 5 acres that he owns, in his case equaling 10 houses. However, if Elmer clusters all of his development on 10 acres, he will be allowed to double his density to 20 houses. In exchange for the increased density Elmer is required to put a conservation easement on 40 acres, ensuring that it can never be developed.

Elmer hires an appraiser, who determines that the value of the 50 acres before he agreed to the cluster and the easement was $1 million, and that after the agreement and easement the property was worth only $750,000. Elmer claims a tax deduction of $250,000 for the easement.

The IRS agrees that the easement is worth $250,000 but disallows the deduction on the grounds that the easement was not the result of any charitable intent; it was given pursuant to Cracker County regulations requiring the easement in order to obtain the increased density. That is a quid pro quo transaction.

Note that it doesn't matter that Elmer gave more than he got in this exchange. The fact that the easement was mandated by governmental regulations precludes any donative intent.

Example Two: Suppose Elmer put the easement in place prior to seeking cluster approval from Cracker County. In this case the deduction might have held up, because the easement would have been contributed independently from county approval.

This example raises several additional issues. First, was the easement written to allow the acreage subject to the easement to be used for purposes of density calculation for development outside of the easement? If so, the appraisal would be required to reflect that retained value. Second, would Cracker County allow the "transfer" of density from the easement land to unrestricted land? Generally, because conservation easements held by private organizations are entirely private contracts, localities do not have the authority to enforce them (which is, in effect, what the county would be doing if it denied Elmer the right to transfer density from the easement property).

I am aware of some easements granted as part of a regulatory requirement in which the grantor of the easement successfully claimed a deduction based on an appraisal indicating that the value of the easement exceeded the value of the additional development potential received in exchange. In other words, the landowners in these cases have treated the conveyance of an easement in response to a governmental regulation as a dual purpose contribution; whether they succeeded in their claims because they were not audited or because their argument for a deduction was persuasive is not known.

The Regulations, which provide that the value of an easement is deductible to the extent of the excess of the value of the easement over the value of any economic benefit received in exchange for the easement (Regulations section 1.170A-14(h)(3)(i)), lend support to this dual purpose approach.

There are also some judicial decisions that uphold the proposition that a person conveying land, or interests in land, to a governmental agency in exchange for governmental approval may, to the extent that the value of the conveyance to the agency exceeds the value of the governmental approval, claim a deduction. See, for example, *Allen v. U.S.* 541 F.2d 786 (C.A. Cal. 1976), in which the U.S. Circuit Court of Appeals upheld the grant of a tract of 9.2 acres of redwoods as part of a cluster development approval as a charitable contribution.

121

2. Reciprocal Easements

When one landowner agrees to grant a conservation easement over his land in exchange for his neighbor's grant of an easement, the contractual obligation to grant the easement precludes donative intent if the agreement is legally enforceable. Performance of a contractual obligation owed to a private individual does not constitute a charitable gift.

Example One: The Blacks and the Whites own adjoining farms. For years each has considered contributing a conservation easement. The only thing keeping them from going forward with the contribution is the fear that once the easement is in place, the other family will develop its land to take advantage of its neighbor's land protection. Finally, Black and White agree with each other that if one donates an easement, the other will follow suit. They sign an agreement to that effect and contribute their respective easements.

Because the easements were granted pursuant to the agreement between them, no deduction is allowed. That is because Black and White were discharging a legal obligation by conveying their easements, not making a charitable contribution.

There is another way to accomplish what Black and White want that would probably (there are no rulings on this plan) preserve their deductions. When a land trust seeks to obtain conservation easements from several landowners to advance a conservation goal that could not be met by the piecemeal contribution of easements, the land trust may agree to escrow easements until it has received enough of them to accomplish its goal. Such an arrangement does not preclude donative intent because the agreement runs between the landowner and the land trust, rather than between landowners. Note that, until the easements are put to record, no deductible gift has been made. Note also that it would be important for the land trust in such a case to have a legitimate conservation justification for the plan.

Example Two: It turns out that the Black and White farms (from the preceding example) comprise a historic Civil War battlefield. Events of considerable national significance happened on both farms. The local land trust has been approached by the Black family to protect its farm. However, being purists, the land trust's board members say that they really aren't interested in protecting just a portion of the battlefield; they want both farms.

For fear that the Blacks will change their mind while it is working on the Whites, the land trust asks the Blacks to put their easement in escrow (essentially in trust) with an independent third party (the escrow agent); typically, the escrow agent is an attorney or title company. The easement would be held by the escrow agent according to a contract that provides that the easement will be held in escrow until the land trust has obtained an easement from the White family. When the White easement is obtained, the escrow agent would release the Blacks' easement to the land trust, which then would put both easements to record.

The escrow agreement further provides that in the event the land trust is unsuccessful in obtaining a satisfactory easement from the Whites within one year of deposit of the Black's easement into escrow, the escrow will terminate and the Blacks' easement will be returned to them.

Within six months of deposit of the Blacks' easement in escrow the land trust has a satisfactory easement from the Whites in hand. The trust records both easements, and both Black and White get a tax deduction.

Because the escrow agreement ran to the benefit of the land trust, which is a tax-exempt organization, conveying the easement pursuant to the terms of that contract should not affect the deductibility of the easement contribution. That is because, as a general proposition, complying with an enforceable pledge to make a charitable contribution, where the pledge is made directly to a charity, does not preclude donative intent. The pledge and the performance of the pledge, having been made out of charitable motives and without any expectation of receiving, or right to receive, any economic benefit in exchange, should be accepted as acts done with donative intent. Here again, this is an untried solution.

3. Conservation Buyer Transactions

Occasionally, a landowner decides to offer his land for sale only to a buyer who will place a conservation easement on the property after closing. When the sales contract imposes an obligation on the buyer to convey the easement after closing, the grant of the easement constitutes performance of a contractual obligation to a private individual, not a charitable contribution. This is true even though the buyer receives no compensation for the easement grant.

123

A variation of the foregoing occurs when the seller grants an option to a land trust to acquire a conservation easement on his land and the land is sold subject to the option. In such a situation, the option is a feature of the title to the property and, therefore, a binding part of the private contract between the buyer and the seller. Furthermore, the buyer, who is obligated to honor the option, did not grant the option; thus, any charitable intention that may have been part of the option grant cannot be attributed to the buyer. For this reason, conveyance of the easement pursuant to the option is the discharge of a private contractual obligation, not likely to be recognized as a charitable contribution.

Until recently, it was believed by many that there would be a different outcome if the prospective buyer herself granted an option to a land trust, exercisable by the land trust *if* the buyer completed the purchase. Similarly, it was believed that a binding pledge to a land trust by a prospective buyer prior to closing to contribute an easement after closing would not preclude a deduction for the contribution. In both cases it was believed that the option, or the pledge, being made directly to a public charity by the person who would make the contribution and claim the deduction, would not preclude a deduction for the contribution pursuant to the option or pledge. The IRS has (unofficially) said that a pledge made prior to the acquisition of title constitutes a restriction on the land that must be considered by the easement appraiser in the event that an easement is later contributed. This is likely to preclude any significant value in the easement.

a. IRS Notice 2004-41 and Conservation Buyer Transactions

In July 2004, the IRS published Notice 2004-41 highly critical of certain types of conservation buyer transactions. A copy of the notice appears in appendix D. The notice states in part, "Some taxpayers are claiming inappropriate charitable contribution deductions under section 170 [of the Code] for cash payments or easement transfers to charitable organizations in connection with the taxpayers' purchases of real property" (emphasis added).

The notice specifically criticizes a type of two-step conservation buyer transaction. In this type of transaction a land trust would sell property and retain a conservation easement. In order to recover what it paid for the property, in spite of the easement, the land trust would require the buyer to make two payments, one for the property, equal to its appraised value as restricted by the easement, the second a cash contribution equal to the value of the easement. In this way the land trust would be able to recover the full, unrestricted value of the property, and the buyer would be able to deduct the value of the easement (without any of the complications associated with easement contributions).

However, the notice said that, in such cases, the IRS would treat both payments (i.e., the payment of the purchase price *and* the cash contribution) as payment for the property and deny the purchaser any charitable deduction for the cash contribution.

Example: The Blue Land Trust bought Blue Acre Farm for $2 million. It later sold the farm, retaining a conservation easement on it. The buyer paid the trust $2 million for the property, the value of which, subject to the retained easement, had already been established by a qualified appraisal to be $1 million. The trust formally acknowledged to the buyer that the buyer had "overpaid" for the property by $1 million, which both buyer and trust acknowledged was intended as a charitable contribution. The buyer successfully claimed a $1 million deduction for the charitable contribution to the Blue Land Trust represented by his overpayment for the land.

According (unofficially) to an IRS representative, the buyer in this example is entitled to a charitable deduction for the $1 million overpayment because the structure of the transaction provides the IRS with information that allows it to evaluate whether the overpayment was based on a valid easement and easement valuation. Furthermore, this is an example of a dual purpose contribution, like the purchase of the ticket to the charity ball, described previously. In the type of two-step transaction criticized by Notice 2004-41 the IRS had no way of knowing that the cash contribution was connected with the acquisition of property or a conservation easement and no way of knowing whether the buyer was claiming more of a deduction than was appropriate (e.g., the buyer could pay the land trust $500,000 for the restricted property that is really worth $1 million and make a cash contribution of $1.5 million for which the buyer claims a deduction, thereby converting $500,000 of what should have been a nondeductible payment into a claimed charitable deduction).

Few land trusts have the resources to acquire land and resell it. More frequently, land trusts try to match conservation-worthy land with conservation-minded buyers who are willing to commit to protect the land if they acquire it. Unfortunately, Notice 2004-41's rather vague and generalized condemnation of all easement conveyances made in connection with the acquisition of real property has cast doubt on those sorts of transactions, as well. As a result, enforceable commitments by prospective buyers to protect land once it is acquired may result in the denial of any deduction for an easement contribution made pursuant to the commitment.

Notice 2004-41 also raises questions about *any easement granted in connection with the purchase of real property*. Again, the language of the notice that creates the issue is this: "Some taxpayers are claiming inappropriate charitable contribution deductions under section 170 [of the Code] for cash payments or easement transfers to charitable organizations *in connection with* the taxpayers' purchases of real property" (emphasis added).

"In connection with" is very broad language. It is unlikely that such language condemns all conservation buyer transactions in which a buyer formally commits to a land trust that he will protect property after he acquires it. However, IRS personnel responsible for the notice have refused to provide any clarification, or to agree that any type of conservation buyer transaction involving an enforceable commitment, other than that described in the preceding example, is beyond the reach of the notice. Therefore, the landowner advisors with whom I am acquainted (including me) are recommending to their landowner clients not to enter into *any* form of agreement to protect land before they have actually acquired that land.

Underscoring this issue, Form 8283 (see section II, A of chapter 6) now requires a statement from the easement donor as to whether the easement described in the form was granted to obtain a governmental approval or as part of a contractual arrangement. Obviously, affirmative answers to that question will alert the IRS to easements conveyed pursuant to contract. That would include charitable, but enforceable, pledges or options, *regardless of when the pledge or option is granted*—that is, either before or after the donor has acquired title. While I am not aware of any basis on which the IRS could successfully challenge a conservation easement granted pursuant to a charitable pledge or option agreement, provided that the pledge or option agreement is made after the donor acquires title, the reporting requirement still compels disclosure of such commitments.

In addition to the disclosure required of donors on Form 8283, Form 990, an information return that land trusts and other exempt organizations are required to file with the IRS, now requires land trusts to disclose whether they engaged in any transactions described in Notice 2004-41 during the preceding tax year. See Form 990, Schedule A, Part III, line 3c. Note that the Land Trust Alliance's position on this requirement is that it requires land trusts to report only transactions in which the buyer makes a cash contribution to a land trust in connection with the acquisition of property from the land trust. However, the transactions covered by the notice are not limited to such transactions.

b. Promissory Estoppel and Conservation Buyer Transactions

An unexplored issue relating to conservation buyer transactions has to do with the doctrine of *promissory estoppel* (also known as the doctrine of detrimental reliance). The principle is simple. If person number one promises something to person number two, and person number two relies on that promise to her detriment, person number one must keep the promise. For example, you ask me to paint your garage, so I go out and buy the paint. You change your mind and say you've gotten a better deal from someone else. You are bound by your promise, even though there was no formal contract, simply because I relied on your promise in buying the paint.

Now let us consider this concept in the context of a conservation buyer deal. A number of conservation buyer transactions are based on a handshake. There is no formal contract. However, let us suppose that a buyer has given a handshake promise to a seller that if the seller will sell the land to the buyer, the buyer will place a conservation easement on it after the purchase has been concluded. After the closing the buyer changes his mind and refuses to put an easement in place. The seller, who relied on the buyer's handshake promise to protect the land after the closing, sues the buyer on the grounds that he would never have sold the land to the buyer had the buyer not promised to protect the land. In effect, the seller is arguing that he relied on the buyer's handshake promise to his detriment (he sold the property to the buyer in reliance on the buyer's promise), and now the buyer must perform.

There are several issues here. It is the law in most, possibly all, states that any agreement pertaining to the conveyance of real property or any interest in real property must be in writing to be enforceable. This rule is part of the "statute of frauds." Can promissory estoppel take an oral promise regarding the conveyance of land or an interest in land outside of the operation of the statute of frauds? In theory, yes. If so, does that mean that when the buyer is forced to contribute the easement that he promised the seller he would contribute, he is not entitled to a tax deduction because he lacks donative intent? Arguably, yes.

These are questions that are only raised, not answered, here. However, depending on the answers, detrimental reliance could shed a whole new light on handshake conservation buyer transactions. For a technical discussion of the effect of promissory estoppel on transactions that are subject to the statute of frauds, the reader is directed to volume 10 of *Williston on Contracts*, 4th ed., section 27:14.

c. Conditions in Land Sales Contracts May Affect Deductions

When an appraiser values easement property in the before-easement part of an easement appraisal, he must consider everything that affects the value of that property. Among the factors that may affect value include the terms of a contract for the sale of land. Such terms may lead to some unplanned consequences, as described in the following example.

Example: Developer and buyer enter into a contract for the sale of land. The contract stipulates that the property will be sold subject to a conservation easement to be granted prior to closing by the developer. The easement is being granted because protecting the property being sold is critical to the remainder of the developer's project, and the developer plans to claim a deduction. The contract price reflects the reduced value due to the proposed conservation easement restrictions. The developer executes the contract with the buyer and promptly thereafter conveys the conservation easement, for which it claims a deduction equal to the difference in the value of the property unrestricted by the easement and restricted by the easement.

The IRS could challenge the deduction on these grounds: When the easement was conveyed, the property was subject to a binding contract of sale that provided that the property would be sold restricted by a conservation easement, and the price agreed to in the contract reflected the value of the property after the easement was in place. Because the contract was in place at the time the easement was conveyed, the IRS could argue that the contract established the value of the property prior to contribution of the easement. Because the contract price already reflected the reduction in value due to the easement, it is likely that the value before the contribution of the easement but after the signing of the contract, and after the contribution of the easement was the same, providing grounds for the IRS to challenge the deduction.

III. The Conveyance of a Conservation Easement Reduces the Basis of the Easement Property: Regulations Section 1.170A-14(h)(3)(iii)

The donor of a conservation easement is required to reduce his basis in the easement property to reflect the value of the contributed easement (basis is, essentially, what was paid for the property; see the discussion of basis in section I, H of this chapter). The reduction in value must equal the proportion of the unrestricted fair market value of the land represented by the value of the easement on the date of the contribution.

Example: Mr. Brown contributed an easement on his land. Before the easement was imposed, the land was valued at $1 million. After the easement, the land was valued at $700,000. Therefore, the value of the easement was $300,000 ($1,000,000 − $700,000). Mr. Brown's basis in his land was $100,000 before the contribution. The easement represents 30 percent of the unrestricted value of the land when the contribution was made ($300,000 / $1,000,000). Therefore, Mr. Brown's adjusted basis after the easement contribution will be $70,000 ($100,000 − [.30 × $100,000]).

As noted in section II, C of chapter 5, basis adjustment does not reflect "enhancement" of adjoining unrestricted land. See example (11), Regulations section 1.170A-14(h)(3)(iii). Even though enhancement may reduce an easement reduction, it does not affect the appraised value of the easement itself; therefore the value of the easement before subtraction of enhancement must be used to adjust the donor's basis. The result is different where the donor contributes a conservation easement over only part of his land. In such a case the appraiser is required to value the entire parcel before and after the contribution of the easement (both the portion covered by the easement and the portion not covered by the easement) to determine the net value of the easement. In such a case, the value of the easement directly incorporates the appreciation in the unprotected balance of the donor's land, reducing the value of the easement itself and, therefore (it would appear), reducing the adjustment in the donor's basis.

129

It is logical that basis reduction is required whether or not the grantor of the easement contributed the easement, sold it for fair market value, or sold it for a bargain price. In each case the easement represents an interest in the property that has been conveyed away, and the remaining property interest has been, accordingly, reduced. The basis reduction in the case of a full cash sale is equal to the price received for the easement. In the case of the grant of an easement in a bargain sale, the basis reduction is equal to the appraised value of the easement on which the bargain sale deduction was based.

IV. Treatment of Easement Contributions by Real Estate Developers

An increasing number of real estate developers are viewing conservation easements as an important part of real estate development. They (correctly) view easements as enhancing the value of a project and its desirability to buyers, and as generating tax deductions to offset the proceeds of lot sales (which is not necessarily correct). However, tax deductions for easement contributions by developers are complicated.

A. Deductions for Contributions of a Conservation Easement on "Inventory Property" Will Be Limited to Basis

First, tax deductions for easement contributions by real estate developers may be limited to the developer's basis in the easement, just as in the case of the contribution of a conservation easement on land owned by the donor for one year or less (see section I, H of this chapter). When a developer places an easement on land "held for sale in the ordinary course of business," that land is considered "ordinary income property," or "inventory" (Regulations section 1.170A-4(b)(1)). That characterization means that the property is not capital gain property; therefore, any deduction for a contribution of an easement over the property will be limited to the donor's basis in the easement.

Technically speaking, a deduction for a contribution of ordinary income property (e.g., lots held for sale by a developer) must be reduced by the amount of gain that would not have been considered long-term gain had the property been sold on the day of the contribution (Regulations section 1.170A-4(a)(1)). Because the sale of ordinary income property generates ordinary income rather than capital gain, this rule essentially limits the deduction to the dealer's basis in the easement.

It is possible for a dealer in real estate to hold property primarily as investment property (a capital asset) and not for sale to customers (inventory). The contribution of a conservation easement on a capital asset will not be limited to basis.

Example: Jack Hoyle is a real estate developer. He has developed 50 lots for sale but has identified 100 acres of the development property, which have never been offered for sale, for open-space protection. On his books Jack carries the 50 lots as inventory and the 100 acres as a capital asset.

Five years go by, and after having sold 40 lots, Jack decides to start a new project and wrap this one up. He agrees with a local land trust to donate a conservation easement on the remaining 10 lots plus the 100 acres. His basis in the portion of easement on the 10 lots is $100,000, and his deduction cannot exceed that amount for that portion of the easement, even though the easement on the lots is appraised at $2 million. That portion of the easement on the 100 acres is appraised at $5 million.

Jack will be allowed to deduct $100,000 for the contribution of the easement on the lots because his deduction relates to the contribution of ordinary income property. He will be allowed to deduct the full $5 million on the 100 acres because that property was clearly not held for "sale to customers in the ordinary course of his trade or business" and is treated as a capital asset held for investment (Regulations section 1.170A-4(b)(1)).

B. Enhancement to the Development

Another complication for the contribution of a conservation easement by a developer is enhancement (see the discussion of enhancement in section II of chapter 5). If the developer protects one portion of his land and develops another, the easement will increase the value of the development portion, requiring an offset to his deduction. The "related party" rules with respect to enhancement require an offset for enhancement when the developed and protected portions of a project are owned by parties related by blood or by business interests. If the easement covers a portion of property under common ownership, the value of the entire property, both before and after the easement, must be appraised to determine the value of the easement. In either case, the increase in value of unrestricted property due to the easement will affect the amount of the deduction for the easement.

C. Quid pro Quo Problems

Complex mixed-use developments are sometimes required to be rezoned, often as a "planned unit development," or according to some other master plan. Open space is often presented within such plans as an integral part of the project and a selling point for its approval by the locality. If the open-space component is approved as part of the development, its preservation may be considered mandated by the governmental approval, making the open-space preservation a government mandate and precluding a deduction on quid pro quo grounds (see the discussion of quid pro quo in section II, B of this chapter).

This is not to say that a developer cannot, or should not, use conservation easements as part of planned development projects. But to be deductible, an easement should be incorporated in the very early planning of a project. Furthermore, to preserve deductibility, a developer will almost always have to be willing to contribute the easement with no strings attached—that is, no commitment of any type of development approval may be included as part of the contribution. Without such a "gap" between the contribution and approval of the project, the IRS is likely to view the contribution as part of a quid pro quo deal that precludes a deduction.

D. New Reporting Requirements

The IRS has become very skeptical of conservation easements granted as part of development projects. Form 990 now requires land trusts to report if they hold any easements on golf courses or within adjoining developments (although it is understood that this information will no longer be required on 2008 Form 990s). The information provided will help the IRS investigate deductions for conservation easement grants arising out of such projects.

Example One: The Lost Path Ranch was conceived by developer Jay Brown as a high-end, high-amenity, low-density residential development. Lots would be limited to only 10 percent of the ranch; the remainder of the ranch would be secured by private covenants running to the benefit of the lot owners, and by a conservation easement. Brown hired an expensive land planning firm specializing in this type of project. Early in the planning process the firm encouraged Brown to place an easement on the open-space portion of the property prior to starting the development approval process. However, Brown was convinced that if he did that, he would be giving up substantial value without any assurance that the development approval would follow. He therefore instructed the planners to proceed with the planning process and put the easement contribution on hold.

The final plans for the project turned out much as Brown originally envisioned, and the locality, thrilled with the inclusion of so much open space, approved the project quickly. The final master plan incorporated in the rezoning clearly showed 90 percent open space.

Before selling any lots, Brown conveyed the easement over the open space shown on the approved plan, and it became a major part of his sales pitch. He later obtained an appraisal indicating that the development potential of the 90 percent open space eliminated by the easement was worth $30 million, and the increase in value resulting to the remainder of the project amounted to $10 million (see the discussion of enhancement in section II of chapter 5), allowing a $20 million deduction. The Pipeslope Land Trust, which holds the easement, reported on its Form 990 for the year in which it received the Lost Path Ranch easement that it held an easement as part of a development. Brown also reported, as required, on a schedule attached to his Form 8283, that the easement was granted in connection with a development approval.

The IRS followed up the next year with an inquiry about all of Pipeslope's easements held as part of development projects and learned of the Lost Path Ranch project. The result was that the IRS denied Brown's deduction on the grounds that the land protected by the easement was already zoned as open space pursuant to the master plan. Although the master plan did not require the contribution of the easement—it was not a quid pro quo transaction—the zoning approval limited the use of the open space to noncommercial recreational use and agriculture. Because the easement mirrored the zoning limitations, the before and after values of the easement land were the same, and the easement had no deductible value.

Example Two: Had Brown taken the planners' advice and granted the conservation easement prior to submitting the master plan for review and approval of the local government, the difference between the before and after values would have reflected the fact that the protected property could have been intensely developed. Of course, there would have been enhancement to the unprotected remainder, but Brown could have put the entire property under easement, not just the open space, and thereby limited the amount of development to which enhancement could be attributed. Such an approach would have provided a solid basis for an easement deduction.

However, if the easement had been granted prior to master plan approval, the open space would already have been secured. Indeed, committing the open space so early in the project might have hampered approval of the development and would certainly have limited the developer's ability to respond to local concerns. Furthermore, it is possible that the locality would have seen no real incentive for granting the master plan approval if the open space was already permanently in place.

The use of conservation easements by developers *with the expectation of reaping substantial tax benefits* poses some tough choices.

V. Corporations, Partnerships, Limited Liability Companies, and Trusts

The amount that may be deducted for the contribution of a conservation easement by an artificial entity may be different than the amount an individual may deduct for the same contribution. The following is a brief description of the rules governing limitations on deductions associated with corporations, partnerships, limited liability companies, and trusts. This is a very complex area of tax law, and no one should proceed in this area without the assistance of tax counsel who has a comprehensive understanding of these rules, which extend considerably beyond what is described here.

A. Corporations

There are two types of corporations for purposes of taxation: C corporations (C-corps) and S corporations (S-corps). A C-corp is a corporation whose income is taxed at the corporate level, not the shareholder level. An S-corp is taxed at the shareholder level, not the corporate level.

1. C Corporations

A C-corp's deduction for the contribution of a conservation easement is limited to no more than 10 percent of its taxable income. In 2006 Congress created an exception from the 10 percent limit for a C-corp whose stock is not publicly traded, provided that more than 50 percent of the corporation's income is from the "business of farming." See section I, C, 1, b, 2 of this chapter for a description of the 2006 law's application to corporations. As previously noted, the 2006 law has now expired and is applicable only to corporate easement contributions in 2006 and 2007.

Getting property out of a C-corp and into the hands of the stockholders in order to avoid the 10 percent of taxable income limitation is not easy. Typically, distribution of a C-corp's assets to its shareholders is a taxable event and will significantly offset, or eliminate, any tax benefit that the shareholders might realize from the subsequent contribution of a conservation easement.

2. S Corporations

[Note: The law has been clarified regarding S corporations since press time. See Appendix E for the clarifications.]

The deductions of an S-corp are passed through to the shareholders in proportion to their ownership interest in the corporation. S-corp deductions are further limited by the shareholders' basis in their stock in the corporation. The shareholders' basis is a function of what they paid for the stock, along with subsequent adjustments to reflect items of income and loss (including deductions) allocated to each shareholder. In general, a shareholder may not deduct more than her basis in the stock of the S-corp, plus the amount of any debt owed by the S-corp to the shareholder; and any debt of the S-corp for which the shareholder is personally liable (Code section 1366(d)(1), Regulations section 1.1366-2(a)(1)).

In 2006, as part of the enhancements for easement contributions it enacted, Congress *supposedly* enacted a provision that eliminated most of the limitations imposed on the ability of an S-corp shareholder to take a deduction for a conservation easement contribution (see Code section 1367(a)(2)). It was believed by some practitioners that the law was amended to allow S-corp shareholders to deduct their entire proportionate share of a conservation easement contribution, based on their ownership interest in the S-corp, without regard to their basis in the S-corp's stock.

A careful reading of the new law regarding charitable contributions by an S-corp suggests, however, that the only change made was the amount by which S-corp shareholders are required to adjust their stock basis to reflect a charitable contribution by the corporation of property. The old rule required a shareholder to reduce her stock basis by her pro rata share of the value of the gift. The new rule limits the basis adjustment to the shareholder's pro rata share of the corporation's adjusted basis in the property that was contributed. This rule reduces the amount that the shareholder must recognize as gain in the event of a future sale of stock in the corporation.

However, the examples provided by the Joint Committee on Taxation accompanying its explanation of the new law suggest that the law eliminates the requirement that shareholders may deduct no more for a charitable contribution made by the S-corp than their basis in their stock in the corporation. A number of authorities believe that Congress intended, with the changes to the foregoing rules, to allow S-corp shareholders to take deductions for charitable contributions made by S-corps without regard to the shareholders' basis in the stock of the corporation, as reflected in the foregoing example. On close reading, however, the new law seems at odds with the committee's example.

So that readers may come to their own conclusions, here is what Congress said (the italicized last paragraph is the new language added in 2006):

1367. Adjustments to basis of stock of shareholders, etc.

(a) General rule.—

(1) Increases in basis.—The basis of each shareholder's stock in an S corporation shall be increased for any period by the sum of the following items determined with respect to that shareholder for such period:

(A) the items of income described in subparagraph (A) of section 1366(a)(1),

(B) any nonseparately computed income determined under subparagraph (B) of section 1366(a)(1), and

(C) the excess of the deductions for depletion over the basis of the property subject to depletion.

(2) Decreases in basis.—The basis of each shareholder's stock in an S corporation shall be decreased for any period (but not below zero) by the sum of the following items determined with respect to the shareholder for such period:

(A) distributions by the corporation which were not includible in the income of the shareholder by reason of section 1368,

(B) the items of loss and deduction described in subparagraph (A) of section 1366(a)(1),

(C) any nonseparately computed loss determined under subparagraph (B) of section 1366(a)(1),

(D) any expense of the corporation not deductible in computing its taxable income and not properly chargeable to capital account, and

(E) the amount of the shareholder's deduction for depletion for any oil and gas property held by the S corporation to the extent such deduction does not exceed the proportionate share of the adjusted basis of such property allocated to such shareholder under section 613A(c)(11)(B).

The decrease under subparagraph (B) by reason of a charitable contribution (as defined in section 170(c)) of property shall be the amount equal to the shareholder's pro rata share of the adjusted basis of such property. The preceding sentence shall not apply to contributions made in taxable years beginning after December 31, 2007. [Emphasis added.]

And, to give equal time, here is the explanation of this provision provided by the Joint Committee on Taxation:

> The provision provides that the amount of a shareholder's basis reduction in the stock of an S corporation by reason of a charitable contribution made by the corporation will be equal to the shareholder's pro rata share of the adjusted basis of the contributed property.
>
> Thus, for example, assume an S corporation with one individual shareholder makes a charitable contribution of stock with a basis of $200 and a fair market value of $500. The shareholder will be treated as having made a $500 charitable contribution (or a lesser amount if the special rules of section 170(e) apply), and will reduce the basis of the S corporation stock by $200. (Technical Explanation of H.R. 4, the Pension Protection Act of

2006, as Passed by the House on July 28, 2006, and as Considered by the Senate on August 3, 2006.)

This new tax benefit, whatever it may have been, expired December 31, 2007. The only reason for including a discussion of it here is that it does apply to easement contributions made during 2006 or 2007, and it may be renewed (hopefully in less ambiguous form) by Congress in the future. If the 2006 law does what the committee example suggests, here is an expanded example of how it should work:

Example: The Blinkers Corporation, an S-corp, made a contribution of a conservation easement on land that it had owned for more than one year. The value of the easement was $1 million. The corporation's basis in the property subject to the easement was $500,000. Jerry Johns owns 75 percent of the stock of Blinkers Corporation, for which he paid $375,000. Over the years he has taken losses, and other deductions, amounting to $250,000, the result of which has been a downward adjustment in his basis in the stock of the corporation to $125,000 ($375,000–$250,000). Under the law prior to 2006, Jerry could deduct only $125,000 in connection with the corporation's gift of the easement, because his basis in the Blinkers Corporation stock was only $125,000.

However, the 2006 law (supposedly) allowed S-corp shareholders to deduct their pro rata share of the value of a contribution of property (including conservation easements) made by the corporation without regard to their stock basis. In other words, under the 2006 law, Jerry may (depending on one's reading of the law) deduct $750,000 in connection with the corporation's easement contribution. Of course, his basis in his stock would be reduced to zero as a result.

B. Limited Liability Companies and Partnerships

Limited liability companies (LLCs) have some of the attributes of corporations (e.g., protection from corporate liabilities for members) but are taxed like partnerships (see IRS Pub. 1066, rev. July 2003, pp. 1–16). Both partnerships and LLCs pass deductions through to the owners of the entity. (See Code section 702(a)(4) and Regulations sections 1.702-1(a)(4) and 1.703-1(a)(2)(iv).) The owners are called members in the case of LLCs and partners in the case of partnerships.

Partnerships and LLCs allow partners/members to allocate

interests in the entity in a manner other than equal shares, provided that allocation has "economic substance." For example, one member may have contributed more money to an LLC, or accepted liability for an LLC debt, and may therefore be entitled to a larger ownership interest in the LLC. Code section 704 and Regulations section 1.704-1 cover the determination of a partner's "distributive share" of a partnership.

Limited partnerships (LPs) have a "general partner" and one or more "limited partners." The general partner manages the business of the partnership and is solely liable for its actions. The limited partners do not play a management role but provide the capital for its operations. They receive income and deductions from the operations of the LP according to a partnership agreement that allocates income and deductions between the general and limited partners, and among the limited partners. Tax deductions, including charitable deductions, are allocated according to the agreement, provided that the agreement has "economic substance."

Example One: The Blue Lake Limited Liability Company owns a 500-acre farm that includes a 100-acre lake. There are 10 members of the LLC. John Jay, the original owner of the property, set up the LLC and originally was the sole member. Over the years he has given membership interests in the LLC to his five children and their four spouses. Each family member has received a 5 percent interest in the LLC. Thus, John owns 55 percent of the LLC, and each of his children and their spouses own 5 percent individually.

The Blue Lake LLC donated a conservation easement on the farm. The easement is valued at $2 million. Therefore, John is entitled to a deduction of $1.1 million ($2,000,000 × .55), and each of the other members in the LLC are entitled to a deduction of $100,000 ($2,000,000 × .05). The same results would occur if the farm had been owned by a family partnership.

Example Two: The Scam LLC owns a 5,000-acre ranch in northern Montana. Scam's sole member is Jim Scam. Scam LLC paid $500,000 for the ranch in 1985. Jim does not want to sell the ranch, but he does want to get some money for a portion of his interest in the LLC. Therefore, he offers to sell a 49 percent interest in the LLC for $1 million to Jonas Schuyler, who had a bang-up year on the stock market and, accordingly, had ordinary income of $10 million for the year. Jim convinces Jonas that for $1 million, Jonas can obtain a $5 million tax deduction that will save him $2.2 million in federal and California income taxes (resulting in a combined top rates of 44 percent). This is because Scam LLC plans to contribute a conservation easement to a local land trust, and the estimated value of the easement is $10.2 million (of which, as a 49 percent owner, Jonas would be entitled to $5 million). Jim also requires that Jonas grant an option to Jim to reacquire the 49 percent interest for $90,000 within two years. Taking into account the net loss in membership value, if the option were exercised, Jonas would still net $1,290,000 ($2,200,000 – $910,000).

The only problem with this scenario is whether Jonas's 49 percent interest in an LLC worth at least $10 million, for which Jonas paid only $1 million, has any economic substance. Even given the discount for a minority interest, and the obligation to resell the stock, it is likely that 49 percent is far too big a percentage for the $1 million payment. It is also likely Jonas would have a great deal of difficulty explaining a rationale for such a deal other than tax avoidance. In other words, the IRS is likely to "collapse" this deal using the Step Transaction Doctrine (see chapter 2, section VI) and successfully argue that the only purpose of the transaction was tax avoidance.

139

C. Trusts (Other Than Charitable Remainder Trusts)

Other than "charitable remainder trusts," qualified under Code section 664 and not governed by the rules described below, there are three types of trusts, and each type is treated differently for taxation purposes.

1. Grantor Trusts

Grantor trusts are trusts in which the person creating the trust (the grantor) retains certain rights or interests in the trust. Most typically, the grantor retains the right to amend or terminate the trust at will. People often create grantor trusts to avoid probate. Grantor trusts are ignored for most purposes of taxation, including federal income and estate taxes. (See Code section 671 and Regulations sections 1.671-1 and 1.671-3(a)(1).)

Therefore, if a grantor trust makes a charitable contribution of a conservation easement on land owned by the trust, the tax deduction passes through the trust directly to the persons who are deemed to be the owners of the trust, as though they themselves had made the contribution.

The income and deductions generated by a grantor trust are taxed entirely to the owner of the trust. The owner of the trust is the person who has a power exercisable solely by herself to appropriate the income or principal of the trust to her personal use (see Code section 677 and Regulations section 1.677(a)-1). It is possible for more than one person to be treated as owner of a grantor trust (Code section 678 and Regulations section 1.678(a)-1).

Example: Jon creates a trust and conveys his farm to the trust. In the trust instrument he retains the full right to revoke or amend the trust. The trust is, therefore, a grantor trust. Jon is the sole trustee and sole beneficiary of the trust until his death. As sole trustee he makes a charitable contribution of a conservation easement to the JY Land Trust. The value of the easement is $500,000. Jon, as the 100 percent owner of the trust, is entitled to a deduction for $500,000, as though the trust did not exist.

Note that even if Jon were not the trustee and sole beneficiary but held the right to amend or revoke the trust, he would still be deemed the owner of the trust.

---

2. Personal Residence Trusts and Qualified Personal Residence Trusts

Grantor trusts include personal residence trusts and qualified personal residence trusts (QPRTs). Most conservation easements will not pertain to personal residence trusts or QPRTs, because the tax law strictly limits the amount of land that may be included in such trusts. It is therefore unlikely that there is sufficient land in such trusts to merit conservation. However, it does not appear that the conveyance of a conservation easement by such a trust would violate the requirements of the tax code. (See, generally, Code section 2702 and Regulations section 25.2702-5.) There are also several private letter rulings (PLRs) that confirm that a residence subject to a conservation easement may be placed into a personal residence trust or QPRT. (See, e.g., PLR 199916030 (1999).)

3. Simple and Complex Trusts

Trusts other than grantor trusts are classified by federal tax law as either "simple trusts" or "complex trusts." Simple trusts are required to distribute all of their income annually, they can make no charitable contributions, and they do not distribute any of the trust principal during the tax year (Regulations section 1.651(a)(1)). A trust that is not a simple trust is a complex trust (Code section 661). Complex trusts are allowed to accumulate income.

Neither simple nor complex trusts pass deductions through to the beneficiaries of the trust. Income and deductions are determined and taxed at the trust level. However, "distributable net income" paid to beneficiaries is taxable to the beneficiaries and is deductible to the trust. Complex trusts are allowed a deduction against trust *income* for payments out of the income of the trust directed by the trust instrument to be paid for charitable purposes (Code section 642(c)).

However, if the trust instrument does not expressly authorize payment of trust income for charitable purposes, no deduction under Code section 642(c) is allowed. (See Rev. Rul. 2004-5.) More important, *no deduction is allowed for the contribution of a conservation easement* regardless of whether the trust instrument authorizes such a contribution. This is because federal tax law allows no deduction for a payment out of the "corpus" (the principal) of a trust. Deductions are limited to amounts paid from income only, and conservation easements are considered part of trust corpus, not income. Thus, other than grantor trusts, trusts are not allowed a deduction for the charitable contribution of a conservation easement because a conservation easement is considered a gift of principal, not income. See *Goldsby v. C.I.R.,* T.C. Memo 2206-274 (U.S. Tax Court, December 27, 2006), and Rev. Rul. 2003-123.

Example: Under the terms of the Dalmatian Trust the trustee is permitted to accumulate income and is authorized to make charitable contributions of cash and property to public charities recognized under Code section 501(c)(3). The trustee makes a $200,000 cash contribution to a local church for a new building and contributes a conservation easement over a farm owned by the trust. The conservation easement is valued at $1 million. The Dalmatian Trust had income of $400,000 during the year of these contributions. The trustee also makes a distribution to the beneficiaries of the trust in the amount of $200,000.

The Dalmatian Trust is permitted a deduction against the trust's $400,000 of income in the amount of $200,000 for the contribution to the church. The trust is also allowed a deduction of $200,000 for the distribution to the beneficiaries. Thus, the trust has no income tax liability for the year. The beneficiaries have collective taxable income from the trust of $200,000. However, no deduction is allowed for the contribution of the conservation easement to the trust, because the contribution was made out of the principal, not the income, of the trust. Furthermore, no charitable contribution for the value of the easement passes through to the beneficiaries of the trust. Thus, the value of the deduction for the easement contribution is lost.

VI. Federal Tax Treatment of State Tax Credits for Easement Contributions

A number of states provide credits against state income tax for easement contributions. Tax credits are much more powerful incentives for easement contributions than deductions, because credits directly offset tax liability, whereas deductions only reduce income against which tax is imposed. The following discussion is intended not to describe the various state credit programs but to summarize how tax credits are treated under federal tax law. It must be emphasized that there are a number of unknowns in this area, and neither the Congress nor the IRS has provided answers to all of the outstanding questions. Furthermore, state tax credit programs frequently change.

Some states allow tax credits to be transferred from the original easement donor to other taxpayers. The tax treatment of credits in the hands of the original recipient of a credit and in the hands of the transferee of a credit differs.

A. Treatment of the Original Credit Recipient

All of the information available about the treatment of tax credits comes from administrative publications of the IRS. There have been no cases or regulations on the topic of the treatment of conservation easement tax credits.

1. The Credit Is Not Taxable If Used Against the Original Recipient's Tax Liability

The IRS has consistently stated that, to the extent that a conservation easement tax credit is used to offset the original recipient's state tax liability, it is not taxable. The most recent statement came in IRS AM (Chief Counsel Attorney Memorandum) 2007-002. (AMs are not supposed to be used or cited as precedent; i.e., the information in an AM cannot be relied upon as binding the IRS.) However, the recipient's federal itemized deduction allowed under Code section 164 for the payment of state taxes will be reduced to the extent that state income tax liability is offset by the use of such credits.

Example: Jordan contributed a conservation easement on land in Virginia. Jordan is a Virginia taxpayer, and his easement contribution made him eligible for a Virginia income tax credit equal to 40 percent of the value of the easement. The value of the easement was $250,000; therefore, Jordan was entitled to a credit against his Virginia income tax of $100,000 ($250,000 × .40). Jordan's Virginia income tax liability for 2006 was just over $200,000 (Virginia's top rate is 5.75 percent, and Jordan's 2006 income was approximately $3,500,000). Jordan filed his 2006 Virginia income tax return and used the tax credit to "pay" $100,000 of his 2006 tax liability of $200,000. He sent along a check for $100,000 to cover the balance. When he files his federal return for 2007 and itemizes his deductions, he may claim a deduction of only $100,000 for his 2006 Virginia income tax payment because he "paid" $100,000 of his $200,000 tax liability with the credit.

---

2. Proceeds from the Sale of a Tax Credit Are Taxable As Ordinary Income

In the same AM 2007-002 referenced above, the IRS stated that the sale of a tax credit by the original recipient to another taxpayer is a taxable event under Code section 1001. The IRS also said that the original recipient's basis in the credit is zero, making the entire sales price received taxable. In another pronouncement (IRS CCA 200211042, a Chief Counsel Advisory, also not to be cited as precedent), the IRS ruled that a state tax credit is not a capital asset within the meaning of Code section 1221, and therefore the sale of a credit results in ordinary income, not capital gain, regardless of how long the seller has held the credit.

Example: Assume that Jordan, in the preceding example, sold his credit rather than using it against his Virginia income tax liability. He received $75,000 in 2007 for the credit (a 25 percent discount, which is not uncommon). He had held the credit for two years prior to the sale. He is required to report the $75,000 as income on his 2007 return and pay tax at the ordinary rate (assume 35 percent in Jordan's case), resulting in a tax on the credit sale of $26,250 ($75,000 × .35).

---

3. Does the Receipt of a Tax Credit Affect the Federal Deduction for the Contribution of the Easement?

The answer to the question of whether the receipt of a tax credit affects the federal deduction for the contribution of the easement is not yet known. The IRS has been considering whether receipt of a tax credit constitutes a quid pro quo that precludes the required donative intent (see IRS CCA 200238041). To date the IRS has issued no advice on this point. There are three obvious alternative answers to this question (and possibly more that are less obvious): (1) The credit is a payment for the easement that precludes donative intent, and no deduction is permitted. (2) The conveyance of an easement resulting in receipt of a tax credit is treated as a "bargain sale," and the amount of the credit must be subtracted from the value of the easement to determine the amount of the deduction. (3) The credit has no effect on the amount of the easement deduction.

It would seem unlikely and illogical that the IRS would rule that the receipt of a credit precludes any deduction for the easement at all. Whether, or when, the IRS will issue any additional comments on the questions raised in CCA 200238041 is unknown at this time.

B. Treatment of Transferees of Credits

Here again, there is very little to guidance when it comes to the income tax treatment of the transferees of state income tax credits.

1. Credit Transferees May Deduct State Taxes Paid with Credits

Use of a tax credit to pay state income tax by someone who acquired the credit from the original recipient of the credit results in a deduction under Code section 164(a) for payment of state income tax. This is different than treatment of use of a credit by the original recipient, which use reduces the deduction allowed under Code section 164(a) (see section VII, A, 1 of this chapter).

2. Taxable Gain (or Loss) May Result from Use of a Credit by a Transferee

The IRS has ruled that the transferee of a state income tax credit has acquired property with a basis equal to the purchase price of the credit (IRS AM 2007-002). The ruling also states that use of the credit may result in gain or loss under Code section 1001. However, the IRS has not said whether gain on the sale or use of a credit by a transferee would be taxed as ordinary income or capital gain.

VII. Tax Treatment of Expenses Incurred in Contributing a Conservation Easement

A frequent question is what expenses incurred by a donor in making an easement contribution are deductible. Typical expenses include legal fees, appraisal fees, surveyor's fees, recording fees, costs incurred for preparation of the natural resources inventory, and payments to land trusts to cover future stewardship expenses. As the reader will note, the discussion that follows is couched in such terms as "arguably" and "probably," because there is no formal IRS guidance or case law covering these matters (sound familiar?).

Code section 212(3) allows an individual to deduct expenses incurred "in connection with the determination, collection, or refund of any tax." Arguably, but based on no formal IRS rulings, this provision covers most of the expenses likely to be incurred by an easement donor in making a contribution, such as legal fees (insofar as those fees are incurred to ensure that the easement is in compliance with federal or state tax requirements); appraisal fees (because the appraisal is a tax code requirement); surveyor's fees (because a survey may be necessary to ensure that the easement is enforceable, which is a tax code requirement); recording fees (tax law requires that easements be recorded to be deductible); and costs incurred in preparation of a natural resources inventory (an express requirement of tax law). In other words, these expenses are all expenses arguably incurred "in connection with the determination . . . of . . . tax."

However, while *voluntary* contributions made to a land trust to assist it in monitoring and enforcing its easements are deductible under Code section 170, a payment *required* by the land trust as a condition of accepting the easement probably does not qualify as a charitable contribution because there is no donative intent (see section II of this chapter). Furthermore, because a payment made to provide for the monitoring or enforcement of conservation easements is not a payment made "in connection with the determination . . . of . . . tax," and because such a payment does not qualify under any other tax code provision as deductible, it is unlikely that such a payment is deductible.

Policy Update

As this book was going to press, the following provision of the "Food, Conservation, and Energy Act of 2008" was enacted by Congress over a presidential veto in May 2008, extending the tax incentives for conservation easement contributions enacted as part of the Pension Protection Act of 2006:

SEC. 15302. TWO-YEAR EXTENSION OF SPECIAL RULE ENCOURAGING CONTRIBUTIONS OF CAPITAL GAIN REAL PROPERTY FOR CONSERVATION PURPOSES.

(a) IN GENERAL.—

(1) INDIVIDUALS.—Section 170(b)(1)(E)(vi) (relating to termination) is amended by striking "December 31, 2007" and inserting "December 31, 2009".

(2) CORPORATIONS.—Section 170(b)(2)(B)(iii) (relating to termination) is amended by striking "December 31, 2007" and inserting "December 31, 2009".

(b) EFFECTIVE DATE.—The amendments made by this section shall apply to contributions made in taxable years beginning after December 31, 2007.

CHAPTER FIVE:

Easement Valuation

One of the most critical and frequently challenged aspects of easement deductions is the valuation of the easement. In my experience few conservation easement appraisals comply satisfactorily with the requirements of the Code and Regulations. Therefore, it is strongly recommended that every easement donor seeking a deduction have the easement appraisal reviewed by tax counsel familiar with the requirements of the Code and Regulations pertaining to conservation easement appraisals.

   Several methods of easement valuation are accepted by the Code and Regulations. They are described below.

I. Valuation Methodologies and Requirements

There are a number of appraisal methodologies in use today. The three most commonly used are the comparable sales method, the replacement value method, and the income approach. However, only the comparable sales method is appropriate for the valuation of conservation easements. In fact, there are two approaches to valuing conservation easements recognized by the Regulations. One is the comparable sales method, which I will call the direct comparable sales method. The other uses comparable sales indirectly as part of a before-and-after valuation of the property subject to the conservation easement being valued. These two methods and the important require-ments that pertain to the before-and-after method are described in this section I.

A. The Comparable Sales Method: Regulations Section 1.170A-14(h)(3)(i)

The Regulations provide that the preferred means of determining the value of a conservation easement for tax deduction purposes is the comparable sales method. This method determines the value of an easement by using recent sales of easements containing similar provisions over land comparable to the subject easement parcel. Assuming that the comparable easements were purchased at fair market value in "arm's-length" transactions (i.e., transactions uninfluenced by personal relationships and into which neither party is compelled to enter for any reason), their sale prices should be the best evidence of easement value.

Example: Haley Sears donated a conservation easement on a 500-acre farm just outside of Expensive, Pennsylvania. Pursuant to the Cheap County (within which Expensive lies) open-space program, there have been a number of conservation easement purchases. The current value being paid for a conservation easement comparable to the one contributed by Sears is $10,000 per acre. Assuming that there is nothing significant differentiating the easement donated by Sears and the other easements being purchased in the area (e.g., none have been sold as bargain sales for which a charitable deduction was sought, and the easement terms are all similar), the value of Sears's easement is $5 million ($10,000 × 500).

The Regulations recognize that in many cases there will not be a "substantial record" of comparable easement sales, and in such cases the Regulations allow easement valuations based on the "before-and-after" method described in the next section. However, if there is a substantial record of comparable easement sales, it can be expected that use of the before-and-after method will be challenged by the IRS.

B. The Before-and-After Valuation Method: Regulations Section 1.170A-14(h)(3)(i)

In the before-and-after approach to valuing an easement, the value of the easement property is determined before the easement is in place and after the easement is in place, using comparable sales for the unrestricted and restricted property. The difference between the two values represents the value of the contribution for deduction purposes (Regulations section 1.170A-14(h)(3)(i); Rev. Rul. 73-339, 1973-2 C.B. 68; and *Thayer v. Commissioner*, T.C. Memo 1977-370).

Example: Joan contributed a conservation easement on 100 acres. Her appraiser determined that before the easement was in place, the property was worth $700,000, based on comparable properties in the area. He also determined that after the easement was in place the same property is worth $100,000 (the easement allows no development and limits future use to agriculture). Therefore, the easement is worth $600,000 ($700,000 – $100,000).

1. Factors Required to Be Considered in the Before-and-After Method: Regulations Section 1.170A-14(h)(3)(ii)

Note that in the direct comparable sales method the value of the easement is determined directly using other easement values, while the before-and-after method derives the value of the easement indirectly by valuing the change in the property that is subject to the value of the easement being appraised. This opens the door to abuse when assumptions about the property subject to the easement are made that exaggerate its value. To minimize the potential for such abuse, the Regulations require that the determination of the fair market value of easement property before contribution of the conservation restriction must take into account *all* of the following factors:

- The current use of the property.
- An objective assessment of how immediate or remote the likelihood is that the property, absent the restriction, would in fact be developed. (Note that in this consideration it is likely that if the highest and best use of the property is as a farm for farming purposes—say a highly productive farm in the middle of Iowa, far removed from development pressure—this objective assessment would conclude that there is little likelihood of development whether or not a conservation easement is contributed. Such a conclusion would likely lead an appraiser to conclude that the before-and-after values of the easement property are essentially the same so that the easement has no deductible value.)
- Any effect on the value of the property resulting from zoning, conservation, or historic preservation laws that already restrict the property.

2. The Development Method of Determining the Before Value

Appraisers will occasionally use what is known as the "development method," or "build-out" method, to determine the highest-and-best-"before" easement value of property. While this method is not prohibited by tax law, it lends itself to abuse because of the significant number of assumptions on which it depends. Essentially, the method determines what the value of the property would be if it were fully developed into residential lots, rather than in its actual state.

In order to use the development method to determine the highest-and-best-use value, an appraiser is required to consider the following factors:

- *Legally permissible uses.* The appraiser *may not* consider uses that are not allowed by current zoning and subdivision regulations applicable to the property. The appraiser must consider restrictions imposed by other laws (e.g., the Endangered Species Act, federal wetlands regulations), as well as private restrictions such as restrictive covenants.
- *Physically possible uses.* The appraiser must take into account the physical characteristics of a property that limit its development potential. For example, an appraiser cannot assume that land on a 75 percent sandy slope is developable.
- *Financially feasible (and marketable) uses.* The appraiser must take into account the actual costs of development and sales, as well as the rate at which the local market will absorb any lots that may be developed. The appraiser must discount the projected selling price of lots to reflect such costs and absorption time.

Example: Joe Dokes owns 200 acres of land. At least 60 percent of the land is swamp, and the remainder is in slopes in excess of 50 percent. Local land-use regulations place Joe's land in the environmentally sensitive category, which allows one subdivision lot per 50 acres; however, no development is allowed in wetlands or on slopes in excess of 25 percent. Undaunted, Joe contributed a conservation easement to help overcome his reputation in the community as a convicted drug smuggler. He has a buddy from his prison days who has become an appraiser. Joe convinced his buddy that he could easily obtain a rezoning of the 200 acres to agricultural use, permitting 1 lot per 2 acres, and that he could develop at least 75 lots by draining the swamp. The easement allowed only one home site. The appraiser figured that if Joe could create the lots, each would sell for $100,000, making the total value of the 200 acres $20 million. The appraiser also figured that, limited to just one home site, the land is worth only $1 million, justifying a $19 million deduction. In exchange for the appraisal, Joe agreed to give his buddy 20 percent of his net tax savings from the anticipated deduction.

Needless to say, the IRS had been keeping a close eye on Joe and audited his return. Of course, sharing a percentage of the tax benefits with an appraiser is strictly prohibited and, in itself, discredits the appraisal. However, the appraiser's "extraordinary" assumptions with respect to valuation flew in the face of most of the rules. The IRS presented its own appraisal, which assumed that, given current regulations and the physical condition of the property, only one home site, the one reserved in the easement, could be built on the property in its unrestricted (before-easement) state. Therefore, it disallowed the entire deduction.

Appraisals using the development approach should be carefully documented. It is possible for an appraiser to include "extraordinary assumptions" in an appraisal, provided that there is a legally justifiable basis for such assumptions. For example, in appraising a property that is zoned agricultural but surrounded by residentially zoned land, an appraiser could obtain a written opinion from a qualified zoning lawyer that the subject property is legally entitled to a rezoning to residential use based on the zoning of the surrounding land.

3. The Problem of the After Value

One of the biggest challenges in the before-and-after method is finding comparables for the subject property in its after-easement condition. The best means of determining that value is to use comparable properties that have sold subject to conservation easements, provided that those other easements are comparable to the easement being appraised. Of course, this can be almost as difficult as finding comparable easement sales. Appraisers confronted with a lack of comparable properties sold subject to comparable easements often rely on sales of property that are restricted in some other fashion—for example, a wetland that cannot be developed, or farmland in a region where there is no market for residential development.

Another approach used by some appraisers is to collect a large base of sales data for property subject to conservation easements and to determine from that data the average percentage reduction in prices versus prices of unrestricted property. I understand that the use of such a database has been found to be acceptable evidence of value in at least one judicial review of an audit. However, it would seem advisable to use real comparable sales whenever possible.

4. Paired Sales Analyses

The before-and-after value method typically relies on the "comparable sales method" to determine the value of easement property before and after an easement is in place. This method requires the appraiser to determine the value of the easement property by looking at what comparable properties are selling for. A comparable property is one similar to the property being appraised in terms of zoning, physical access, proximity to services, physical characteristics, amenities, and size. It is possible to adjust the sales of properties that are not comparable to the subject property to make them more comparable. This is typically done using a "paired sales analysis." In a paired sales analysis the sales prices of properties that are comparable except for one characteristic—for example, one has a great view and the other has no view—are compared. The difference in values is assumed to be attributable to the one characteristic that the two properties do not have in common. Using a number of such comparisons, appraisers are able to determine how much to adjust the values of comparable properties to compensate for distinctions between them.

It is also necessary to adjust the value of comparable sales to reflect time elapsed from those sales to the present. This is done by computing the rate of change in sales prices over time and applying that rate to comparable sales to adjust them to reflect such change.

Example: In an earlier example, Haley Sears donated a conservation easement on a 500-acre farm just outside of Expensive, Pennsylvania. For this example, assume that there is no substantial record of comparable easement sales for the appraiser to draw on. Land comparable to the Sears farm in terms of zoning, physical access, proximity to services, and physical characteristics was, at the time of the easement contribution, selling for approximately $50,000 per acre. The Sears farm has exceptional views over a large public reservoir and park. A paired sales analysis has determined that such a view increases the property value by about

10 percent. Therefore, the appraiser can estimate the before value of the property at $55,000 ($50,000 × 1.10) per acre. However, the comparable sales are all derived from parcels smaller than the Sears parcel, the comparables averaging only 50 acres each. The appraiser is required to discount the Sears parcel to reflect that difference (smaller parcels generally have a higher per-acre value than larger ones) and so applies a 30 percent discount. Thus, the final before value of the subject property is determined to be $38,500 ([$50,000 x 1.10] × .70) per acre, or $19,250,000 ($38,500 × 500).

Determining the after-easement value also depends on the use of comparable sales. It happens that in the Expensive region, there have been a number of properties sold subject to conservation easements similar to the one contributed by Sears. Those properties have sold for an average of $2,500 per acre, essentially their value for agricultural use. (No paired sales analysis was necessary in determining the value of the property as restricted by the easement.) However, those sales all occurred five years earlier. The appraiser determined that the value of such property has been increasing at a rate of 3 percent per year, on average, during the five-year period. He applied this factor to the prior sales and determined that the current sales prices of such properties equates to $2,898 per acre ($2,500 × 1.03 × 1.03 × 1.03 × 1.03 × 1.03). Thus, the value of the Sears property, after the easement is in place, is $1,449,000 (500 × $2,898).

The difference between $19,250,000 (the before value) and $1,449,000 (the after value) is the value of the easement: $17,801,000.

153

C. Date of Appraisal: Regulations Section 1.170A-13(c)(3)(i)(A)

Appraisal of a conservation easement must be done no earlier than 60 days prior to the contribution of the easement and no later than the due date for the tax return on which the deduction is first claimed. However, regardless of when the appraisal is made, it must reflect the value of the easement *on the date of the conveyance* (Regulations section 1.170A-13(c)(3)(ii)(I)).

D. The Use of Preliminary Appraisals

An experienced appraiser can estimate the value of a potential easement contribution by knowing the terms of the proposed easement and assuming it is in place. Such precontribution estimates can be a valuable tool for helping prospective easement donors design a protection plan that will make the most efficient use of potential tax deductions. They are especially helpful in conservation buyer transactions in which prospective buyers plan to use the tax savings from a conservation easement deduction to help finance their purchase.

Example One: Susan has intended for many years to contribute a conservation easement on her family farm of 300 acres. She decides to do so in 2007. Her income averages around $100,000 per year, so, under the 2006 law provisions relating to the percentage of income against which she can claim a deduction and the length of the carry-forward period, she figures that she can use a charitable contribution deduction in the amount of $600,000 (which is conservative, as, in theory, she could use an $800,000 deduction, assuming she could deduct up to $50,000 per year and carry the deduction forward for 15 years). She consults a local appraiser for a preliminary valuation of the easement. When she goes to see the appraiser, she already has in hand the terms of the conservation easement.

The appraiser checks the zoning and physical characteristics of the land and researches the market for comparable properties (there is no substantial record of comparable easement sales). Based on what he finds, the appraiser determines, considering the restrictions proposed in the easement, that if the easement is conveyed, it will reduce the value of Susan's farm by $2 million.

That is far more of a tax deduction than Susan can use. She renegotiates the conservation easement with the local land trust so that it applies to only 100 acres. In this case the preliminary valuation allowed Susan to maximize, without wasting, the tax benefits from the conservation of her farm.

Example Two: After several years of looking, the Rush family has found the exact farm they have been looking for. The asking price for the farm is $2 million, which is about $500,000 more than they figure they can afford, even though they have a substantial annual income. Their realtor, knowing that they have no intention of developing the place, suggests that they consult a local land trust about the prospect of a conservation easement. The Rushes do that and come away enthusiastic about protecting the farm as well as reducing their income tax liability sufficiently to make up the $500,000 that they need to buy the place.

The Rushes consult an appraiser, knowing that they can agree to a conservation easement that limits future use of the farm to one residential compound, farming, and noncommercial recreation use. Considering all of the relevant factors, the appraiser provides the Rushes with a preliminary estimate that the proposed conservation easement will reduce the value of the farm to $800,000, generating a tax deduction of approximately $1.2 million.

The Rushes are residents of California, so between their state and federal income tax, they are paying a top "marginal rate" (recognizing that a taxpayer typically pays several rates of tax on his income, the marginal rate is the highest rate of the different rates paid) of 44 percent (35 percent + 9 percent) on an annual income of $600,000. The family figures that the deduction will save them about $132,000 per year ([$600,000 × .50] x .44) in state and federal income tax over a period of nine years if they contribute the easement in 2007 ($1,200,000 / $132,000). This reduction in annual income tax liability allows the Rushes' mortgage lender to increase by $500,000 the amount it is willing to loan to the Rushes to purchase the farm.

II. Enhancement: Regulations Section 1.170A-14(h)(3)(i)

It is a fairly well-established fact that conservation easements "enhance" the value of other property in the vicinity of the easement. This value varies according to the nature of the local real estate market. Some folks believe that, rather than reducing the value of land subject to an easement, conservation easements actually enhance the value of that land. However, that belief confuses the *effect of the easement on the easement property* and the *effect of the easement on other property in the vicinity* of the easement. No rational buyer would pay more for property whose future use was restricted than for property that was unrestricted. However, a buyer will pay more for property that adjoins or is near property that is restricted. For that reason, where a number of landowners in a given area have put their land under easement that land may, in fact, have higher value than other unprotected property. Nevertheless, that is still a reflection of the fact that people will pay more for property that adjoins or is in the vicinity of protected property.

Because conservation easements typically increase the value of property in their vicinity, the Regulations require that, where such increases benefit the donor of the easement, or a member of the donor's family, the easement deduction must be reduced. This is known as the "enhancement rule."

The enhancement rule applies in two distinct situations. First, where a donor contributes a conservation easement over only a portion of contiguous property owned by the donor and the donor's family, the unprotected portion of that property is likely to increase in value. Second is where the donor, or a related party, owns *noncontiguous* property that is enhanced in value due to the contribution of the easement. In the second case it does not matter where the enhanced property is located, as long as it is enhanced in value due to the contribution of the conservation easement.

For purposes of contiguous property owned by the donor and members of the donor's family, the term *family members* means the donor's brothers and sisters (whole or half blood), spouse, ancestors, and lineal descendants (Code section 267(c)(4)).

The definition of *related party* is far more expansive and in addition to family members as defined above includes corporate and trust relationships, partnerships, estates, and so forth. For a detailed list, see Code sections 267(b) and 707(b). Put simply, virtually any familial, business, or trust relationship falls within the definition.

A. Dealing with Contiguous Property

The appraiser is required to calculate differently the value of enhancement to contiguous property and enhancement to noncontiguous property, even though the result of the calculations may be the same. In the case of contiguous property, the appraiser is required by the Regulations to value the *entire* property before and after the easement, not just that portion of the property being placed under the easement. In this process the appraiser will reflect any enhancement in the value of that portion of the contiguous property that is not subject to the easement in determining the after value of the entire property. The requirement to appraise an entire contiguous property even though only a portion is placed under easement is sometimes overlooked by appraisers and landowners alike because they cannot see the sense of determining the value of the easement by looking at property that isn't subject to the easement. However, failure to do that means that whatever increase occurs in the unprotected contiguous property is not captured; it also is a violation of a clear requirement of the Regulations and a red flag for an audit.

The effect of enhancement on contiguous property is to reduce the value of the *easement*.

Example: Sonny Jacobs owns a 500-acre farm in western Pennsylvania. He decided to contribute a conservation easement over the eastern 250 acres. Local zoning allows Sonny to divide and develop houses on the remaining acreage at a density of one unit per 5 acres. The unrestricted portion of the property overlooks the eastern 250 acres, which includes a river and a series of springs and wetlands. There are four potential home sites on the eastern portion of the property under local zoning regulations.

The appraiser valued the eastern 250 acres at $4,000 per acre before the easement (a total of $1million) and at $500 per acre after the easement ($125,000). Sonny was pleased with the $875,000 deduction ($1,000,000 – $125,000), because he thought it would help him offset the proceeds from development of the unrestricted balance of the property.

The IRS audited Sonny's return, however, and denied all but $125,000 of his claimed deduction. The IRS appraiser, following the con-tiguous parcel rule, valued Sonny's entire 500-acre farm before and after the easement. She found that before the easement the western 250 acres of the farm were worth $6,000 an acre ($1,500,000) and the eastern por-tion was worth $4,000 an acre ($1 million). However, after the easement she found that the western portion was worth $9,000 an acre ($2,250,000) because of the protection of the eastern portion, over which the western portion looks. The IRS agreed that the eastern portion after the easement was worth only $500 per acre. The net result, according to the IRS, is that the entire 500-acre property was worth $2,375,000 after the easement. Thus, the easement was worth only $125,000 ($2,500,000 – $2,375,000).

The IRS also imposed a severe penalty on Sonny and Sonny's appraiser because the appraisal "grossly overvalued" the easement. In fact, the appraisal overvalued the easement by 700 percent, far more than the 200 percent overvaluation that triggers the gross overvaluation penalty. (See the discussion of penalties in section I, C of chapter 6.)

The language of the Regulations dealing with contiguous prop-erty is somewhat ambiguous and appears to require valuation of an entire contiguous property only if the entire parcel is owned by the donor *and* members of the donor's family. This suggests that if the entire parcel is owned solely by the donor, the entire parcel need not be valued to deter-mine the value of the easement. However, that makes no sense, and the Regulations are applied as though they read "the donor *and/or* members of the donor's family." In other words, the entire contiguous parcel should be valued, whether the donor owns the balance of the property with other family members or by himself. It is also likely that when the Regulations speak of "encumbered property," they intend to refer to the entire property, even if only a portion is encumbered by the easement.

B. Dealing with All Other Enhanced Property

When noncontiguous property is enhanced in value due to the contribution of a conservation easement, the appraiser is required to do *four* separate appraisals. First, he must appraise the value of the easement property before the easement; second, he must appraise the value of the easement property after the easement; third, he must appraise the value of any other property that is owned by the donor, or a member of the donor's family, that may be enhanced in value due to the contribution of the easement before the easement is in place; and fourth, he must value that other property after the easement is in place to determine the amount of enhancement. The amount of enhancement to noncontiguous property should be separately accounted for in the appraisal and then subtracted from the value of the easement to obtain the actual net value of the contribution.

The effect of enhancement on noncontiguous property is to reduce the amount of the *deduction*, not the value of the easement, as is the case with contiguous property.

Example: The Jordan family owns a large farm. The farm has been divided into four parcels, two of which are located about a quarter of a mile from the other two. Sara and Sam own two parcels, and John and Eddie own the other two. John's and Eddie's parcels form a beautiful entrance, including a long tree-lined drive, to Sara's and Sam's parcels. John and Eddie decide to contribute a conservation easement over their two parcels and specifically provide for the protection of the tree-lined drive and maintenance of the pastures on either side of the drive.

The appraiser determines the value of the conservation easement to be $500,000. After visiting the property, he asks John and Eddie if there is any other property owned by them or members of their family in the area. John and Eddie point down the drive to Sara's and Sam's parcels. After viewing all four parcels and considering the impact on Sam's and Sara's parcels of protecting the beautiful entrance to their property, the appraiser realizes that he has an enhancement situation. After he explains the need for additional work, John and Eddie authorize him to proceed.

The appraiser values Sara's and Sam's property both before and after the easement is placed on John's and Eddie's parcels and determines that Sara's and Sam's parcels increase in value by $100,000 (10 percent of their value before the easement) due to the protection of the entrance to their parcels. The appraiser subtracts the enhancement in Sara's and Sam's property from the $500,000 easement value, resulting in a net charitable deduction for John and Eddie of $400,000.

C. The Effect of Enhancement on Basis Adjustment

The following discussion is based on a logical application of the law. Unfortunately, there is no case law or administrative guidance available. One might conclude from this to ignore the following until there is an official explanation.

As described in chapter 4, section III, the donor of a conservation easement is required to adjust her basis in the easement property to reflect the contribution of a portion of that property in the form of an easement. The enhancement rule plays a role in this adjustment *if* the enhancement is to *contiguous property*. In such a case the value of the easement is directly offset by the appreciation in the contiguous property without the need for a separate calculation. This reduces the amount by which the donor is required to adjust her basis. However, where enhancement occurs to *noncontiguous property*, the appraiser comes up with an easement value that does not inherently reflect enhancement, so the easement value is higher. The amount of enhancement reduces the donor's deduction but does not reduce the value of the easement. Therefore, the basis adjustment will not be reduced by the amount of enhancement.

Example: Harry contributes an easement on half of his 200-acre ranch. The appraiser determines that the value of the 200 acres before the easement is $2,000,000 and after the easement is $1,500,000. The easement is worth $500,000 and represents 25 percent of the unrestricted value of the ranch, requiring Harry to reduce his basis by 25 percent.

Now suppose that Harry owned only 100 acres and his sister owned the adjoining 100 acres. The appraiser determines that Harry's land is worth $1,000,000 before the easement and $250,000 after the easement. Thus, the easement has reduced the value of Harry's ranch by 75 percent, and he must reduce his basis in the ranch by 75 percent. However, in a separate appraisal the appraiser determines that the value of Harry's sister's ranch has increased by $250,000 due to Harry's easement. Harry is required per the enhancement rule to reduce his deduction by $250,000, to $500,000, but this does not affect his basis. While the net result is the same in both cases, because of the way the basis adjustment rule works, Harry suffers a much greater basis adjustment in the first case than in the second.

D. Why Not to Disregard Enhancement

Appraisers will sometimes take the position that, even though there is noncontiguous property owned by the donor or the donor's family in the vicinity of the easement property, there is no enhancement. This is almost always a mistake. First, it is more likely than not that there is enhancement. Second, the IRS will assume that there is enhancement and view the failure to account for it as a defect in the appraisal, justify-

ing an audit. Third, it is much easier for the IRS to successfully challenge a deduction where the appraiser has failed to reflect any enhancement, than to challenge one where the appraiser has calculated enhancement, even though the amount of enhancement calculated is very low. This third point is true because it is easier for the IRS to make an effective case on a point of law (that a legal requirement—the requirement to compute and subtract enhancement has been ignored) than on a point of fact (that the value of enhancement as determined by the appraiser is incorrect).

Form 8283 now requires the easement donor to declare whether or not property owned by any person related to the donor is located in proximity to the easement for which the deduction is claimed. This is to alert the IRS to any possible enhancement that has not been reflected in the valuation summarized on Form 8283.

III. Financial Benefits Received Must Be Subtracted from the Deduction: Regulations Section 1.170A-14(h)(3)(i)

In addition to the adjustments required for enhancement in property values, the Regulations require that the amount of any easement deduction be reduced by any cash payment or other economic benefit received, or reasonably expected, by the donor or any "related person" as a result of the contribution of the easement. (See also the discussion of donative intent in section II of chapter 4.)

Example One: Mr. Blue agrees with the ABC Land Trust that he will contribute an easement over his land if ABC will acquire and protect a parcel of land adjoining Mr. Blue's land. ABC agrees to do that. The acquisition by ABC enhances the value of Mr. Blue's land by $150,000. The value of Mr. Blue's easement is $400,000. ABC is required to notify Mr. Blue that, in exchange for his easement contribution to ABC, he has received $150,000 in "goods and services" from ABC, thereby reducing the amount of Mr. Blue's deduction to $250,000 ($400,000 – $150,000).

Example Two: Ms. Brown agrees with the XYZ Land Trust to sell a conservation easement to XYZ on land that she owns adjoining one of XYZ's most important holdings. The agreed price for the easement is $50,000. An appraisal of the easement shows that its value is $150,000. Ms. Brown is allowed a deduction of $100,000 ($150,000 – $50,000) for this qualified bargain sale. (See Code sections 170 and 1011(b) for provisions regarding bargain sales.)

Example Three: Mr. Green contributes a conservation easement to the UVW Land Trust. The land trust agrees to pay the costs Mr. Green incurred in the transaction, which include obtaining legal counsel, an appraisal, and a survey and preparation of the natural resources inventory. The costs amount to $5,000. The land trust is required to notify Mr. Green that, in exchange for his easement contribution, he has received $5,000 in goods and services. Mr. Green must reduce his deduction by the $5,000 amount. However, Mr. Green may be able to deduct most of the $5,000 he spent on legal and appraisal fees in connection with his contribution (see chapter 4, section VII for a discussion of the deductibility of expenses incurred in making the contribution).

CHAPTER SIX

Substantiation Requirements and Penalties

Any claim for a deduction for the contribution of property (as opposed to cash) exceeding $5,000 must be supported by a "qualified appraisal" (Regulations section 1.170A-13(c)(2)), conducted by a "qualified appraiser" (Regulations section 1.170A-13(c)(3); see section 1.170A-13(c)(5) for a definition).

The definitions of a qualified appraisal and appraiser were revised by Congress in 2006 in an effort to curb appraisal abuses (Code section 170(f)(11)(E)). The new law provides new requirements for qualified appraisals, qualified appraisers, and declarations of appraisers and imposes new penalties for "substantial" and "gross" misstatements of value. See IRS Notice 2006-96 for "interim guidance" on the implementation of the new law. Note that this part of the 2006 law did not expire and remains in effect.

I. New Statutory Requirements

The Pension Protection Act of 2006, in addition to providing (temporarily) for new conservation easement tax benefits, provided permanent changes to the rules governing appraisals of conservation easements.

A. Qualified Appraisal and Appraiser: Regulations Sections 170(f)(11)(E)(i) and (ii)

The 2006 law, as interpreted by IRS Notice 2206-96, provides (1) that an appraisal is treated as a qualified appraisal if it complies with the Regulations or "other guidance prescribed by the Secretary of the Treasury," and (2) that a qualified appraiser of real property must be licensed or certified to appraise the type of real property being appraised in the state where the property in question is located.

Neither the Code nor the notice addresses qualifications for appraising conservation easements. However, because conservation easements are a real property interest, it is likely that being licensed or certified to conduct appraisals of real property is sufficient qualification for appraising a conservation easement, even though conservation easement appraisals can be somewhat more complex than normal real estate appraisals.

B. New Declaration Provision: Regulations Section 1.170A-13(c)(5)(i)

The 2006 law requires an addition to the appraiser's declaration already required by Regulations section 1.170A-13(c)(5)(i). The declaration must now include a statement that the appraiser understands that a substantial or gross valuation misstatement resulting from an appraisal of the value of property that the appraiser knows, or reasonably should have known, would be used in connection with a return or claim for refund may subject the appraiser to a civil penalty under Code section 6695A.

C. New Penalty: Code Section 6695A

If an appraiser knew, or should have known, that an appraisal was to be used in connection with a tax return or claim of a tax refund; if the appraisal is of the value of property; and if the appraisal misstates that value by 150 percent or more, it is considered a "substantial" misstatement of value. If the misstatement is 200 percent or more, it is considered a "gross" misstatement of value. Substantial or gross misstatements of value can result in a penalty for the appraiser. The Code provides that in either case the penalty shall be equal to the greater of (1) 10 percent of the amount of underpayment of tax resulting from the misstatement; (2) $1,000; or (3) 125 percent of the gross income received by the appraiser for conducting the appraisal.

The penalty provisions are new and do not expire, unlike some other provisions of the 2006 law. There is no question that incentives for more accuracy in appraising conservation easements are needed and little question that the penalty provisions will create such an incentive. However, as most people who work with conservation easements are aware, it is already difficult to locate more than one or two appraisers in an area willing to conduct a conservation easement appraisal. Exposing appraisers' work to the rigors of audit and imposing potentially substantial financial penalties for overvaluing conservation easements are not likely to increase the number of appraisers willing to undertake such appraisals.

II. Other Requirements

In addition to requiring an appraisal of the value of the conservation easement, the law requires documentation of the contribution from both the donor and the land trust.

A. Form 8283: Regulations Section 1.170A-13(c)(4)

The law requires that any tax return that includes a deduction for the contribution of property valued at over $5,000 be accompanied by Form 8283, Noncash Charitable Contributions, which includes a summary of an easement appraisal. If the value of the property contribution exceeds $500,000, the law now requires that Form 8283 be accompanied by the complete appraisal of the easement, not just a summary. Clearly, having the actual easement appraisal on hand increases the likelihood that someone at the IRS will actually read it.

In order to address certain "oversights" in the valuation process, Form 8283 now requires the donor of the easement to attach a statement that does the following:

- identifies the conservation purposes furthered by the easement;
- shows the value of the property subject to the easement, both before and after its contribution;
- states whether the contribution was made to obtain a permit or other governmental approval and whether the contribution was required by a contract; and
- states whether the donor, or any related person, has any interest in other property near the easement property and, if so, describes that interest.

Form 8283 requires that the recipient of the contribution acknowledge receipt of that contribution, the date of receipt, and that the organization is qualified under Code section 170(c). However, the form expressly states, "This acknowledgement does not represent an agreement with the claimed fair market value." This is an extremely important caveat. There is considerable discussion in the land trust community today about the responsibility of a land trust·for the deductions claimed by easement donors. The IRS, and a number of land trust personnel, would like land trusts to review easement appraisals and either approve or disapprove the values being claimed.

It is my opinion that this is neither necessary nor required of a land trust. In fact, I believe that land trusts that seek to second-guess appraisers about the value of conservation easements are encroaching on an area that requires expertise that land trust staff typically does not have. Furthermore, the land trust that involves itself in reviewing and approving or disapproving easement appraisals unnecessarily exposes itself if its assessment of the appraisal is incorrect.

I believe that the sole responsibility of a land trust with respect to Form 8283 is to acknowledge receipt of a deductible contribution (there is no reason for the land trust to sign the form other than confirmation of receipt of such a contribution). If the land trust believes that a deduction is being claimed for a contribution that is, flat out, not deductible, it should not sign the form. If the land trust believes that a deductible contribution has been made but the value claimed is substantially in excess of what it believes the contribution was worth, it can (but should not feel obligated to) communicate its concern to the donor prior to signing the form.

B. Acknowledgment of the Contribution: Regulations Section 1.170A-13(f)(2)

In addition to Form 8283, the law requires that an organization receiving a charitable contribution in excess of $250 in value must acknowledge the gift and state whether the donor received any "goods or services" from the organization "in consideration, in whole or in part, for" the contribution. The acknowledgment in the case of a cash gift must state the amount of the gift; in the case of a noncash gift, it must generally describe the property received. Failure by the donee organization to provide such an acknowledgment is grounds for disallowance of the donor's claim of a charitable deduction. The acknowledgment is required to be provided before the earlier of (1) the date the donor files the return on which he claims the deduction, or (2) the due date (plus extensions) of the return on which the donor is required to report the deduction.

The Regulations provide that "goods or services" means cash, property, services, benefits, and privileges. The Regulations also define the phrase "in consideration for" as follows: "A donee organization provides goods or services in consideration for a taxpayer's payment if, at the time the taxpayer makes the payment to the donee organization, the taxpayer receives or expects to receive goods or services in exchange for that payment. Goods or services a donee organization provides in considera-tion for a payment by a taxpayer include goods or services provided in a year other than the year in which the taxpayer makes the payment to the donee organization."

PART IV

Estate and Gift Tax Benefits

The estate tax remains part of the U.S. Tax Code in spite of years of efforts to repeal it. It weighs particularly heavily on people whose primary asset is land, such as farming and ranching families. This is because land, which is the principal asset of such families, represents taxable value, and, in many parts of the country, land has increased in value out of all proportion to its value for agricultural use. However valuable land may be, it is not easily liquidated to pay taxes, and, where the land in question is the family farm or ranch, liquidating it to pay estate taxes can force an unwanted and significant change in life style. For families who want to keep their land intact, and for whom land is the primary asset, a conservation easement may make the difference between keeping the land and being forced to sell it to pay estate taxes.

There are two specific types of estate tax benefits. One is a reduction in the value of easement property resulting from the restrictions of the conservation easement. The reduction eliminates taxable value from a decedent's estate and can represent substantial savings to the decedent's family. The second benefit is exclusion from an estate of a portion of the value of easement land. The exclusion is figured against the value of easement land as reduced by the easement. The exclusion also reduces the taxable value of a decedent's estate: an additional saving.

Furthermore, a decedent's heirs may direct the executor of an estate to contribute a conservation easement on estate property, and, if it is contributed before the date the estate tax return is due, such a contribution allows the estate to qualify for the easement-related estate tax benefits as though the decedent had contributed the easement before dying. A conservation easement also controls the future use of property in the hands of a decedent's heirs more effectively than any other technique available.

For all of these reasons, conservation easements complement and increase the power of many estate planning techniques. In addition, the substantial estate tax benefits associated with conservation easements are important tools for estate planning.

In 2001 Congress repealed the federal estate tax (but not the gift tax), effective in 2010. Between 2001 and 2010 the estate tax is being phased out. However, in 2011 the tax is scheduled to be automatically reinstated, as it existed in 2001. What will actually happen is hard to predict. It is unlikely that Congress will allow full reinstatement, but it is also unlikely that Congress will make the repeal permanent. The Republican-controlled Congress tried and failed, in 2006, to make the repeal permanent; it is less likely that permanent repeal will occur with a Democratically controlled Congress.

The two principal components of the estate tax are (1) the rate of tax imposed, and (2) the exemption of assets from the estate for taxation purposes (the "Exclusion Amount" for purposes of this discussion, to distinguish it from the "exclusion" of a portion of the value of easement land described above). These components will be changing over the next five years as follows:

- In 2008 the Exclusion Amount is $2 million; the tax on assets over $2 million is 45 percent.
- In 2009 the Exclusion Amount increases to $3.5 million; the tax on assets over $3.5 million remains 45 percent.
- In 2010 the estate tax is fully repealed.
- In 2011 the estate tax is reinstated, and the Exclusion Amount drops to $1 million; the top rate of tax is increased to 55 percent.

CHAPTER SEVEN:

Basic Estate Tax Concepts

The federal estate tax is not an "inheritance tax," which is a tax on inheritances received from a decedent. It is a tax levied on a decedent's estate, and it is paid by a very small percentage of estates. According to "The State of the Estate Tax as of 2006," an article by Joel Friedman and Aviva Aron-Dine published by the Center on Budget and Policy Priorities in 2006, only 13,000 decedents' estates, approximately 0.5 percent of all decedents' estates, were liable for federal estate tax that year. In 2009 the number of decedents' estates anticipated to be subject to tax drops to 7,000, about 0.3 percent of all decedents' estates expected in 2009.

The estate tax has a disproportionate effect on farmers and ranchers because of the dramatic appreciation in land values over the past several decades and because farmers and ranchers typically have few liquid assets (however, the Congressional Budget Office, as cited in the article just referenced, projects that with the reductions in the estate tax enacted in 2000, by 2009 only 100 family-owned businesses and 65 family farm estates will be subject to the estate tax). Payment of estate tax by farming and ranching families may actually require the sale of the family farm or ranch. In some cases cashing out the family farm or ranch may be a boon to children anxious to lead a different life than their parents. In other cases, however, such sales force unwilling families out of a cherished way of life.

Due to the increased shelter for estates provided by the estate tax, which is now up to $2 million, with an increase to $3.5 million scheduled for 2009, and with the relatively simple estate planning techniques available, a farm or ranch family should be able to pass along land worth many millions of dollars without paying estate tax. The projection of the number of family-owned businesses and farms that will be subject to estate tax in 2009 contained in the preceding paragraph assumes certain basic estate planning. However, even the simplest techniques are often not used.

This chapter provides an explanation of basic estate tax concepts and planning tools and discusses the role that conservation easements can play. While the estate tax will be phased out by 2010, unless Congress acts, it is scheduled to be reinstated in its 2000 form in 2011. It seems unlikely that Congress will allow the estate tax to entirely disappear, so planning for the tax is prudent.

I. Estate and Gift Taxes

The Code imposes two taxes on the transfer of property from an individual. The so-called estate tax is imposed on transfers of property that result from the death of an individual. The gift tax is imposed on transfers of property made during an individual's lifetime. The intention is to tax all transfers of wealth made by an individual, except for charitable contributions and transfers to a spouse. Charitable contributions to governmental agencies and public charities, whether lifetime gifts or testamentary bequests, are deductible for estate and gift tax purposes and are not taxed. Transfers of property between a husband and wife, whether made during a person's lifetime or at death are also deductible and are not taxed (see the discussion of the "marital deduction" in section I, A, 5 of this chapter).

The Code excludes from the estate tax up to $2 million of property value transferred at a person's death (by will or by the laws of intestate succession if there was no will). However, the law excludes only up to $1 million for property transferred by gift during a person's lifetime (plus an annual exclusion of $12,000, described in section I, B, 1 of this chapter).

A. The Estate Tax

The following discussion is intended to provide an explanation of basic estate tax principles and the role of conservation easements in estate planning. However, it is important to remember that estate planning is a multifaceted undertaking that may require the expertise of a number of experts including attorneys, accountants, land planners, and appraisers.

1. The Gross Estate: Code Section 2031

An important concept in estate tax law is the "gross estate." The gross estate is different from the "taxable estate," described below. The gross estate includes everything titled in a descedent's name, as well as any other property over which the decedent had discretionary control for her personal benefit.

For example, if a decedent was the trustee of a trust and had the authority to direct the use of the assets of the trust for her own benefit, the assets of the trust must be included in her gross estate. If a decedent owned life insurance and controlled the cash value or the designation of beneficiaries, or other "incidents of ownership" of the policy, the proceeds of the policy would be included in her estate.

In addition, interests in limited liability companies, trusts, corporations, partnerships, limited partnerships, and the like would be included in the decedent's estate to the extent of her ownership in such entities. Property owned by the decedent through a "revocable trust" (one she had the right to amend or terminate at will) would be included in her gross estate.

a. Jointly Owned Property

The treatment of jointly owned property is an important factor in determining the size of the gross estate. Code section 2040(b) provides that property owned by a husband and wife jointly as "tenants by the entireties" or jointly with right of survivorship (provided that no one other than the husband and wife is a joint owner of the property) will be treated as owned one-half by the husband and one-half by the wife. This is known as a "qualified joint ownership."

Code section 2040(a) provides that each owner of jointly owned property with right of survivorship, acquired by gift or inheritance, owns an equal undivided interest in such property. In other words, if there were three joint tenants of a property acquired by gift or inheritance, each owner would be considered by the law to own one-third.

On the other hand, Code section 2040(a) also provides that if the jointly held property was acquired by purchase, each owner would be considered to own a share equal to the percentage of the purchase price she contributed. In other words, if there were three joint owners and one owner contributed one-fifth and the other two owners contributed two-fifths each, the owner that contributed one-fifth would be considered to own one-fifth of the joint property, and each of the two who contributed two-fifths would be considered to own two-fifths each.

b. Eliminating Property from the Gross Estate

One of the principal goals of estate planning is to remove property from a person's estate so that it will not be subject to the estate tax (or, ideally, the gift tax). In order to ensure that property owned in almost any manner is excluded from the owner's estate, the person must completely divest herself from all rights to any personal enjoyment or control over that property. The exception to this rule (and it is only a partial exception) is for property placed irrevocably in trust for the benefit of another. "Irrevocably" means that the gift cannot be reversed.

In the case of property irrevocably placed in trust, such property would be considered to have been removed from the estate of the person placing it in the trust (typically called the grantor or "settlor"), even though the settlor retains control over investment of the trust property and over the manner in which the trust assets are used. However, it must be impossible for the settlor to use the trust property for her own benefit, or direct that the property be used for her benefit by someone else, or the trust property would be considered part of her estate.

176

A person should assume that virtually everything she owns or may control for her personal benefit is included in her gross estate.

Property is included in a decedent's estate at its value measured on the date of her death or, if the decedent's executor makes a special election to do so, on a date six months after the decedent's death. The six-month deferral of valuation protects the estate from dramatic downward changes in asset values occurring shortly after a person dies. The valuation of estate property is obviously an extremely important aspect of the estate tax.

2. The Taxable Estate: Code Section 2051

The taxable estate is the gross estate reduced by all allowed estate tax deductions. Deductions are allowed for the following: costs of estate administration; executor's fees; funeral expenses; debts of the decedent, including mortgage debt; taxes, including state death taxes; charitable contributions provided for in the decedent's will; and the value of all property passing to the decedent's spouse (whether by the terms of the will or by operation of law and including survivorship accounts, real property owned jointly with right of survivorship, etc.).

3. Stepped-Up Basis

One of the only silver linings in the federal estate tax is that assets that are subject to the estate tax receive a "stepped-up basis" when they pass into the hands of a decedent's beneficiaries. Recall that basis is, essentially, what someone pays for property plus the value of any improvements made to that property. Basis is important because it is the difference between a person's basis in property and the sales price of that property that is subject to income tax; the higher a person's basis relative to the sales price, the less income tax due on the sale. See the discussion of basis in section I, H of chapter 4.

Stepping up the basis on property that has passed through a decedent's estate (whether that estate is taxable or not) means that the decedent's basis in the property is increased to the fair market value of that property on the date of the decedent's death. This means that when a beneficiary of the property sells it, either the income tax due on the sale will be significantly less than if the decedent had sold it or there will be no tax due at all.

Example: Selby bought a ranch in 1980 for $200,000. His original basis in the ranch was $200,000—what he paid for it. Over the years he paid $100,000 to improve the ranch with new fencing, barns, and stables. Therefore, his "adjusted basis" was $300,000—the amount of his original basis plus the cost of the improvements. When Selby died in 2007 the ranch was appraised for estate tax purposes at $2 million. Had Selby sold the ranch for $2 million before his death, his taxable gain on the sale (the difference between his adjusted basis and the sales price) would have been $1.7 million ($2,000,000—$300,000). At current rates the income tax on that gain would have been $255,000 ($1,700,000 × .15).

However, Selby didn't sell the property, and it was included in his estate and passed to his son Junior. Junior hated ranching and promptly sold the ranch for $2 million. Fortunately for Junior, because the ranch had passed through his father's estate, it received a stepped-up basis to reflect the fair market value of the ranch as included in Selby's estate: $2 million. Because the stepped-up basis and sales price were the same, Junior did not have to pay any income tax on the sale.

Remember, only assets that pass through a decedent's estate receive a stepped-up basis. Assets that are not included in the decedent's estate—for example, gifts made during the decedent's lifetime, either outright or in trust—do not receive a stepped-up basis. Assets that are transferred by gift have a "carryover basis." Carryover basis is the same as the basis of the property in the hands of the person making the gift; in other words, the gift maker's basis is "carried over" to the person receiving the gift.

Example: Had Selby, in order to avoid the estate tax, given the ranch to Junior before he died, Junior's basis in the ranch would be the same as his father's: $300,000. Because Selby's basis in the ranch is carried over to Junior, when Junior sells the ranch, he will have to pay income tax on the difference between the $300,000 carry-over basis and the sale's price.

---

4. The Unified Credit

As already noted, the Code excludes from estate tax a certain amount of every decedent's estate (the "Exclusion Amount"). The Exclusion Amount actually results from a credit against the tax due on the estate. Technically speaking, every dollar of a decedent's taxable estate is subject to tax. However, the credit against the tax effectively excludes, in 2008, the first $2 million in assets (i.e., the tax on $2 million in estate assets would be $780,800 and the credit available in 2008 against estate tax is $780,000).

The credit against estate and gift taxes is called unified because it applies to transfers of property made at death *and* to gifts made during a person's lifetime. It is applicable to both types of transfers. However, the gift tax Exclusion Amount is $1 million, while the estate tax Exclusion Amount is $2 million. The unified credit can be used only once, against either estate or gift tax—for example, a person may use $1 million of the credit against lifetime gifts, but if she does, she will have only $1 million in credit left to cover estate tax liability.

The Exclusion Amount (for estates only) increases in 2009 to $3.5 million. The gift tax exclusion remains at $1 million for 2009.

Example: Suppose that Mr. Jones made taxable gifts during his lifetime amounting to $800,000 (over and above the annual gift tax exclusion of $12,000; see section I, B, 1 of this chapter). When he died, his taxable estate amounted to $2 million. Assuming he died in 2008, the unified credit would shelter only $1.2 million of his estate because a portion of the unified credit would already have been used to shelter the $800,000 in lifetime taxable gifts. In this example, Mr. Jones's estate would be liable for $360,000 in estate tax, based on the 2008 top rate of 45 percent ($800,000 x .45).

---

5. The Marital Deduction

The estate tax code allows a decedent's estate to deduct the total value of all assets passing to the spouse upon the decedent's death. This is known as the marital deduction, and it is unlimited. In other words, Bill Gates could leave his entire estate to his wife, Melinda, and it would pass to her tax free. Of course, when Melinda dies, there would be a tax on her estate unless she remarried and passed all of her property on to her new husband. If her new husband survived her, he could remarry and so forth. Remarriage actually makes for an interesting and, from a tax standpoint, foolproof, estate tax–avoidance technique.

a. Overqualifying for the Marital Deduction

If a person dies and is survived by his spouse, all assets passing to the spouse pass free from the estate tax under the unlimited marital deduction. For that reason it may seem like a good idea to have all assets pass to your spouse when you die. In many cases that is exactly what people do with their wills: Everything goes to the surviving spouse or, if there is no surviving spouse, to the children (there may be estate tax on the transfer to children, which is not subject to an unlimited deduction). Such wills are sometimes referred to as I-love-you wills. I-love-you wills may be a nice sentiment, but they can be very bad estate planning. If everything passes to a surviving spouse under the marital deduction, nothing passes under the $2 million Exclusion Amount. Therefore, the Exclusion Amount is wasted.

Furthermore, when the surviving spouse dies (assuming that he didn't spend everything received from the first decedent's estate), the amount subject to tax will include what was received from the first decedent—and, unless there has been a subsequent marriage, none of it will be eligible for the marital deduction. This is called overqualifying for the marital deduction because it was not necessary for the entire amount of the first decedent's estate to pass under the marital deduction to avoid the estate tax, and because doing that has increased the combined tax on the husband's and wife's estate.

Example: Jane and Bill have joint net assets of $6 million. Jane owns exactly one-half of those assets in her own name, as does Bill. (This is typically not the case, but it helps illustrate the point of this example.) Jane's will directs that all of her assets go to Bill when she dies, or to their children if Bill predeceases her. Bill's will provides that all of his assets go to Jane when he dies or to their children if Jane predeceases him. Jane dies first. There is no estate tax on her estate because all of the assets passing to Bill pass under the marital deduction. When Bill dies, all of his assets ($6 million) go to their children. The estate tax is $1,800,000 ([$6,000,000 – $2,000,000] × .45).

Had Jane directed that $2 million of her estate pass directly to her children—or to a trust for the benefit of (but not subject to the control of) Bill and then to her children—and $1 million directly to Bill, there would have been no tax on her estate. This is because $2 million of her estate would have been sheltered by the Exclusion Amount of $2 million, and $1 million would be sheltered by the marital deduction. When Bill died, he would have owned $4 million in assets (assuming neither appreciation nor depreciation in those assets), and the tax on his estate would have been $900,000 ([$4,000,000– $2,000,000) × .45).

By "overqualifying" for the marital deduction—that is, by arranging that everything would pass to Bill without taking advantage of the Exclusion Amount of $2 million—Jane and Bill caused the collective estate tax on both estates to be $900,000 higher than necessary.

It isn't enough for a husband and wife merely to make provisions in their wills intended to avoid overqualifying, because many assets owned by a husband and wife are jointly owned. When assets are titled in the joint names of husband and wife, they automatically pass by operation of law to the survivor, regardless of the provisions of the decedent's will. To effectively avoid overqualifying, it is often necessary to retitle some (or all) jointly owned property so that it passes according to the terms of the owner's will, rather than automatically as a matter of title. Note that the rules governing joint ownership described in section I, A, 1, a of this chapter dictate how joint assets are owned during the period of joint ownership. Those rules do not dictate how jointly held assets pass on the death of a joint owner.

Example One: Suppose that George and Mary jointly own $3 million in assets. When George dies, everything passes to Mary (regardless of what George's will provides, because the title—not the joint owner's will—dictates the disposition of jointly held assets). There is no estate tax due because George's entire estate is sheltered by the marital deduction. When Mary dies, everything goes to the couple's two children, according to the terms of her will. The tax (assuming that Mary dies in 2006 with a taxable estate of $3 million) will be $460,000 ([3,000,000 – 2,000,000] × .46).

Example Two: Now let's assume that George and Mary divide their joint property so that each owns $1.5 million outright in their own name without any survivorship provision. They each have a will that provides that their estate will be placed in a trust at their death. Each provides that the trust income be paid entirely to the survivor and that the trust assets be available for the use of the survivor during his or her lifetime, but not subject to the survivor's control. Upon the survivor's death, what is left in the trust is to be distributed outright to the two children.

When George dies, his entire estate goes into the trust, and the entire estate is covered by the $2 million Exclusion Amount, so there is no tax. When Mary dies, her entire estate will go directly to the two children because the trust was required only if she was survived by George. Again, Mary's estate is entirely sheltered by the $2 million exclusion, so there is no tax on it, either. The result is that, rather than having to pay $460,000 in estate tax, the children receive the entire $3 million tax free.

The foregoing example illustrates what are known as "bypass trusts." Bypass trusts are designed to provide benefits to a surviving spouse while bypassing the surviving spouse's estate and passing assets, after the survivor's death, directly to the children. The same tax result could be accomplished by simply giving property outright, or in trust, to the children without providing for the other spouse, except that there would be no guarantee that the surviving spouse would receive benefits.

b. Underqualifying for the Marital Deduction

In attempting to avoid overqualifying for the marital deduction, it is important not to fail to take full advantage of it. Remember that the Exclusion Amount is limited to $2 million (through 2008). Every dollar over $2 million in a decedent's assets that does not qualify for the marital deduction will be taxed at the top rate of estate tax.

Example: Max and Minnie own property worth $5 million. They divide their ownership to eliminate any survivorship joint ownerships, so that their wills control the disposition of their property when either of them dies. They then provide for bypass trusts in their respective wills, and each provides that all of the assets that he or she owns be transferred to a bypass trust if he or she is the first to die. Minnie dies first. Her gross estate includes $2.5 million. All of it goes to a bypass trust; none goes to Max. The $2 million Exclusion Amount shelters the first $2 million of her estate. However, that leaves $500,000 subject to tax—$230,000 in 2006 (based on the 2006 top estate tax rate of 46 percent). Had Minnie left everything in excess of the $2 million Exclusion Amount to Max, there would have been no tax because of the marital deduction.

To maximize the shelter of the first decedent's estate, everything over $2 million should go to, or be made subject to the control of, the surviving spouse. This arrangement maximizes use of the Exclusion Amount and marital deduction, thus eliminating any tax on the first decedent's estate.

Example: Assume the same facts as the preceding example, except that Max and Minnie both provide in their respective wills that everything over the Exemption Amount (and wills typically speak in terms of the "Unified Credit Amount" rather than the Exemption Amount and rather than spelling out a specific dollar amount, because the Exemption Amount changes over the next several years) is to pass outright to the surviving spouse, or in a so-called marital deduction trust for the benefit of the surviving spouse. Such an arrangement guarantees no tax on the estate of the first spouse to die and minimizes the amount of tax on the estate of the second spouse to die.

---

6. Estate Tax Returns and Tax Payment

An estate tax return (Form 706) is required to be filed with the IRS within nine months of a decedent's death. Six-month extensions of the return date are allowed on a discretionary basis for up to six months. Six-month extensions are automatic if (1) the extension application is filed before the normal due date for the return; (2) the application is filed with the proper IRS office; and (3) the application includes an estimate of the amount of estate tax due. Returns are required to be filed only by estates whose value exceeds the Exclusion Amount ($2 million through 2008; $3.5 million in 2009).

The estate tax must be paid nine months after the decedent's death, even if an extension for filing is granted (unless the extension expressly extends the time for payment). After that date interest will begin to accrue, and penalties for late payment may apply.

a. Fourteen-year Installment Period for Farms and Closely Held Businesses

If the decedent's estate included interest in a farm or closely held business, and that interest was at least 35 percent of the gross estate or 50 percent of the taxable estate, the estate is allowed 14 years in which to pay the estate tax pertaining to the farm or closely held business.

b. Other Installment Agreements

The IRS is authorized to enter into an installment payment agreement with a decedent's estate that provides for the payment of tax, with interest, in installments over time. Such agreements are not uncommon and are allowed in any case in which the IRS determines that the agreement will facilitate the payment of tax. Such agreements can cover payment of the entire amount of tax due or a portion of the tax due. However, whether or not to enter into such an agreement is discretionary with the IRS.

7. Life Insurance

Life insurance is a particularly useful tool for payment of the estate tax. This is because life insurance provides a payment of cash at the time when estate tax liability occurs. Furthermore, properly handled, life insurance is subject to neither income tax nor estate tax. If the policy holder places the insurance into a trust created during his lifetime and relinquishes all of the "incidents of ownership" (that is, the right to change beneficiaries, borrow against the policy, terminate the policy, draw down the cash value of the policy, etc.), the proceeds of the policy will be excluded from the decedent's gross estate. However, the face value of an insurance policy transferred by a person within three years of his death will be included in his estate for estate tax purposes. (Code section 2035(h)(2).)

183

8. A Caution about Estate Planning

It is important to keep estate taxes in perspective. It is possible to come up with a perfect estate plan that saves lots of tax but is completely unworkable for a family. For example, it rarely makes sense to put a personal residence in a bypass trust, even though it may save estate tax, because the surviving spouse should not have to work with a trustee and trust structure for her day-to-day living arrangements. The same can be said for other basic assets necessary for the normal conduct of the surviving spouse's life.

B. The Gift Tax

In 2008 the rate of the gift tax after the first $1 million of gifts was 45 percent. In 2010 the gift tax rate will be reduced (not eliminated, as with the estate tax) to 35 percent for all gifts in excess of $500,000.

1. The Annual Gift Tax Exclusion

While it is not the purpose of this book to discuss the federal gift tax, a little background on it is needed because its provisions play an important role in estate planning, with particular relevance to landowners and conservation easements. One important feature of the federal gift tax is the $12,000 annual exclusion from the tax.

The $12,000 gift tax exclusion, unlike the $1 million gift tax exemption, is allowed annually for each gift made to a different individual. In addition, gifts made jointly by a husband and wife are considered a separate gift for each spouse and are each eligible for a $24,000 exclusion ($12,000 × 2).

The $12,000 exclusion effectively avoids not only the gift tax, but also the estate tax by removing assets from a person's estate prior to his death, and therefore from liability for estate tax. The Code requires the annual exclusion to be adjusted for inflation. Because many assets are subject to appreciation in value, and therefore increasing estate tax over time, it may make sense to gift them, thus paying tax at the current value of the gift rather than the potentially higher value when the owner dies.

Example: Don and Jean have three married children and four grandchildren. By using the annual exclusion and making joint gifts, they can make gifts sheltered by the gift tax exclusion amounting to $240,000 per year. This can be done by making a $24,000 joint gift to each child (amounting to $72,000); similar joint gifts to the spouse of each child (also amounting to $72,000); and four $24,000 joint gifts to each of the four grandchildren (amounting to $96,000).

The annual exclusion is a very important part of many basic estate plans. Annual gifts to children (typically made to a trust set up for children, or through the Uniform Gift to Minors Act), if started while parents are relatively young, can, over the years, effectively transfer substantial amounts tax free. While it is easier to transfer liquid assets (stocks, bonds, or cash), it is also possible to transfer land.

---

a. Gifts of Land

Because land is not "liquid" like cash or stocks and bonds, and because dividing land and valuing the resulting portions is difficult, it merits a bit of additional discussion.

There are several ways in which land may be gifted. The most obvious way is to make the gift outright in "fee simple." The problem with that type of gift is that existing parcels of land are unlikely to fit within the annual $12,000 gift tax exclusion (or the joint gift exclusion for husbands and wives of $24,000). It is typically necessary to divide land into smaller parcels based on an appraised per-acre value, which is not very practical and may be further complicated by local land-use regulations.

One alternative is to gift an undivided percentage interest in land (typically called a "tenancy in common"). For example, if a ranch is worth $2 million, an undivided 1.2 percent interest in the ranch would equal $24,000 (actually less, because there would be a substantial discount in value for such a small minority interest; see the discussion of "discounting" in section I, B, 1, b of this chapter).

Another alternative is to transfer the ranch to an entity such as a family limited partnership (FLP) or a limited liability company (these entities are described in chapter 4, section V). These entities allow property interests to be divided fairly simply. The "division" takes place in the form of membership interests in an LLC or limited partner shares in the FLP, leaving the property itself intact. This type of division does not require the actual physical division of the land. In addition, these entities allow a form of centralized decision making (by the general partner in an FLP or the managing member in an LLC), so that the parents, for example, may continue to control the ranching operation.

185

LLCs and FLPs (as opposed to corporations) are often called "pass-through" entities because they allow the income and deductions associated with any property held by the entity to pass through to the limited partners or members in proportion to their ownership interests. So-called S corporations (see section V of chapter 4 for a description of corporation types) have some of the attributes of pass-through entities, but they are more complex and have tax aspects that can be less advantageous to shareholders.

b. Discounting

One important consequence of making annual gifts is that by transferring a portion of the interest in family land (or a family business) to children, the value of the interest retained by the parent may be reduced by considerably more than the percentage interest actually transferred. This is due to "discounting" rules. The tax law considers that the marketability, and therefore the value, of an asset is significantly less if it is only partially owned or controlled by a person than if wholly controlled by that person.

Therefore, by transferring a 25 percent interest in the family ranch LLC to children, the parents may have reduced the value of the ranch in their estates by considerably more than 25 percent, without increasing the value transferred to the children (unless the transfer gives them a majority interest, which may affect the taxable value of what they receive). The "lost" value resulting from lost control is not picked up by the children to whom the gift is made because they don't obtain the control that the parents have given up (also reducing the taxable value of what they receive). Discounting through partial interest transfers is a complex business and should be undertaken *only* with qualified tax counsel. Any further discussion is beyond the scope of this book.

c. Other Issues with Annual Gifts

In addition to the complexity of making annual gifts of land, there are other important considerations regarding gifts. Probably the most important is whether it is advisable, as a family matter, to transfer (ultimately) control over the family ranch to the children during the parents' lifetimes. This will depend a great deal on family dynamics. How should a family divide land when some children are working on the ranch and some are not? When some love the ranch and others hate it? The point here is this: Tax planning is important but not always as important as what will happen to the family when the parents begin to shift control of major family assets to other family members.

Another point to keep in mind is that assets transferred by gift do not receive a stepped-up basis as do assets that pass through a decedent's estate (see the discussion in section I, A, 3 of this chapter). Therefore, when gifted property is sold, the tax on the gain is likely to be considerably higher than if the property passed at death and thereby received an increased basis.

In addition, property transferred by gift is not eligible for the 40 percent estate tax exclusion provided by Code section 2031(c) for land subject to a conservation easement. (Code section 2031(c) is discussed in detail in chapter 8, section IV.)

2. Other Gift Tax Exemptions

All gifts between a husband and wife are sheltered by the marital deduction (see section I, A, 5 of this chapter), and are therefore exempt from the gift tax. In addition, payments made for tuition (but not room, board, books, etc.) and for medical expenses on behalf of another person (whether or not a family member) are exempt from the gift tax, regardless of the amount paid (Code section 2503(e)).

186

II. Special Use Valuation: Code Section 2032A

As previously noted, the estate tax is particularly troublesome for farmers and ranchers (and anyone else for whom real property makes up a substantial part of a trade or business that is, essentially, family owned). This is because farmers and ranchers often have valuable estates due to the value of the farm or ranch but little in the way of cash or other liquid assets, such as stocks and bonds that can easily be converted to cash to pay estate taxes. Recognizing this problem, Congress has provided that the executors of estates in which the real and personal property included in a farm, ranch, or other family-owned business makes up at least 50 percent of the value of all of a decedent's assets may elect to have the farm or ranch assets valued based on the income that the farm or ranch can generate as an agricultural operation, not on its development potential.

There are a number of complex requirements for qualifying for this election. They are found in Code section 2032A and are beyond the scope of this book. However, two of the most important are (1) the decedent must have "materially participated" in the farm or ranch operation or closely held business for a certain period of time before he died; and (2) a member of the decedent's family must agree to operate the farm, ranch, or closely held business for at least ten years after the decedent's death without selling or otherwise transferring title to any of the specially valued property.

In the event that the property subject to the election is converted from farm or ranch use, or from the closely held business, or is transferred out of the family, a "recapture tax" equal to the estate tax reduction due to the special valuation is imposed. This tax is imposed if the conversion occurs within 10 years of the decedent's death. The tax is prorated if only a portion of the property is converted. The Code does exempt from the penalty the conveyance of a conservation easement during the 10-year period (Code section 2032A(c)(8)).

In addition, there is a limit to the amount of value that may be eliminated from a decedent's estate by this provision. In 2007 the maximum reduction in value allowed by section 2032A was $940,000. The Code provides for the adjustment of this limitation to reflect inflation.

Example: John owned Two-Rivers Ranch, which he operated with his son, Bill, for over 20 years. John had been divorced for many years. He died in 2006 and left the entire ranch to his son. The appraised value of the ranch, taking into consideration its development potential (it has over two miles of scenic frontage on a nationally recognized trout stream) was $3 million. John also had $200,000 in equipment and $50,000 in cash and no debt. Therefore, his gross estate amounted to $3,250,000.

The first $2 million of John's estate was covered by the Exclusion Amount. His executor elected the special valuation treatment for the ranch allowed by section 2032A. The value of the ranch, as a ranch, using the valuation method provided in the tax code, was only $1 million, not $3 million. The reduction in value due to section 2032A was, therefore, $2 million ($3,000,000 – $1,000,000). However, the maximum reduction for estate tax purposes allowed by section 2032A is $940,000. Therefore, between the $2 million Exclusion Amount and the $940,000 reduction under section 2032A, John's taxable estate was $310,000 ($3,250,000 – $2,000,000 – $940,000). The estate tax in 2007 on $310,000 was $139,500 ($310,000 × .45). The 2032A election saved Bill $423,000 ($940,000 × .45) in estate tax.

III. Generation-Skipping Transfer Tax

Generation-skipping transfers (GSTs) are subject to special estate tax rules. A GST occurs when a person (the grantor) transfers property through the use of a trust (created during the grantor's lifetime or by the grantor's will) to a member of a generation at least twice removed from the grantor's own generation—for example, to a grandchild, great-grandchild, grandniece or grandnephew. Typically, GST trusts provide for payment of income and a possibility of enjoying some of the trust principal for educational or other uses stipulated in the trust and within the control of the trustee, for the intervening generation. The original purpose of GSTs was to allow the intervening generation (the "skip generation") to enjoy the income from a decedent's assets without subjecting those assets to estate tax, and then pass them on to the next generation.

The tax law assumes that the normal way to transfer property from one generation to another is one generation at a time, without skipping over intervening generations. In other words, generation one passes property on to generation two for its use, generation two passes on what is left of the property to generation three, and so forth. A generation-skipping transfer, by contrast, is one in which generation one passes property directly, or in trust, to generation three or four, skipping over generation two.

Example: Mary, a widow, has $1 million in stocks and bonds. She dearly loves her three children but considers that they have plenty of money already. She has one granddaughter, Susie, age four. Mary provides that upon her death, the $1 million in stocks and bonds will be placed in a trust. The terms of the trust are that all income from the trust is to be distributed equally to her three children on a quarterly basis. She also provides that in the event of a financial emergency, the trustee may distribute up to $100,000 of the trust to the child experiencing the emergency. Finally, the trust provides that when all three of Mary's children die, the balance of the trust is to be distributed outright to Susie, provided that Susie is then at least 25 years old. If she isn't yet 25, the trust remains in force until she reaches that age.

The transfer of property from one generation to the next, to the next, and so on generates a tax at each step. The GST skips one or more generations, thereby eliminating the tax on the generations that have been skipped.

The tax on GSTs is intended to generate, more or less, what would have been the tax if the property had passed from one generation to the next without any skips. There is an exemption from the GST tax equivalent to the $2 million Exclusion Amount, which (like the Exclusion Amount) is scheduled to increase to $3.5 million in 2009. The exclusion from the GST replicates the exclusion that would have been applicable to the second generation's transfer to the third, had the second generation not been skipped. The tax on the GST is also equivalent to the unified estate and gift tax amount, currently 45 percent.

Example: In the preceding example of Mary, there would be no tax because of the $2 million generation-skipping tax exclusion. However, if Mary had put $3 million into the GST trust for Susie's benefit, there would have been a tax of 46 percent (in 2006) on the $1 million by which the trust exceeded the $2 million exclusion.

The GST tax rules are highly complex, and anyone contemplating a GST of any sort *must* consult qualified tax counsel.

CHAPTER EIGHT:

Conservation Easements and Estate and Gift Taxes

I. Two Types of Conservation Easement Estate Tax Benefits

In addition to generating income tax benefits, conservation easements can result in substantial estate tax savings. Two kinds of estate tax benefits arise from the conveyance of a conservation easement. First, when land subject to a conservation easement is included in a decedent's estate, the determination of the value of that land takes into account the restrictions imposed by the easement (I will call this benefit the "reduction"). Second, under Code section 2031(c) the decedent's executor is allowed to exclude 40 percent of the value of the easement land as restricted by the easement, up to a maximum exclusion of $500,000. I will call this 40 percent exclusion the "2031(c) exclusion," not to be confused with the Exclusion Amount described in chapter 7. A husband and wife can easily double the 2031(c) exclusion to $1 million (see section IV, C, 1 of this chapter).

The "reduction" in estate value attributable to a conservation easement is a simple concept: Any land subject to a conservation easement that meets the requirements of Code section 170(h) included in a decedent's estate is valued as restricted by the easement, not at its unrestricted value.

Example One: John's estate includes a 300-acre farm. The farm is subject to a qualified conservation easement. The value of the farm subject to the easement is $1 million. Had the farm been unrestricted, its value would have been $5 million. The easement has reduced the size of John's estate by $4 million.

The following example shows the operation of the estate tax in a situation where there is no conservation easement.

Example Two: Sally and Bill own Polecat Ranch, which includes about 2,000 acres near Cody, Wyoming. The ranch has tremendous resource values, beautiful views, spring creeks, and a great trout stream. Sally and Bill run the ranch as a dude ranch. Their two children, Susan and Doug, live on the ranch with their families and help with its operation. Because of its high "amenity values," the ranch is worth $10 million for large-lot, "trophy home" development.

In addition to the ranch, Sally and Bill have about $500,000 in investments and another $250,000 in equipment. Therefore, their gross estate is $10,750,000. Sally and Bill have done some basic estate planning: The ranch is titled 50 percent in Sally's name and 50 percent in Bill's name as tenants in common (not a "survivorship" interest). Each has a will providing that no more than $2 million (or whatever amount is equivalent to the Exclusion Amount allowed for the year of death) in assets owned by the first to die will go to a bypass trust for the benefit of the survivor, then to the children. In this fashion Sally and Bill have each maximized use of the Exclusion Amount. All of the assets of the first to die, other than the assets passing to the bypass trust, pass outright to the surviving spouse. In the event there is no surviving spouse, all of the assets go directly to Susan and Doug. (All of the concepts included in this example are explained in chapter 7.)

Bill dies in January of 2006; he is the first to die. His gross estate is valued at $5,750,000. This is one-half of the value of the ranch, plus all of the other assets (owned jointly). However, there is no tax payable on his estate because the entire estate is sheltered by either the $2 million Exclusion Amount or the marital deduction.

Sally dies in August of 2006. Her estate is valued at $8,750,000. This is the entire value of both Sally's and Bill's estates, less the $2 million that passed under Bill's estate to the bypass trust. After subtracting debts, administrative expenses, and so forth, Sally's taxable estate amounts to $8.5 million. Taking the $2 million Exclusion Amount into account, the estate tax that will be due on Sally's estate is $2,990,000 ($6,500,000 × .46, the applicable rate in 2006).

Example Three: Now let's assume that Sally and Bill donated a conservation easement on the ranch before they died. The easement allowed continued operation of the dude ranch and agricultural use. It also allowed the ranch to be divided into four parcels, each with one home site, guesthouse, barns, etc. The easement reduced the value of the ranch from $10 million to $5 million. This dramatically changes the estate tax liability.

Bill's gross estate now amounts to $3,250,000. In addition, Bill's executor elects the 2031(c) exclusion. That election removes another $500,000 from Bill's gross estate, bringing it down to $2,750,000. Another $2 million goes into the bypass trust, and the remaining $750,000 goes directly to Sally, sheltered from tax by the marital deduction. There is no tax due on Bill's estate.

When Sally dies in August, her gross estate amounts to $3,250,000. Sally's executor also elects the 2031(c) exclusion on her portion of the ranch, reducing her gross estate by $500,000, from $3,250,000 to $2,750,000. After payment of debts, administration expenses, etc., Sally's taxable estate amounts to $2,500,000. Taking the $2 million Exclusion Amount into account, the estate tax on Sally's estate is $230,000 ($500,000 × .46). The conservation easement saved Susan and Doug $2,760,000 in estate taxes, making it possible for them to keep the ranch.

II. The Reduction in Value

When a person dies, his executor (or administrator if he dies without a will) is responsible for collecting and valuing the property he owned when he died. As part of that valuation process, the executor is required to consider all of the factors affecting property value, including conservation easements.

A. Demonstrating Savings

If a landowner conveyed a conservation easement prior to his death, that easement must be taken into account by the executor in determining the value of the estate. Because easement land comes into a decedent's estate with the restrictions in place, it also comes in at a reduced value, which reflects those restrictions. To demonstrate the actual estate tax savings attributable to a conservation easement, you must compare the potential estate tax as though the land were not restricted, with the estate tax taking into account the easement restrictions. Of course, an executor has no need to demonstrate savings, only to include the easement land at its restricted value.

B. The Reduction Increases over Time

The reduction in the value of a landowner's property due to a conservation easement may be much greater when he dies than when the easement was conveyed, because land values may have appreciated since the conveyance. As the development potential eliminated by a conservation easement appreciates, the reduction in value attributable to the easement, and therefore the estate tax savings, also increases.

Example: Deborah contributed a conservation easement on her farm in 1990. At that time the unrestricted value of the farm was $300,000, and the value of the farm as restricted by the easement was $125,000. Deborah died in 2007. The farm was included in her estate and valued at $500,000, reflecting the existence of the conservation easement. Deborah's children complained that the easement failed to save any estate taxes because the value of the land appreciated by 400 percent in spite of the easement. However, Deborah's executor pointed out that if there had been no easement in place, the value of the farm would be $2 million; thus, the easement removed $1,500,000 from Deborah's estate.

Some of Deborah's children were happy to have the farm and the savings in estate taxes; others were unhappy not to have the additional $1,500,000 in assets, even though estate taxes would have reduced that amount 45 percent. However, Deborah loved her farm and her children. The easement allowed her, and them, to keep the farm intact and prevented an inter-family fight over the future use of the farm.

C. Reduction Applies to Easements That Are Sold

As noted, a conservation easement on real property included in a decedent's estate reduces the value of that property for estate tax purposes. This "reduction" in value is applicable regardless of whether the easement was sold or contributed. The value of real property subject to a conservation easement will be determined at the same time as other estate assets: on the date of the decedent's death or six months after the death if the executor elects the alternate date.

Example One: Mrs. Smith's land was worth $4 million at her death. That was the value of her land without considering the effect of the conservation easement that she contributed prior to her death. When the effect of the easement was taken into account, the value of the land was only $2 million. Thus, the easement reduced the size of her taxable estate by $2 million. Because the other assets in her estate were substantial enough that the entire $2 million in land value removed by the easement would have been taxed at the top estate tax rate of 45 percent, the estate tax savings due to the easement was $900,000 ($2,000,000 × .45).

Example Two: Mr. Blue sold a conservation easement in 2000 for $550,000. The easement reduced the value of the easement land by $1 million. Mr. Blue is entitled to a bargain sale deduction for the difference between what he received for the easement and what it was worth: $450,000 ($1,000,000 − $550,000).

Mr. Blue died in 2007. At his death the value of his land was $2,500,000, taking into account the restrictions of the easement. If the land had been unrestricted, the value in 2007 would have been $5 million. Therefore, the easement reduced his taxable estate by $2,500,000, generating estate tax savings of $1,125,000 ($2,500,000 × .45). However, Mr. Blue bought stock with the $467,500 (net of taxes) that he received from the sale of the easement. At his death, the stock had a value of $1 million. The estate tax on that value was $450,000 ($1,000,000 × .45).

Taking into account the tax savings due to the restrictions imposed by the conservation easement, and the tax on the stock purchased with the proceeds of sale of the easement, the net estate tax savings to Mr. Blue's estate was $675,000 ($1,125,000 − $450,000).

D. The Effect of Restrictions Other Than Conservation Easements: Regulations Section 25.2703-1(a)

Generally, restrictions on real property (e.g., options, restrictions on use, the right to acquire or use property for less than fair market value) *cannot* be taken into account by an estate in valuing the property for estate tax purposes. However, qualified easements, pursuant to Code section 170(h), granted during a decedent's lifetime are exempt from this provision (Regulations section 25.2703-1(b)(4)), and are also deductible for gift tax purposes under Code section 2522(d). In addition, easements qualified under Code section 170(h) that are conveyed by the terms of a decedent's will are qualified for estate tax deductions under Code section 2055(f) (but without regard to Code section 170(h)(4)(A)), as noted in section III, C of this chapter.

Certain other restrictions are also permitted to be considered for estate valuation purposes, provided that all of the following requirements are met:

- the restrictions are the result of a "bona fide business arrangement";
- the restrictions are not a device to transfer the property to family members for less than adequate consideration; and
- the terms of the restriction are comparable to similar arrangements entered into by persons in an arm's-length transaction (Regulations sections 25.2703-1(b)(1) and (2)).

Example: Mr. Brinkman sells a "scenic easement" over Greenacre to his neighbor, the owner of Brownacre. The easement expires after 50 years. The easement is, in effect, a restrictive covenant benefiting Mr. Brinkman's neighbor and any future owners of Brownacre during that period. The scenic easement prohibits construction over an area of some 200 acres within view of Brownacre. It also reduces the value of Greenacre by 25 percent.

Although this scenic easement does not qualify as a conservation contribution within the meaning of Code section 170(h), it does meet the three requirements of Regulations section 25.2703-1(b)(1) and (2) described above. Therefore, when Mr. Brinkman dies, his executor is allowed to take into account the effect of the scenic easement on the value of Greenacre.

III. Gift and Estate Tax Deductions for Conservation Easements

In addition to the reduction and 2031(c) exclusion, the Code allows a deduction from the federal estate tax for conservation easements bequeathed by a decedent's will. The Code also allows a deduction from the federal gift tax for lifetime transfers of conservation easements. These deductions are described below.

A. The Gift Tax Deduction

This may be a bit less confusing if you recognize that there are several different types of taxes involved here. The earlier chapters of this book focused on the federal income tax and how conservation easements that qualified as charitable contributions may be deducted from income in computing income tax. Now I am talking about a different type of tax, the tax on gifts made during a person's lifetime. Such transfers are subject to the federal gift tax. So there are really two deductions that figure into this section: the income tax deduction *and* the gift tax deduction. To qualify for the gift tax deduction, a conservation easement must also qualify for the income tax deduction.

Generally, all gifts made during a person's lifetime are subject to the federal gift tax. This tax applies to contributions that are not recognized as charitable—for example, gifts to children. Even gifts to charity are subject to the gift tax if those gifts are not qualified as charitable contributions—for example, a partial interest gift that does not fall into one of the four exceptions described in section I, A of chapter 3.

However, Code section 2522(d) allows a gift tax deduction for gifts that are deductible as charitable contributions. In other words, the Code allows an income tax deduction for the lifetime contribution of a conservation easement *and* excuses such a contribution from the gift tax.

B. The Estate Tax Deduction

Sometimes a landowner is reluctant to make an easement contribution during his lifetime because of concern that his plans or needs for the land might change. Such a landowner could provide for the contribution of a conservation easement in his will, figuring that he can always change his will to eliminate the easement provision if needed. Contributions of conservation easements made by will *are not eligible for federal or state income tax deductions*. However, such contributions are eligible for an estate tax deduction under Code section 2055(f). The amount of the deduction is equal to the value of the easement, determined in the same way as an income tax deduction for the contribution of a conservation easement (see chapter 5).

The estate tax benefit for an easement contributed by will takes the form of a deduction because the property to be placed under easement comes into the decedent's estate unrestricted and, therefore, at full fair market value. Section 2055(f) allows the estate to deduct the value of the easement, netting the same result (for estate tax purposes) as if the decedent had contributed the easement prior to death.

C. The Conservation Purposes Test Does Not Apply

Both the gift tax deduction and the estate tax deduction for a conservation easement are allowed *regardless* of whether the easement meets the
"conservation purposes" requirement imposed by Code section
170(h)(4)(A) for federal income tax deductions (see section I, D of chapter 3). Presumably, if a conservation easement is not required to meet the
conservation purposes test, it would not be subject to the prohibition on
the retention of rights that are inconsistent with conservation purposes
(see section II of chapter 3 regarding inconsistent uses), although this is
only logical speculation.

 According to the official 1986 explanation of the gift and estate
tax easement deductions, the reason for exempting gifts and bequests of
easements from the conservation purposes requirement was to avoid a situation in which a decedent made an irrevocable bequest of a conservation
easement but, because the easement failed to meet a technical standard of
the tax code, the property subject to the easement was taxed in the decedent's estate at full value, even though it was permanently restricted. See
the Committee Reports on P.L. 99-514 (Tax Reform Act of 1986).
Regulations have not been promulgated, nor cases decided, under this
provision to give further guidance.

 It is also possible that an easement that fails to meet the conservation purposes test might constitute a restriction on the use of real property that a decedent's executor could take into account in valuing such
property for estate tax purposes under Code section 2703, as discussed in
subsection D of this section II.

Example One: Mr. Brown, a farmer, has a very large estate because of the
value of his farmland, but he has only a small income. An income tax
deduction is not going to do him much good. His children love the farm,
and neither they nor he want it to be sold out of the family. Because of the
uncertainty of his financial situation, Mr. Brown doesn't want to restrict
his ability to sell the farm for top dollar while he is living (Mrs. Brown left
years earlier, thoroughly disgusted with farming). Therefore, Mr. Brown
provides in his will for the contribution of a conservation easement on the
farm (incorporating into the will a complete draft of the easement, so that
his executor doesn't have to guess what it should contain).

 The executor values the farmland on the date of Mr. Brown's
death at $4 million before the easement and at $2 million after the easement. The executor is able to deduct the $2 million value of the easement

under Code section 2055(f). That saves Mr. Brown's children $900,000 in estate taxes because the entire $2 million would have been subject to the 45 percent marginal rate (the top rate in 2007). Due to the $2 million estate tax exemption in 2007, and the 2031(c) exclusion, the easement entirely eliminates the estate tax on Mr. Brown's estate.

Note: Under the terms of Code section 2031(c)(9), even if Mr. Brown hadn't made a provision in his will for the easement, his heirs could have directed the executor to donate a "post-mortem" easement that would have given the estate the same tax benefits as the testamentary easement. See the discussion of post-mortem easements in section IV, T of this chapter.

Example Two: The easement provided for in Mr. Brown's will simply stated that its purpose was preservation of the family farm. It did not prohibit a number of farm-related uses that were harmful to the valuable wildlife habitat that occupied a portion of the farm; in fact, it allowed future owners to eliminate that habitat if desired to expand the farming operation.

While these provisions of Mr. Brown's easement clearly fail to meet the requirements of Code section 170(h)(4)(A) regarding conservation purposes, because the easement was conveyed pursuant to his will at his death, it is exempt from those requirements. A deduction from the estate is, therefore, allowed in the amount of the value of the easement.

IV. The 2031(c) Exclusion

In addition to recognizing the reduction in the value of real property resulting from the restrictions of a conservation easement, federal tax law allows 40 percent of the value of land (but not improvements) subject to a qualified conservation easement to be excluded from a decedent's estate (note that the exclusion must be affirmatively elected by a decedent's executor; see section IV, M of this chapter). To date, no regulations or cases concerning the 40 percent exclusion are available to provide guidance. Note that this exclusion applies to the value of easement land as already reduced by the restrictions of the conservation easement.

The exclusion started out as a simple and compelling concept: If a landowner contributed a conservation easement that qualified under Code section 170(h), the entire value of that land would be excluded from his estate for estate tax purposes. However, the legislative process had its way with that concept, and the result is a more complex, and less compelling, provision. An amendment of Code section 2031(c) that would increase the amount of the exclusion substantially has been proposed in Congress. How it will fare is unknown.

A. Qualified Conservation Easements:
Code Section 2031(c)(8)(B)

The 2031(c) exclusion does not apply to all qualified conservation contributions, as do the deductions under Code sections 170(h) and 2055(f); it applies only to "qualified conservation easements." There are several differences between qualified conservation contributions and qualified conservation easements.

First, the term *qualified conservation easement* excludes certain types of contributions that are considered as *qualified conservation contribution* (see chapter 3, section I, B). Second, a qualified conservation easement must meet requirements that a qualified conservation contribution does not: (1) the easement must apply to land held by the decedent or a member of the decedent's family for at least a three-year period immediately preceding the decedent's death; (2) the easement contribution must have been made by the decedent or a member of the decedent's family (as defined in the law); (3) the conservation purposes of the easement cannot be limited to historic preservation; and (4) the easement can allow no more than a "de minimis commercial recreational use." These requirements are discussed in more detail in section IV, P of this chapter.

Again, the 2031(c) exclusion should not be confused with the Exclusion Amount described in section I, A, 4 of chapter 7. The 2031(c) exclusion is allowed *in addition to* the Exclusion Amount.

B. Extent of the 2031(c) Exclusion: Code Section 2031(c)(2)

Code section 2031(c)(2) provides that a decedent's executor *may elect* to exclude 40 percent of the value of land subject to a qualified conservation easement. In other words, the exclusion applies to the value of the land, *taking into account* the restrictions of the easement. Values (for estates of decedents dying after December 31, 2000) are determined as of the date of the decedent's death, or six months thereafter if the executor elects the "alternate valuation date" (Code section 2031(c)(2)).

Example: Before he died, Mr. Brown contributed a conservation easement on his farm that reduced the value of the farm from $3 million to

$1 million. The value of the farm on the date of his death remained at $1 million, taking into account the restrictions of the easement. Mr. Brown's executor elected to exclude 40 percent of the restricted value of the farm (the $1 million) from his estate under Code section 2031(c). Therefore, $400,000 ($1,000,000 × .40) may be excluded. The easement reduced the taxable value of the land in Mr. Brown's estate by $2,400,000: $2 million from the initial reduction in value and $400,000 due to the exclusion. Taken together, the reduction and the exclusion saved Mr. Brown's heirs $1,080,000 ($2,400,000 × .45) in federal estate tax.

C. The Exclusion Is Limited to $500,000 per Estate: Code Section 2031(c)(3)

Regardless of how much value is represented by 40 percent of land subject to a qualified conservation easement, the amount that may be excluded is limited to $500,000 *per estate*. The limitation was phased in beginning in 1998, in $100,000 increments. The $500,000 limit applies to the estates of decedents who die after December 31, 2001.

Example: James owns land subject to a qualified conservation easement. The value of the land, as restricted by the easement, is $2 million. James dies in 2007. Forty percent of the value of the restricted land is $800,000 ($2,000,000 × .40). However, the maximum amount that may be excluded by James's estate is $500,000; thus, James's executor may exclude only $500,000.

---

1. The Benefits of the Exclusion May Be Multiplied

Because the $500,000 limitation on the exclusion applies per estate, not per easement (Code section 2031(c)(1)), one conservation easement can generate multiple exclusions.

Example One: Mr. Green and his wife own land as tenants in common, with each entitled to a 50 percent share. In a tenancy in common, the interest of the first decedent does not automatically pass to the surviving tenant, as it does with joint tenancies and tenancies by the entirety. In their wills each of the Greens provides that his or her share of the land goes directly to their children rather than to the surviving spouse. The Greens put extensive easements on the land, reducing the value of the land overall from $6,500,000 to $2,500,000. Accordingly, the 50 percent share of the land owned by each, as restricted by the easement, is worth $1,250,000. The exclusion available to each of the Greens' estates would be $500,000 ($1,250,000 × .40). Dividing the ownership of the land and keeping it separate enabled the Greens to exclude an aggregate $1million from their estates by qualifying each estate to use the exclusion up to the $500,000 limit.

Example Two: Four brothers own a ranch inherited from their parents as equal tenants in common. They donate a qualified conservation easement on the ranch. The value of the ranch before the easement was $20 million; after the easement it was $10 million. The brothers all die in a blizzard in 2007. Their executors each elect to take advantage of the 40 percent exclusion. Each estate receives the decedent brother's 25 percent interest in the ranch, worth $2,500,000 ($10,000,000 × .25), taking into account the restrictions of the easement. The value of the exclusion available to each estate prior to the $500,000 limitation is $1 million ($2,500,000 × .40). Each estate may elect to exclude up to $500,000 of its share of the ranch. Therefore, the total value of the ranch that may be excluded is $2 million ($500,000 × 4). In this manner one conservation easement qualified for four separate exclusions of $500,000 each.

The net effect of the conservation easement in this example was to reduce the taxable value of the entire ranch by $12 million. This is the combination of the initial reduction in value due to the restrictions of the conservation easement ($20,000,000 − $10,000,000 = 10,000,000) and the exclusion of $500,000 available to each brother's estate ($500,000 × 4 = $2,000,000). Assuming that all of the value thus removed from the four brothers' estates would have been taxed at the 45 percent federal estate tax rate, total estate tax savings between the four estates would amount to $5,400,000 ($12,000,000 × .45). Due to the $2 million exemption from estate tax available in 2007, none of the brothers' estates would be taxable.

Note: If the brothers had held their interests in the ranch as partners in a partnership, as members in a limited liability company, or as stockholders in a corporation, the result would not have been the same. Because each brother would have owned less than 30 percent of the partnership, limited liability company, or corporation, their estates would not have been eligible for the exclusion. Code section 2031(c)(10) allows the exclusion for partnership, corporation, and trust interests held by a decedent only if the decedent owned at least 30 percent of such entity (see section IV, S of this chapter).

D. The Easement Must Meet the Requirements of Code Section 170(h) to Qualify for the Exclusion: Code Section 2031(c)(8)(B)

The easement must meet the requirements of Code section 170(h) for a qualified conservation contribution, described in chapter 3, *including* the conservation purposes test. Therefore, while it is possible for an easement that does not meet the conservation purposes test of Code section 170(h)(4)(A) to be deductible for estate and gift tax purposes (see section III, C of chapter 8), and possible for other permanent restrictions on the use of property to reduce the value of that property for estate tax purposes under Code section 2703, such easements or restrictions *will not* qualify for the exclusion because they do not comply with Code section 170(h).

E. The Exclusion Applies to Land Only: Code Section 2031(c)(1)(A)

The exclusion applies only to the value of land, not to improvements on the land.

Example: Mrs. White died owning a 200-acre farm subject to a qualified conservation easement. The easement allows only agricultural use of the land and imposes architectural standards on the house, a certified historic structure. Without the easement the land would be worth $1 million and the house and outbuildings $350,000. Taking the easement into account, the land is valued at $750,000 and the house and outbuildings at $300,000 for estate tax purposes. Mrs. White's executor elected the Code section 2031(c) exclusion. As a result he could exclude $300,000 of the restricted value of the land ($750,000 × .40). The exclusion does not apply to the house and outbuildings. Thus, for estate tax purposes, the conservation easement resulted in a total reduction of $600,000 in the value of Mrs. White's farm. This is due to a reduction of $250,000 in the value of the farmland, a reduction of $50,000 in the value of the structures, and the exclusion of $300,000 in the value of the farmland as restricted by the easement. The easement saves Mrs. White's heirs $270,000 in federal estate tax ($600,000 × .45), assuming that all of the value removed by the easement was subject to tax.

F. The Exclusion Does Not Apply to the Gift Tax

As noted, the Code taxes gifts made during an individual's lifetime as well as transfers at death. However, the exclusion *does not apply* to the gift tax. For this reason estate-planning strategies based on lifetime transfers of property should carefully evaluate the effect of making a lifetime gift of easement land. A lifetime gift of easement land that is subject to a conservation easement, and otherwise qualifies for the exclusion, will waste the exclusion. However, there may be other overriding reasons to make a lifetime transfer of such land.

Example: Mr. Smith donated a conservation easement on 100 acres. The value of the land as restricted by the easement is $200,000. Before he dies Mr. Smith gives the land to his son. The gift is subject to the full federal gift tax on a $200,000 gift (which could be as much as $90,000), and none of the value of the land can be excluded under Code section 2031(c).

If Mr. Smith had transferred the land to his son by will, only $120,000 of the value of the land would have been subject to tax. That is because the exclusion would reduce the taxable value by $80,000 ($200,000 × .40). Assuming that both the lifetime gift and the bequest would have been taxed at 45 percent (the maximum estate and gift tax rate in 2007), transferring the land by lifetime gift rather than by will would cost Mr. Smith $36,000 ($80,000 × .45) in gift tax over and above what the estate tax would have been had the transfer been made at death.

G. The Exclusion Does Not Apply to Easements Whose Sole Conservation Purpose Is Historic Preservation: Code Section 2031(c)(8)(B)

The exclusion does not apply if the *sole* conservation purpose of the easement is preservation of the historic character of the land (historic structures, being improvements rather than land, aren't eligible for the exclusion, either). However, the fact that land is historic does not disqualify an easement over the property for the exclusion if there is another bona fide conservation purpose for the easement.

Example: Sally owns a historic 18th-century New England farm. The land is identified in the local comprehensive plan and zoning ordinance as prime agricultural land and is accorded a special reduced real estate tax assessment because of its agricultural value. Sally donates a conservation easement protecting the historic and agricultural characteristics of the farm. When she dies, her executor may elect to exclude 40 percent of the value of the land making up the farm after taking the value of the easement into account. Even though the easement has a historic purpose, it also has the purpose of preserving open space pursuant to "a clearly delineated governmental conservation policy" (i.e., farmland preservation).

If the sole purpose of the easement and the only significant characteristic of the farm were its historical significance, the exclusion would not be available. However, assuming that the easement is a qualified conservation contribution, the easement would qualify for an income tax deduction. In addition, such an easement would reduce the value of Sally's property for estate tax purposes.

205

H. The Exclusion Is Available for the Estates of Decedents Dying after 12/31/97

Regardless of the date on which a decedent contributes a qualified conservation easement, the exclusion will be available to her estate if she dies after December 31, 1997, which was the effective date of Code section 2031(c).

Example: Mary donated an easement in 1980 that is a qualified conservation easement. She died December 1, 2000. Because she died after December 31, 1997, her estate may elect to use the exclusion.

I. Three-Year Holding Period Required: Code Section 2031(c)(8)(A)(ii)

One of the many concerns of the staff of the Joint Committee on Taxation that controlled the drafting and "scoring" (determining the loss in tax revenues attributable to "tax breaks") of the legislative proposal that led to the 2031(c) exclusion was that the 2031(c) exclusion would become a tax shelter, inducing people to cash in securities and other types of assets and buy land to make their estates eligible for the exclusion. While this seems a bit unlikely, the concern led to the requirement that to qualify for the exclusion, the easement land had to have been held by the decedent, or a member of the decedent's family, for at least three years prior to the death. For purposes of this provision "member of the decedent's family" includes the following:

- an ancestor of the decedent;
- the spouse of the decedent;
- a lineal descendent of the decedent, or of the decedent's spouse, or of a parent of the decedent; and
- the spouse of any such lineal descendent (Code section 2032A(e)(2)).

---

206 Example: Joel's father gave him 200 acres. His father owned the land for two years before he made the gift to Joel. Joel promptly donated a conservation easement on the land. He died two years later. The land will qualify for the exclusion because the total period of time that Joel and a member of his family owned the land immediately preceding Joel's death was four years.

J. The Exclusion May Be Used in Conjunction with Other Tax Benefits for Easements

The *exclusion*, the *reduction in value* of a decedent's estate due to the existence of a conservation easement, and the *income tax deduction* attributable to the original contribution of the easement may all be used in connection with the same easement contribution.

Example: Mr. Jones's land is valued at $1 million, and his easement reduces that value to $700,000. Mr. Jones is entitled to a $300,000 income tax deduction; his estate can report the value of the easement-restricted land as $700,000 rather than $1 million, and the executor can elect to exclude $280,000 of the remaining value under Code section 2031(c) ($700,000 × .40). In that manner the easement removes $580,000 ($300,000 + $280,000) from the taxable value of the estate, in addition to generating state and federal income tax deductions.

Assume that all of Mr. Jones's income sheltered by the easement deduction is taxed at the top 2007 federal rate of 35 percent and a state rate of 6 percent, and that the assets in his estate are taxed at the rate of 45 percent. Given these assumptions, contribution of an easement valued at $300,000 would save Mr. Jones and his estate a total of $384,000 in state and federal taxes. These savings are made up of income tax savings of $123,000 ([.35 + .06] × $300,000); estate tax savings of $135,000 due to the reduction in the value of the estate resulting from the conservation easement ($300,000 × .45); and additional estate tax savings of $126,000 due to the exclusion ($700,000 × .40 × .45).

In addition, the exclusion may be layered on top of the Exclusion Amount described in chapter 7, section I, A, 4, and the tax benefits available under the special valuation rules of Code section 2032A for qualified family farms, described in section II of chapter 7.

K. The Exclusion May Be Passed from One Generation to the Next: Code Section 2031(c)(8)(C)

The benefit of the exclusion is available to each succeeding generation of landowners as long as the land remains in the family of the donor. Once the land passes outside of the family, the exclusion is no longer available unless the new owner donates another easement on the land that independently qualifies under Code section 2031(c). If such a contribution can be made, the exclusion will be revived for the estate of the new donor and his heirs, as long as the land remains in that family.

Example One: Mr. Jones donated a qualified conservation easement on his land. When he died, the property passed to his son, John. John married and passed his land to his wife, Sarah, at his death. Sarah had a daughter, Julie, by a subsequent marriage (John died young). Julie inherited the land at Sarah's death, married, and had children who ultimately became beneficiaries of the land. Mr. Jones's estate was eligible for the exclusion, as were the estates of John, Sarah, Julie, and Julie's children (if the land is included in their estates at their deaths).

In addition, the reduction in value due to the restrictions imposed by the easement will be available to future generations in the family of the donor. However, unlike the exclusion, the reduction in value attributable to the restrictions of the easement remains available to owners outside of the family of the original donor in the event that the land is transferred outside of the family.

Example Two: Mr. Green donated a qualified conservation easement on his land, which reduced the development potential on the land from 100 houses to 10, generating a significant public conservation benefit. When Mr. Green died, the land passed to his son, Alfred. Alfred sold the land to his neighbor, Mrs. Brown. Mrs. Brown died, leaving the land to her daughter Melissa. Melissa donated a second conservation easement that eliminated the remaining 10 house sites, so that the land cannot be developed at all. The easement donated by Melissa is a qualified conservation easement. Melissa passed the land on to her daughter Joan, and it was included in Joan's estate at her death.

Mr. Green's estate was eligible for the exclusion. Alfred's estate didn't contain the property, so no exclusion was available and the proceeds of sale that remained in his estate at his death were fully taxable. Mrs. Brown's estate was not eligible for the exclusion because neither she nor any members of her family donated the easement. However, due to the new easement donated by Melissa, Melissa's estate was eligible, as was Joan's estate.

L. The Exclusion Imposes a Carryover Basis: Code Section 1014(a)(4)

To the extent of the exclusion, land received from a decedent has a carryover basis in the hands of heirs, rather than the stepped-up basis that is normally provided for assets passing at death. (See the discussion of stepped-up basis in section I, A, 3 of chapter 7.) As noted, basis is, essentially, what the owner paid for the land plus amounts paid for improvements. The significance of basis is that when property is sold, the seller pays tax on the difference between a property's basis and what the property sold for.

Carryover basis refers to passing on a decedent's basis in his property to his heirs. Normally, land passing from a decedent to heirs receives a stepped-up basis. This means that the decedent's basis in the property is replaced with a new basis reflecting the fair market value of the property when the decedent died. The stepped-up basis substantially reduces or eliminates income tax on sales of property received from a decedent's estate by heirs.

However, if the exclusion is elected, the stepped-up basis is not allowed for that portion of the property that is subject to the exclusion, and the basis in that portion will remain the same as the decedent's basis.

Improvements are not eligible for the exclusion; therefore, improvements will continue to receive a stepped-up basis, regardless of whether the exclusion is elected.

Example: Mr. Smith's estate includes land subject to a conservation easement. The restricted value of the land, as valued by the executor, is $750,000. Mr. Smith's basis in the land (adjusted to reflect the easement contribution; see section III of chapter 4) is $5,000. The exclusion allowed is $300,000 ($750,000 × .40). The carryover basis rule requires that 40 percent of Mr. Smith's $5,000 basis be carried over to the heirs, along with the stepped-up basis on that portion of the value of the land not subject to the exclusion. Thus $2,000 ($5,000 × .40) must be carried over to the heirs. That portion of the value of the land that was not subject to the exclusion, $450,000 ($750,000 – $300,000) will receive a stepped-up basis. The total adjusted basis for the land is therefore $452,000 ($2,000 + $450,000).

The effect of the carryover basis rule, given 2007 income and estate tax rates, is that while Mr. Smith's estate saves $135,000 in estate taxes ($300,000 × .45), the heirs are exposed to increased income tax liability on the sale of his easement property of $44,700 ([$750,000 – $452,000] × .15), assuming 15 percent is the capital gains tax rate when the property is sold.

While the carryover basis applicable to that property subject to the exclusion is a penalty of sorts for electing the exclusion, because estate tax rates are substantially higher than capital gains rates, it almost always makes sense to elect the exclusion if it will save estate taxes.

Because of the carryover basis requirement for land subject to the exclusion, if a decedent's estate is not taxable, *no election for the exclusion should be made*, as it will unnecessarily prevent land subject to the exclusion from gaining a stepped-up basis.

M. The Exclusion Must Be Elected: Code Sections 2031(c)(1) and (6)

In order to take advantage of the exclusion, a decedent's executor or trustee must make an *affirmative* election to use the exclusion before the date the estate tax return for the decedent is due, including extensions. The election is made on Schedule U (Qualified Conservation Easement Exclusion) of Form 706, which is the federal estate tax return.

Federal law requires estate tax returns to be filed within nine months of a decedent's death. Extensions of up to six months are available but are not automatic. Nothing in the current laws says that failure to elect the exclusion precludes subsequent generations from electing the exclusion. Schedule U provides that an executor is deemed to have made this election by filing Schedule U and excluding the value of easement land from the estate on the return.

The election appears to be a trap for the unwary, and it is. However, there is a good reason for requiring that the exclusion be elected, rather than applying it automatically. This has to do with the fact that land subject to the exclusion does not receive a stepped-up basis (see the discussion of the effect of the 2031(c) exclusion on basis in the preceding subsection). For this reason, if a decedent's estate includes easement land but is not taxable, the exclusion *should not be elected*.

N. The Easement Must Reduce Land Value by at Least 30 Percent to Qualify for the Full Exclusion: Code Section 2031(c)(2)

Now here is a convoluted concept: In order to qualify for the full 40 percent exclusion, a conservation easement must reduce the unrestricted value of the easement land by at least 30 percent. And for each percentage point by which the easement fails to meet the 30 percent threshold, the exclusion available is reduced by two percentage points.

The purpose of this provision is to prevent landowners from contributing minimal easements in order to take advantage of the exclusion. Congressional staff envisioned a landowner, for example, who put an easement on her land that reduced its fair market value by 5 percent in order to exclude 40 percent of the value of that land from her estate. This would be a good deal and truly an abuse; hence, the 30 percent "threshold" requirement.

The values for determining compliance with the 30 percent threshold are the values of the land and easement *at the time of the original contribution* of the easement. To determine compliance with the threshold, the executor must, therefore, obtain information about the value of the easement, and the value of the land as restricted by the easement, at the time of the original contribution.

However, if the estate qualifies for the exclusion, the exclusion is applied to the restricted value of land under easement *as of the date of the decedent's death* (or the alternate valuation date if selected).

Example: Mrs. Johnson's land was valued at $1,250,000 before she contributed her easement and $1 million after she contributed her easement. The value of the easement was, therefore, $250,000 ($1,250,000 – $1,000,000). The easement reduced the value of the unrestricted land by 20 percent ($250,000 / $1,250,000), which is 10 percentage points less than the 30 percent reduction in value required by Code section 2031(c)(2). To determine the amount by which the 40 percent exclusion must be reduced, Mrs. Johnson's executor must subtract two percentage points from the exclusion for every one percentage point by which the easement falls short of the 30 percent requirement, in this case 20 percent (2 × .10). Therefore, the executor may exclude only 20 percent of the restricted value of the land.

O. Retained Development Rights Are Not Eligible for the Exclusion: Code Sections 2031(c)(5)(A) and (B)

Any "development rights" retained in the conservation easement are ineligible for the exclusion. However, if those people with an interest in the easement land after the decedent's death agree before the due date for the estate tax return (including any extension) to terminate some or all retained development rights, the exclusion will apply as though the terminated rights never existed. Anyone with an interest in the easement land has two years after the decedent's death to put the agreement to terminate development rights into effect (presumably by recording an amendment to the original easement or recording a supplemental easement).

1. Development Rights Defined

Development rights for purposes of this provision are defined in the law as any right to use the land "for any commercial purpose which is not subordinate to and directly supportive of the use of such land as a farm for farming purposes" (Code section 2031(c)(5)(D)). The definition of "farming purposes" is incorporated from Code section 2032A(e)(5):

> The term "farming purposes" means—
>
> (A) cultivating the soil or raising or harvesting any agricultural or horticultural commodity (including the raising, shearing, feeding, caring for, training, and management of animals) on a farm;

(B) handling, drying, packing, grading, or storing on a farm any agricultural or horticultural commodity in its unmanufactured state, but only if the owner, tenant, or operator of the farm regularly produces more than one-half of the commodity so treated; and

(C) (i) the planting, cultivating, caring for, or cutting of trees, or (ii) the preparation (other than milling) of trees for market. (Code section 2032A(e)(5))

Code section 2031(c)(5) does not incorporate the definition of the word *farm*, but it is likely that, in interpreting that word, a court would look to the same source providing the definition of *farming purposes*. That source (Code section 2032A(e)(4)) defines *farm* as including "stock, dairy, poultry, fruit, furbearing animals, and truck farms, plantations, ranches, nurseries, ranges, greenhouses or other similar structures used primarily for the raising of agricultural or horticultural commodities, and orchards and woodlands."

Exactly how these terms are defined becomes important in trying to determine exactly what kind of rights may be reserved that are not development rights. Rights to maintain a residence for the owner's use, as well as normal farming, ranching, and forestry practices, probably would not be considered retained development rights. Retained rights to sell land for development or establish houses for sale or rent probably would be considered as retained development rights.

Many conservation easements retain the landowner's right to use an existing residence or to construct a new residence for his use. While there are no regulations, cases, or rulings on this point, it would seem that such a retained right is not a retained development right because a right reserved by the landowner to personally use a residence does not constitute a "commercial purpose." To be consistent with this interpretation, the easement should prohibit such a residence from being sold separately from the farm.

Example: A qualified conservation easement reserves the right to develop and sell five home sites, each worth $50,000. The land is valued at $2 million before the easement and $1 million after the easement (including the value of the retained home sites). Before calculating the exclusion, the executor must subtract the value of the retained development rights from the restricted value of the land ($1,000,000 – [5 × $50,000] = $750,000).

The exclusion is then applied to the adjusted value of $750,000. The value that can be excluded from the decedent's estate is therefore $300,000 ($750,000 × .40).

If all the people with an interest in the decedent's land agree to terminate these retained development rights, the exclusion will increase to $400,000 ($1,000,000 × .40). If the value excluded were subject to 45 percent federal estate tax rate of 2007, terminating those rights would save the heirs an additional $45,000 ($100,000 × .45) in estate taxes.

2. Use of the Post Mortem Election to Eliminate Development Rights

It is also possible for people with a legal interest in the decedent's land to take advantage of the "post mortem" easement provisions of Code section 2031(c)(9) (see the discussion of post mortem easements in section IV, T of this chapter) and eliminate the retained development rights by donating a new easement before the estate tax return is due. That would qualify the termination of the retained rights for both an expanded exclusion and an estate tax deduction under Code section 2055(f). The expanded exclusion and deduction would be in addition to the reduction in value already attributable to the restrictions of the easement donated by the decedent during his lifetime.

3. The Effect of the 30 Percent Threshold on High-Value Lands

The 30 percent threshold requirement ceases to have much meaning with very valuable property, unless the easement has reduced the value of that property by 10 percent or less. That is because the value of the land, as restricted by the easement, remains so substantial that even a small percentage of its value exceeds the $500,000 limit on the exclusion. For example, if the value of land as restricted by a conservation easement is $50 million or more, even a 1 percent exclusion will exceed $500,000. In high-amenity markets it is likely that the restricted values of land will remain high enough for easement donors to enjoy the full benefit of the exclusion even though the effect of their conservation easement is to reduce land values by less than the 30 percent threshold.

Example: Mrs. Johnson's conservation easement reduced the value of her farm by only 20 percent. Therefore, her executor may exclude only

20 percent due to the reduction required for easements failing to reduce the value of land by at least 30 percent. However, at Mrs. Johnson's death, the value of the land as restricted by the easement is $2,500,000. Twenty percent of that value is $500,000 ($2,500,000 × .20), which is the maximum amount that can be excluded under section 2031(c) in any event. Therefore, due to the high value of the restricted land, the 30 percent threshold requirement does not penalize the estate at all.

P. Commercial Recreational Uses Must Be Prohibited: Code Section 2031(c)(8)(B)

Any easement in which the right is retained to use the easement land for more than de minimis commercial recreational purposes is not a qualified conservation easement and is disqualified for the exclusion. Congressional staff members were concerned about people taking advantage of the exclusion by contributing conservation easements that allowed commercially valuable uses, such as amusement parks, for example (even though such a use would appear to clearly disqualify the easement as a "qualified conservation easement" for purposes of the exclusion).

The official explanation of this provision given by the Joint Committee on Taxation includes a statement that rights retained in an easement to grant hunting or fishing licenses on land subject to the easement is within the exemption for de minimis uses and does not disqualify the easement for the exclusion. (See Joint Committee on Taxation, "General Explanation of Tax Legislation Enacted in 1997.")

No other official clarification of this provision has been given. From a drafting standpoint, until more information about the meaning of this provision is made available, easement donors intending to qualify for the exclusion should consider including something along the lines of the following language in their easements: "Any commercial recreational use is expressly prohibited, except those uses considered de minimis according to the provisions of Code section 2031(c)(8)(B) of the Internal Revenue Code." An equally effective alternative is a blanket prohibition in the easement against any "commercial recreational" activity or any "commercial activity."

Existing conservation easements that lack such prohibitions should be reexamined and possibly amended. The staff of the Joint Committee on Taxation has verbally taken the position that a prohibition against all but de minimis commercial recreational uses may be supplied by a decedent's executor or trustee in a post mortem amendment to an existing easement (see the discussion of post mortem easements in subsection T of this section IV). If the easement donor is unable to amend the easement, such a post mortem correction may be the only alternative. However, because of the cumbersome process involved in granting a post mortem easement, including the uncertainty of state law, and of obtaining consent from all beneficiaries in a timely fashion, amendment of the easement is a far more reliable approach to compliance with this requirement.

Q. Geographic Limitations on the Exclusion: Code Section 2031(c)(8)(i)

When originally enacted, the exclusion applied only to land in or within a twenty-five-mile radius of a metropolitan statistical area (MSA), national park, or national wilderness area. (See former Code section 2031(c)(8)(i).) That requirement was eliminated by the Economic Growth and Tax Relief Reconciliation Act of 2001 (P.L. 107-16). The current provision requires only that land, to be eligible for the exclusion, be located within the United States or any U.S. possession.

R. Debt-Financed Property: Code Section 2031(c)(4)

If a landowner borrowed to purchase land that is subject to a conservation easement, and his executor elects to claim the 2031(c) exclusion for the land, any amount of that debt (including refinancings) that remains unpaid when the landowner dies must be subtracted from the value of the land before calculating the exclusion. However, the debt is deductible under Code section 2053(a)(4).

If debt were not subtracted from the amount subject to the exclusion, estates containing easement property would be able to "double dip," because they would get the benefit of the exclusion on the debt *and* deduct the debt, as well.

Example: Gerry's land had a $400,000 mortgage on it when he died. The land was subject to a conservation easement, and the value subject to the easement was $500,000. Gerry's executor elects the exclusion and calculates it to be $40,000, because it can apply to only $100,000 of the value of Gerry's land due to the outstanding mortgage ([$500,000 – $400,000] × .40). Had there been no mortgage, the exclusion would have removed $200,000 from Gerry's estate ($500,000 × .40), rather than $40,000. However, the executor is allowed to deduct the $400,000 mortgage under Code section 2053(a)(4), so the estate still obtains a tax benefit for this debt.

S. Property Owned by Partnerships, Corporations, and Trusts: Code Section 2031(c)(10)

If the decedent's interest in land eligible for the exclusion is held indirectly through a partnership, corporation, or trust, his estate may still enjoy the benefit of the exclusion to the extent of his ownership interest in such an entity. However, he must own at least a 30 percent interest in the entity in order for his estate to be able to take advantage of the exclusion.

Although the statute does not speak of limited liability companies, it is likely that such entities will qualify for similar treatment because they have the attributes of a corporation and a partnership, both of which are eligible for the exclusion.

Example: Mrs. Sanders, a widow, placed the family farm into a family corporation in order to facilitate the transfer of interests in the farm to her four children. She donated a conservation easement on the farm before transferring it to the corporation. At the date of her death the farm's land was worth $4 million, taking into consideration the restrictions imposed by the conservation easement. The other assets in the corporation were worth $1 million (farm improvements and equipment). Mrs. Sanders owned 35 percent of the stock of the corporation when she died.

Mrs. Sanders's executor may elect to exclude 40 percent of the value of her stock attributable to the farm's land from her estate because she owned over 30 percent of the stock in the corporation at her death. If we assume that the portion of Mrs. Sanders's stock value attributable to the land value is $1,400,000 ($4,000,000 × .35; remember that the exclusion applies to the value of land only),the executor may exclude $500,000 of that value from the estate. Note that 40 percent of Mrs. Sanders's share of the land is $560,000 ($1,400,000 × .40), but because of the limitation on the amount of the exclusion (see section IV, C of this chapter), her estate can exclude only $500,000.

If Mrs. Sanders's interest in the corporation had been less than 30 percent, her estate would not have been eligible for any of the exclusion. Note that we are assuming that the corporation will qualify for the exclusion, even though neither it nor any member of its "family" contributed the easement or owned the easement for the requisite three-year period immediately preceding the contribution. This may not be a safe assumption. To be completely safe it might be prudent to defer contribution of the easement until after conveyance of the land to the corporation and until the corporation has held the land for at least three years.

T. Easements Donated after the Decedent's Death (Post Mortem Easements): Code Sections 2031(c)(8)(A)(iii) and (C), and 2031(c)(9)

In most cases, once a person dies, the estate tax consequences are locked in and the family must live with them, whatever they may be. However, in some cases post mortem estate planning may still save estate taxes.

Post mortem estate planning refers to actions that can be taken after a person dies that retroactively affect the amount of the decedent's estate and, therefore, the amount of tax due on the estate. There are very few ways in which this can be done. One is the renunciation by a surviving spouse of some or all of the assets passing to him from a deceased spouse (further discussion is beyond the scope of this summary); another is the special-use valuation provision of Code section 2032A discussed in section II of chapter 7.

217

Another important, but little used, estate planning tool is provided by Code section 2031(c) of the estate tax code, the same section that provides the 40 percent exclusion. If a decedent owned conservation worthy land at his death, it is still possible, under this section, for the family to substantially reduce estate taxes by contributing a conservation easement on the land. This is due to a truly useful law that allows an estate to reap the same estate tax benefits from an easement placed on the decedent's land after his death as would have been available had the landowner contributed the easement during his lifetime.

A post mortem easement will qualify for both the exclusion *and* an estate tax deduction under Code section 2055(f), *provided* that no income tax deduction is taken in connection with the conveyance of the easement. The grant of a post mortem conservation easement must be completed prior to the due date for the estate tax return (nine months after the date of the decedent's death), plus any extension granted for filing the return.

See PLR 200418005, confirming use of the post mortem election by a trust.

Example: Sam and Susie had tried for years to get their aging father to put a conservation easement on his farm. The old man never seemed to get around to it and died without donating the easement. At the time of his death the farm's land was valued at $1 million. Sam and Susie, being the only people with any legal claim to the land, directed their father's executor to donate an easement on the farm, and the contribution was completed within nine months of their father's death. The easement reduced the value of the land by $400,000, thereby generating a $400,000 estate tax deduction under Code section 2055(f). The value of the farm's land, taking the restrictions of the easement into account, was $600,000. Therefore, the 40 percent exclusion removed an additional $240,000 ($600,000 × .40) from the estate. Given the value of other assets in the estate, the entire value of the land subject to the easement would have been taxed at 45 percent. Thus, the post mortem election saved Sam and Susie $288,000 ([$400,000 + $240,000] × .45) in estate tax.

Code section 2031(c) merely controls the tax consequences of a post mortem easement contribution; it does not authorize the contribution. *State law, not federal tax law, governs the powers of executors and trustees to make a post mortem easement contribution.* Unless state law specifically allows executors and trustees to donate a conservation easement, a decedent must specifically authorize his executor or trustee to donate the easement in the will. If there is no provision in the decedent's will, and no authority granted by state law, a court order may be required. However, at least three states (Colorado, Maryland, and Virginia) have amended their laws to allow post mortem easements to be donated by an executor or trustee in order to take advantage of the post mortem election.

CHAPTER NINE:

Conservation Easements and Other Estate Planning Techniques

The primary object of most estate planning efforts is to reduce the size of the taxable estate. There are a number of means of doing this. Conservation easements can dramatically reduce a landowner's taxable estate. Of course, this is accomplished by permanently removing value from the easement land. For some families, this is anathema because eventually liquidating land that has been in the family is seen as the key to wealth and independence. For others, however, keeping family land intact is the primary objective, either for sentimental reasons or for reasons of lifestyle and livelihood.

Where the principal goal of a family is to preserve family land, conservation easements should be one of the primary tools used to achieve that goal. By reducing the value of easement land overall, conservation easements make other means of reducing the size of the taxable estate more efficient. For example, the Exclusion Amount (discussed in chapter 7) will shelter many more acres of farmland if that land has first been reduced in value by a conservation easement.

In this chapter we will take a brief look at how conservation easements may be used in concert with other planning tools to help families keep land intact. Remember, if the goal is something other than maintaining family land, conservation easements may be counterproductive. Where keeping land intact is important, easements are key.

I. Use with the Annual Gift Tax Exclusion

As noted in chapter 7, an important estate planning technique is to remove value from a future estate by making annual gifts over a period of time. The gifts can be sized to fit the annual gift tax exclusion (currently $12,000). A husband and wife may make gifts under the exclusion of $24,000 per year per donee. Thus, if a couple has four children, they can gift $96,000 (4 × $24,000) tax free. Such gifts are not subject to the gift tax, and, because they remove value from the estate, they reduce the size of the couple's future taxable estate.

Because conservation easements reduce the value of the easement property, they can play an important role in maximizing use of the annual $12,000 gift tax exclusion. By reducing the value of property subject to the gift, a conservation easement allows transfer of, for example, a family ranch to the children much more quickly than if the property were transferred at its unrestricted value.

In addition, the entire family gains the assurance that, regardless of how different family members may feel about using their share of the ranch, its future use and potential development will be controlled by the terms of the easement, and the easement will control each gift made thereafter.

Example: John is a widower. His son Paul works with him on the family ranch and wants to continue to do so. The value of the ranch is $5 million. Using the annual exclusion, John can transfer 0.24 percent of the value of the ranch to Paul annually ($12,000 / $5,000,000). However, if John placed a conservation easement on the ranch that reduced its value to $2.5 million, he could transfer 0.48 percent annually, double the amount of land. Remember that he only needs to reduce the value of the ranch (including the rest of his estate) to the Exclusion Amount ($2 million in 2008). Even so, at the rate of $12,000 per year, it would take him over 41 years to transfer the $500,000 ($500,000 / $12,000) of value necessary to reduce the estate to the $2 million Exclusion Amount (which will increase to $3.5 million in 2009). In other words, while a conservation easement can accelerate the rate of transfer, the use of the annual exclusion alone to transfer value still can take a very long time.

John's problem of transferring an already valuable piece of land will be compounded by future appreciation in the value of the ranch. While a conservation easement will not eliminate appreciation, it will increase the amount of land John can transfer annually, thus reducing the period during which appreciation will affect John's estate. The easement will also likely reduce the rate of appreciation.

An important question is how to actually make annual gifts of land. Because subdivision is likely to be costly—and may be prohibited by local law—family partnerships, limited liability companies, and corporations are often used to convert land into partnership interests, membership interests, or shares that can be more easily conveyed.

One of the added values of a conservation easement in connection with gifting strategies is that it ensures the future use of the land after the current owners have conveyed a majority interest to their children.

II. Use with the Code Section 2032A Special Valuation Provisions

By reducing overall farm or ranch values, conservation easements can also effectively increase the amount of a farm or ranch that can pass through a decedent's estate under the special-use valuation rules of Code section 2032A (see the discussion of this provision in chapter 7). Section 2032A is currently (in 2008) limited to reducing the value of qualified land by no more than $960,000. A conservation easement can reduce the value of land by an unlimited amount and bring the value of a family farm or ranch much closer to the $2,900,000 that can be sheltered by the combination of the special-use valuation provisions and the Exclusion Amount.

Example: John's ranch is reduced in value from $5 million to $3.5 million by a conservation easement. Under the Exclusion Amount available in 2008, the year of John's death, $2 million of the ranch's value will pass free of estate tax. The exclusion available under Code section 2031(c) removes an additional $500,000, bringing the taxable estate down to $1 million ($3,500,000 – $2,000,000 – $500,000). However, the tax on the remaining $1 million will be $450,000 ($1,000,000 × .45). Paul, John's son, has worked on the ranch all of his life. There are no other assets to pay the tax, and Paul has no intention of doing anything other than operating the ranch in the future. Therefore, Paul elects the special-use valuation allowed under Code section 2032A. The maximum reduction in value of $960,000 allowed under that section reduces the taxable estate to $80,000 ($1,000,000 – $960,000) and the tax to $18,000 ($40,000 × .45). John's estate also qualifies for installment payment of the tax under another section of the Code. The combination of conservation easement, Exclusion Amount, and special-use valuation allows Paul to retain the ranch.

However, if using a conservation easement in combination with Code section 2032A, it is important to be careful not to reduce the value of a farm or ranch in a decedent's estate so that it makes up less than 50 percent of the value of the estate. Doing so would disqualify the estate for use of Code section 2032A.

III. Use with the $2 Million Exclusion Amount

Again, because a conservation easement reduces the value of property, it also allows the transfer of more land under the current $2 million Exclusion Amount.

Example: John wants his ranch to go to his son Paul. The ranch is valued at $4 million. The tax on the ranch, after subtracting the Exclusion Amount, will be $900,000 ([$4,000,000 – $2,000,000]× .45). However, assume that John places a conservation easement on the ranch before he dies. The easement reduces the value of the ranch to $2 million, which is entirely sheltered by the estate tax exclusion of $2 million, making it possible for the ranch to pass to Paul estate-tax free.

IV. Value Replacement

Value replacement is an estate planning technique whereby a person converts the income tax savings resulting from a charitable donation into additional cash for her estate. This works particularly well when the income tax savings results from the contribution of a conservation easement, because such tax savings represent "new money" to the donors (as opposed to the contribution of a liquid asset, such as cash, stocks, or bonds).

Example: Assume that John and Joan are aged 51 and 43, respectively. Assume that they donate a conservation easement worth $1,800,000 and that the income tax deduction resulting from that donation saves them $738,000 in income tax. They spend $58,000 on a new car and buy a "second-to-die" life insurance policy (such a policy pays out when the surviving spouse dies, and premiums are generally lower than on a single-life policy) with the remaining $680,000 of their income tax savings. They place the policy into an inter vivos trust (a trust created during their lifetimes) for the benefit of their children and transfer all of the "incidents of ownership" to the trust.

Assume that a premium payment of $680,000 for a second-to-die policy on a couple John's and Joan's ages will buy approximately $12,500,000 in coverage. If the policy is properly placed in an inter vivos trust, there will be neither income tax nor estate tax on the policy proceeds. Using value replacement, John and Joan have replaced $1,800,000 in land value lost due to the conservation easement with $11,820,000 (face value of the policy less the premium) in tax-free cash payable directly to their children.

Note that investing the $680,000 in stocks or mutual funds transferred to an inter vivos trust could generate substantial results, as well. There are many variations.

CHAPTER TEN:

Other Forms of Charitable Giving and Estate Taxes

In addition to gifts of cash or conservation easements donated by will, already described, a number of other charitable giving methods can generate income and estate tax savings. This summary is not designed to provide an exhaustive description but to present a few examples of ways charitable giving can allow a person to "have his cake and eat it, too."

I. Charitable Remainder Trusts: Code Section 664(d)

Charitable remainder trusts (CRTs) are a vehicle for selling appreciated assets (such as stocks or bonds) tax free, generating lifetime income from the proceeds, and making a charitable contribution of the proceeds at death. This is a tool that works particularly well for wealthy people who can leverage the benefits of the transaction on the ability to use tax deductions.

Example: Frank owns five hundred shares of highly appreciated Microsoft stock. If he sells it himself, he will pay 15 percent of the gain in federal income taxes. Frank really would like to convert this stock to an asset that pays regular income. Plus, he has a substantial income already and could use a tax deduction. Finally, he is a great fan of the University of Wyoming and wants to contribute to it when he dies. By using a charitable remainder trust, he can accomplish all of his goals, including avoiding paying tax on the sale of the Microsoft stock. Here is how it works:

1. Frank's lawyer sets up a charitable remainder trust. Note that there are two types of CRTs, charitable

remainder unitrusts (CRUTs) and charitable remainder annuity trusts (CRATs), the difference primarily having to do with the way income is paid to the trust beneficiary. The trust provides that it will pay income to Frank for as long as he lives; and when he dies, it will pay the amount remaining in the trust to the university. The trust is irrevocable—that is, Frank cannot change the trust, except in limited ways, or revoke it. Also, once he puts assets in the trust, he cannot get them back.

2. Frank contributes the highly appreciated stock to the CRT.

3. The trust sells the stock (there can be no agreement to sell the stock prior to the contribution in order for all of the tax benefits of this arrangement to be available). Because the trust is a charitable entity, it pays no income tax on the sale's proceeds.

4. Frank is entitled to a federal income tax deduction (and a state income tax deduction if he is a resident of a state that imposes an income tax and allows charitable contribution deductions). The tax deduction is equal to the value of the remainder interest in the stock, based on Frank's age at the time of the gift and the value of the stock when he transferred it to the trust.

5. Frank receives income for his lifetime from the trust, based on the terms of the CRT. This income will be greater than if he sold the stock himself and invested the proceeds because the sale's proceeds will not have been reduced by any income tax.

6. The value of the stock will be excluded from Frank's estate for estate tax purposes.

II. Contribution of a Remainder Interest

The Code also allows an income tax deduction for the gift of a remainder interest in a personal residence, farm, or ranch. This allows a landowner to receive a tax deduction for the remainder value of his residence, farm, or ranch on the date the remainder interest is contributed, continue to live on the property for the rest of his life, and effectively remove the value of the property from his estate for estate tax purposes. The gift of a remainder interest must be irrevocable to generate any tax benefits to the donor.

Note that simply contributing the remainder interest to a conservation organization or government agency is no guarantee of preservation. Preservation can only be ensured by placing a conservation easement on the property before making the contribution of the remainder interest. While such a contribution will reduce the tax deduction associated with the contribution of the remainder interest (because the value of the remainder will be reduced by the easement), it will generate an offsetting deduction for the contribution of the conservation easement. Without the conservation easement, the charity receiving the remainder interest has the ability to sell the property for any purpose, including development, as long as it uses the proceeds in a manner consistent with its charitable purposes.

III. Other Charitable Contributions

227

As earlier noted, any contribution made by will to a qualified charity or governmental organization is deductible from the decedent's gross estate for purposes of determining the amount of the taxable estate.

IV. The Use of Trusts

Trusts can be a valuable tool for estate planning. They have income tax, estate tax, and gift tax implications. Among the lists of trusts that are commonly used in estate planning strategies are qualified personal residence trusts (QPRTs), grantor retained annuity trusts (GRATs), qualified terminable interest trusts (QTIPs), and grantor retained unitrusts (GRUTs). The structure and tax aspects of these trusts are far beyond the scope of this summary. Suffice it to say that they are all used to facilitate the transfer of property from one person to another while retaining some rights of the grantor (the person setting up and funding the trust) to use or enjoy the property, while minimizing transfer taxes, either gift or estate.

In addition to estate planning benefits, trusts have the very practical benefit of controlling how property given to children is used until the children are old enough to manage the property for themselves. Without a trust, property transferred to children becomes theirs to manage and use upon their eighteenth birthday.

V. A Note on Estate Planning

It is the not the place of this book to provide a detailed argument for writing a will or undertaking estate planning. However, it is fair to say that without a will, a person who owns a farm or business, or is likely to be survived by young children, does a huge disservice to his family by not having a will—even if the estate is not large enough to be taxable.

A will allows a person to provide some direction as to how her property is to pass to others, and to consider the personalities and abilities of those who will receive that property. Where a person has a potentially taxable estate, a will is almost a necessity to avoid unnecessary imposition of estate tax.

It is hoped that a reader of this summary will take away at least the following: (1) that anyone owning a farm or ranch may have a taxable estate even if they have no money in the bank; (2) if there has been no planning and an estate tax is assessed, it may force the sale of the farm or ranch; and (3) avoiding the payment of estate tax is not difficult or costly (compared to the tax savings that can result) if families are willing to make a little effort and consult an experienced professional.

VI. Conclusion

The federal tax code is an ever-changing set of rules. What has been described in this book about the current state of those rules as they apply to conservation easements and land trusts will inevitably change. One anticipated change is reinstatement of the 2006 law governing the amount of income against which a donor may deduct a conservation easement contribution, and the number of years he may carry unused portions of that deduction forward, will either expire or be extended by Congress on that date.

Many other areas of tax law pertaining to conservation easements are also likely to change. The limit on the amount that may be excluded from a decedent's estate under Code section 2031(c) is proposed (which is a long way from being law) for increase; the entire estate tax is set to expire on December 31, 2009, and then to be reenacted automatically on December 31, 2010; it is hoped that rules now clouding conservation buyer transactions will be clarified; and so on.

What is certain is that for the foreseeable future, the public, the media, the Congress, and many conservation critics are keenly aware of the potential for abuse of charitable deductions for conservation transactions, particularly conservation easements. There will be more IRS easement challenges; indeed, the service has hired an entire new section just to look at charitable abuses. There will be more IRS pronouncements, which have the potential to significantly, and unilaterally, alter the context for voluntary land conservation. There will be, hopefully, more judicial rulings to clarify tax rules that have been undefined for several decades.

It can be expected that criticism of tax incentives for land conservation will increase. Successful movements always draw criticism, which seems sometimes to be directly proportional to the level of success. We can expect to hear more and more about the wisdom of allowing private individuals to permanently "dictate" the future use of land through conservation easements, and the wisdom of maintaining publicly financed incentives for them to do so. However, such criticism must be balanced by an understanding of the extent to which government, through the tax code and many other influential subsidies, supports the development of land, which is just as permanent an allocation of land resources as permanent conservation. In fact, it is more so, as permanent land conservation is the result of a merely legal mechanism, whereas development is fundamental physical alteration of land, its capability for use, and the structure of its ownership. This can easily be understood by considering how easily Johnson County, Wyoming, was able to reverse the permanent protection of Meadowwood Ranch, as reported in the *Hicks v. Dowd* case, compared to the difficulty of reversing a fifty-lot subdivision that has been sold out and developed.

The best protection against future attacks on voluntary land conservation will be land trusts, landowners, and their advisors who know what they are doing with conservation easements and do it well. It is hoped that with more attention, the quality of land trusts, the professional services of landowner advisors, and conservation transactions themselves will improve substantially, so that permanent voluntary conservation will be and will remain a reality and an increasingly meaningful tool for land conservation in the United States.

229

Internal Revenue Code Provisions Governing Conservation Easements

Code Section 170(h): Internal Revenue Code Provisions Governing
Conservation Easements

(h) Qualified conservation contribution.—

(1) In general.—For purposes of subsection (f)(3)(B)(iii), the term "qualified conservation contribution" means a contribution—

    (A) of a qualified real property interest,

    (B) to a qualified organization,

    (C) exclusively for conservation purposes.

(2) Qualified real property interest.—For purposes of this subsection, the term "qualified real property interest" means any of the following interests in real property:

    (A) the entire interest of the donor other than a qualified mineral interest,

    (B) a remainder interest, and

    (C) a restriction (granted in perpetuity) on the use which may be made of the real property.

(3) Qualified organization.—For purposes of paragraph (1), the term "qualified organization" means an organization which—

    (A) is described in clause (v) or (vi) of subsection (b)(1)(A), or

    (B) is described in section 501(c)(3) and—

        (i) meets the requirements of section 509(a)(2), or

        (ii) meets the requirements of section 509(a)(3) and is controlled by an organization described in subparagraph (A) or in clause (i) of this subparagraph.

(4) Conservation purpose defined.—

    (A) In general.—For purposes of this subsection, the term "conservation purpose" means—

        (i) the preservation of land areas for outdoor recreation by, or the education of, the general public,

        (ii) the protection of a relatively natural habitat of fish, wildlife, or plants, or similar ecosystem,

        (iii) the preservation of open space (including farmland and forest land) where such preservation is—

            (I) for the scenic enjoyment of the general public, or

            (II) pursuant to a clearly delineated Federal, State, or local governmental conservation policy,

            and will yield a significant public benefit, or

        (iv) the preservation of an historically important land area or a certified historic structure.

    (B) Special rules with respect to buildings in registered historic districts.— In the case of any contribution of a qualified real property interest which is a restriction with respect to the exterior of a building described in subparagraph (C)(ii), such contribution shall not be considered to be exclusively for conservation purposes unless—

        (i) such interest—

            (I) includes a restriction which preserves the entire exterior of the building (including the front, sides, rear, and height of the building), and

            (II) prohibits any change in the exterior of the building which is inconsistent with the historical character of such exterior,

        (ii) the donor and donee enter into a written agreement certifying, under penalty of perjury, that the donee—

            (I) is a qualified organization (as defined in paragraph (3)) with a purpose of environmental protection, land conservation, open space preservation, or historic preservation, and

            (II) has the resources to manage and enforce the restriction and a commitment to do so, and

        (iii) in the case of any contribution made in a taxable year beginning after the date of the enactment of this subparagraph, the taxpayer includes with the taxpayer's return for the taxable year of the contribution—

            (I) a qualified appraisal (within the meaning of subsection (f)(11)(E)) of the qualified property interest,

            (II) photographs of the entire exterior of the building, and

            (III) a description of all restrictions on the development of the building.

(C) Certified historic structure.—For purposes of subparagraph (A)(iv), the term "certified historic structure" means—

(i) any building, structure, or land area which is listed in the National Register, or

(ii) any building which is located in a registered historic district (as defined in section 47(c)(3)(B)) and is certified by the Secretary of the Interior to the Secretary as being of historic significance to the district.

A building, structure, or land area satisfies the preceding sentence if it satisfies such sentence either at the time of the transfer or on the due date (including extensions) for filing the transferor's return under this chapter for the taxable year in which the transfer is made.

(5) Exclusively for conservation purposes.—For purposes of this subsection—

(A) Conservation purpose must be protected.—A contribution shall not be treated as exclusively for conservation purposes unless the conservation purpose is protected in perpetuity.

(B) No surface mining permitted.—

(i) In general.—Except as provided in clause (ii), in the case of a contribution of any interest where there is a retention of a qualified mineral interest, subparagraph (A) shall not be treated as met if at any time there may be extraction or removal of minerals by any surface mining method.

(ii) Special rule.—With respect to any contribution of property in which the ownership of the surface estate and mineral interests has been and remains separated, subparagraph (A) shall be treated as met if the probability of surface mining occurring on such property is so remote as to be negligible.

(6) Qualified mineral interest.—For purposes of this subsection, the term "qualified mineral interest" means—

(A) subsurface oil, gas, or other minerals, and

(B) the right to access to such minerals.

Income Tax Regulations for Conservation Easements

Regulations Section 1.170A-14: Income Tax Regulations for
Conservation Easements

§ 1.170A-14 Qualified conservation contributions.

(a) Qualified conservation contributions. A deduction under section 170 is generally not allowed for a charitable contribution of any interest in property that consists of less than the donor's entire interest in the property other than certain transfers in trust (see § 1.170A-6 relating to charitable contributions in trust and § 1.170A-7 relating to contributions not in trust of partial interests in property). However, a deduction may be allowed under section 170(f)(3)(B)(iii) for the value of a qualified conservation contribution if the requirements of this section are met. A qualified conservation contribution is the contribution of a qualified real property interest to a qualified organization exclusively for conservation purposes. To be eligible for a deduction under this section, the conservation purpose must be protected in perpetuity.

(b) Qualified real property interest—

(1) Entire interest of donor other than qualified mineral interest.

(i) The entire interest of the donor other than a qualified mineral interest is a qualified real property interest. A qualified mineral interest is the donor's interest in subsurface oil, gas, or other minerals and the right of access to such minerals.

(ii) A real property interest shall not be treated as an entire interest other than a qualified mineral interest by reason of section 170(h)(2)(A) and this paragraph (b)(1) if the property in which the donor's interest exists was divided prior to the contribution in order to enable the donor to retain control of more than a qualified mineral interest or to reduce the real property interest donated. See Treasury regulations § 1.170A-7(a)(2)(i). An entire interest in real property may consist of an undivided interest in the property. But see section 170(h)(5)(A) and the regulations thereunder (relating to the requirement that the conservation purpose which is the subject of the donation must be protected in perpetuity). Minor interests, such as rights-of-way, that will not interfere with the conservation purposes of the donation, may be transferred prior to the conservation contribution without affecting the treatment of a property interest as a qualified real property interest under this paragraph (b)(1).

(2) Perpetual conservation restriction.

A "perpetual conservation restriction" is a qualified real property interest. A "perpetual conservation restriction" is a restriction granted in perpetuity on the use which may be made of real property—including, an easement or other interest in real property that under state law has attributes similar to an easement (e.g., a restrictive covenant or equitable servitude). For purposes of this section, the terms easement, conservation restriction, and perpetual conservation restriction have the same meaning. The definition of perpetual conservation restriction under this paragraph (b)(2) is not intended to preclude the deductibility of a donation of affirmative rights to use a land or water area under § 1.170A-13(d)(2). Any rights reserved by the donor in the donation of a perpetual conservation restriction must conform to the requirements of this section. See e.g., paragraph (d)(4)(ii), (d)(5)(i), (e)(3), and (g)(4) of this section.

(c) Qualified organization—

(1) Eligible donee. To be considered an eligible donee under this section, an organization must be a qualified organization, have a commitment to protect the conservation purposes of the donation, and have the resources to enforce the restrictions. A conservation group organized or operated primarily or substantially for one of the conservation purposes specified in section 170(h)(4)(A) will be considered to have the commitment required by the preceding sentence. A qualified organization need not set aside funds to enforce the restrictions that are the subject of the contribution. For purposes of this section, the term qualified organization means:

(i) A governmental unit described in section 170(b)(1)(A)(v);

(ii) An organization described in section 170(b)(1)(A)(vi);

(iii) A charitable organization described in section 501(c)(3) that meets the public support test of section 509(a)(2);

(iv) A charitable organization described in section 501(c)(3) that meets the requirements of section 509(a)(3) and is controlled by an organization described in paragraphs (c)(1) (i), (ii), or (iii) of this section.

(2) Transfers by donee. A deduction shall be allowed for a contribution under this section only if in the instrument of conveyance the donor prohibits the donee from subsequently transferring the easement (or, in the case of a remainder interest or the reservation of a qualified mineral interest, the property), whether or not for consideration,

unless the donee organization, as a condition of the subsequent transfer, requires that the conservation purposes which the contribution
was originally intended to advance continue to be carried out.
Moreover, subsequent transfers must be restricted to organizations
qualifying, at the time of the subsequent transfer, as an eligible donee
under paragraph (c)(1) of this section. When a later unexpected
change in the conditions surrounding the property that is the subject
of a donation under paragraph (b)(1), (2), or
(3) of this section makes impossible or impractical the continued use
of the property for conservation purposes, the requirement of this
paragraph will be met if the property is sold or exchanged and any
proceeds are used by the donee organization in a manner consistent
with the conservation purposes of the original contribution. In the
case of a donation under paragraph (b)(3) of this section to which the
preceding sentence applies, see also paragraph (g)(5)(ii) of this section.

(d) Conservation purposes—

(1) In general. For purposes of section 170(h) and this section, the
term conservation purposes means—

(i) The preservation of land areas for outdoor recreation by, or the
education of, the general public, within the meaning of paragraph
(d)(2) of this section,

(ii) The protection of a relatively natural habitat of fish, wildlife, or
plants, or similar ecosystem, within the meaning of paragraph
(d)(3) of this section,

(iii) The preservation of certain open space (including farmland
and forest land) within the meaning of paragraph (d)(4) of this section, or

(iv) The preservation of a historically important land area or a certified historic structure, within the meaning of paragraph (d)(5) of
this section.

(2) Recreation or education—

(i) In general. The donation of a qualified real property interest to
preserve land areas for the outdoor recreation of the general public
or for the education of the general public will meet the conservation purposes test of this section. Thus, conservation purposes
would include, for example, the preservation of a water area for the
use of the public for boating or fishing, or a nature or hiking trail
for the use of the public.

(ii) Access. The preservation of land areas for recreation or education will not meet the test of this section unless the recreation or
education is for the substantial and regular use of the general public.

(3) Protection of environmental system—

(i) In general. The donation of a qualified real property interest to
protect a significant relatively natural habitat in which a fish,
wildlife, or plant community, or similar ecosystem normally lives

will meet the conservation purposes test of this section. The fact
that the habitat or environment has been altered to some extent by
human activity will not result in a deduction being denied under
this section if the fish, wildlife, or plants continue to exist there in
a relatively natural state. For example, the preservation of a lake
formed by a man-made dam or a salt pond formed by a man-made
dike would meet the conservation purposes test if the lake or pond
were a nature feeding area for a wildlife community that included
rare, endangered, or threatened native species.

(ii) Significant habitat or ecosystem. Significant habitats and
ecosystems include, but are not limited to, habitats for rare, endangered, or threatened species of animal, fish, or plants; natural areas
that represent high quality examples of a terrestrial community or
aquatic community, such as islands that are undeveloped or not
intensely developed where the coastal ecosystem is relatively intact;
and natural areas which are included in, or which contribute to,
the ecological viability of a local, state, or national park, nature
preserve, wildlife refuge, wilderness area, or other similar conservation area.

(iii) Access. Limitations on public access to property that is the
subject of a donation under this paragraph (d)(3) shall not render
the donation nondeductible. For example, a restriction on all public access to the habitat of a threatened native animal species protected by a donation under this paragraph (d)(3) would not cause
the donation to be nondeductible.

(4) Preservation of open space—

(i) In general. The donation of a qualified real property interest to
preserve open space (including farmland and forest land) will meet
the conservation purposes test of this section if such preservation is—

(A) Pursuant to a clearly delineated Federal, state, or local governmental conservation policy and will yield a significant public
benefit, or

(B) For the scenic enjoyment of the general public and will
yield a significant public benefit.

An open space easement donated on or after December 18, 1980,
must meet the requirements of section 170(h) in order to be
deductible.

(ii) Scenic enjoyment—

(A) Factors. A contribution made for the preservation of open
space may be for the scenic enjoyment of the general public.
Preservation of land may be for the scenic enjoyment of the
general public if development of the property would impair the
scenic character of the local rural or urban landscape or would
interfere with a scenic panorama that can be enjoyed from a
park, nature preserve, road, waterbody, trail, or historic structure
or land area, and such area or transportation way is open to, or
utilized by, the public. "Scenic enjoyment" will be evaluated by

considering all pertinent facts and circumstances germane to the contribution. Regional variations in topography, geology, biology, and cultural and economic conditions require flexibility in the application of this test, but do not lessen the burden on the taxpayer to demonstrate the scenic characteristics of a donation under this paragraph. The application of a particular objective factor to help define a view as scenic in one setting may in fact be entirely inappropriate in another setting. Among the factors to be considered are:

(1) The compatibility of the land use with other land in the vicinity;

(2) The degree of contrast and variety provided by the visual scene;

(3) The openness of the land (which would be a more significant factor in an urban or densely populated setting or in a heavily wooded area);

(4) Relief from urban closeness;

(5) The harmonious variety of shapes and textures;

(6) The degree to which the land use maintains the scale and character of the urban landscape to preserve open space, visual enjoyment, and sunlight for the surrounding area;

(7) The consistency of the proposed scenic view with a methodical state scenic identification program, such as a state landscape inventory; and

(8) The consistency of the proposed scenic view with a regional or local landscape inventory made pursuant to a sufficiently rigorous review process, especially if the donation is endorsed by an appropriate state or local governmental agency.

(B) Access. To satisfy the requirement of scenic enjoyment by the general public, visual (rather than physical) access to or across the property by the general public is sufficient. Under the terms of an open space easement on scenic property, the entire property need not be visible to the public for a donation to qualify under this section, although the public benefit from the donation may be insufficient to qualify for a deduction if only a small portion of the property is visible to the public.

(iii) Governmental conservation policy—

(A) In general. The requirement that the preservation of open space be pursuant to a clearly delineated Federal, state, or local governmental policy is intended to protect the types of property identified by representatives of the general public as worthy of preservation or conservation. A general declaration of conservation goals by a single official or legislative body is not sufficient. However, a governmental conservation policy need not be a cer-

239

tification program that identifies particular lots or small parcels of individually owned property. This requirement will be met by donations that further a specific, identified conservation project, such as the preservation of land within a state or local landmark district that is locally recognized as being significant to that district; the preservation of a wild or scenic river, the preservation of farmland pursuant to a state program for flood prevention and control; or the protection of the scenic, ecological, or historic character of land that is contiguous to, or an integral part of, the surroundings of existing recreation or conservation sites. For example, the donation of a perpetual conservation restriction to a qualified organization pursuant to a formal resolution or certification by a local governmental agency established under state law specifically identifying the subject property as worthy of protection for conservation purposes will meet the requirement of this paragraph. A program need not be funded to satisfy this requirement, but the program must involve a significant commitment by the government with respect to the conservation project. For example, a governmental program according preferential tax assessment or preferential zoning for certain property deemed worthy of protection for conservation purposes would constitute a significant commitment by the government.

(B) Effect of acceptance by governmental agency. Acceptance of an easement by an agency of the Federal Government or by an agency of a state or local government (or by a commission, authority, or similar body duly constituted by the state or local government and acting on behalf of the state or local government) tends to establish the requisite clearly delineated governmental policy, although such acceptance, without more, is not sufficient. The more rigorous the review process by the governmental agency, the more the acceptance of the easement tends to establish the requisite clearly delineated governmental policy. For example, in a state where the legislature has established an Environmental Trust to accept gifts to the state which meet certain conservation purposes and to submit the gifts to a review that requires the approval of the state's highest officials, acceptance of a gift by the Trust tends to establish the requisite clearly delineated governmental policy. However, if the Trust merely accepts such gifts without a review process, the requisite clearly delineated governmental policy is not established.

(C) Access. A limitation on public access to property subject to a donation under this paragraph (d)(4)(iii) shall not render the deduction nondeductible unless the conservation purpose of the donation would be undermined or frustrated without public access. For example, a donation pursuant to a governmental policy to protect the scenic character of land near a river requires visual access to the same extent as would a donation under paragraph (d)(4)(ii) of this section.

(iv) Significant public benefit—

(A) Factors. All contributions made for the preservation of open space must yield a significant public benefit. Public benefit will be evaluated by considering all pertinent facts and circumstances germane to the contribution. Factors germane to the evaluation of public benefit from one contribution may be irrelevant in determining public benefit from another contribution. No single factor will necessarily be determinative. Among the factors to be considered are:

(1) The uniqueness of the property to the area;

(2) The intensity of land development in the vicinity of the property (both existing development and foreseeable trends of development);

(3) The consistency of the proposed open space use with public programs (whether Federal, state or local) for conservation in the region, including programs for outdoor recreation, irrigation or water supply protection, water quality maintenance or enhancement, flood prevention and control, erosion control, shoreline protection, and protection of land areas included in, or related to, a government approved master plan or land management area;

(4) The consistency of the proposed open space use with existing private conservation programs in the area, as evidenced by other land, protected by easement or fee ownership by organizations referred to in § 1.170A-14(c)(1), in close proximity to the property;

(5) The likelihood that development of the property would lead to or contribute to degradation of the scenic, natural, or historic character of the area;

(6) The opportunity for the general public to use the property or to appreciate its scenic values;

(7) The importance of the property in preserving a local or regional landscape or resource that attracts tourism or commerce to the area;

(8) The likelihood that the donee will acquire equally desirable and valuable substitute property or property rights;

(9) The cost to the donee of enforcing the terms of the conservation restriction;

(10) The population density in the area of the property; and

(11) The consistency of the proposed open space use with a legislatively mandated program identifying particular parcels of land for future protection.

(B) Illustrations. The preservation of an ordinary tract of land would not in and of itself yield a significant public benefit, but the preservation of ordinary land areas in conjunction with other factors that demonstrate significant public benefit or the preservation of a unique land area for public employment [sic—should read "enjoyment"] would yield a significant public benefit. For example, the preservation of a vacant downtown lot would not by itself yield a significant public benefit, but the preservation of the downtown lot as a public garden would, absent countervailing factors, yield a significant public benefit. The following are other examples of contributions which would, absent countervailing factors, yield a significant public benefit: The preservation of farmland pursuant to a state program for flood prevention and control; the preservation of a unique natural land formation for the enjoyment of the general public; the preservation of woodland along a public highway pursuant to a government program to preserve the appearance of the area so as to maintain the scenic view from the highway; and the preservation of a stretch of undeveloped property located between a public highway and the ocean in order to maintain the scenic ocean view from the highway.

(v) Limitation. A deduction will not be allowed for the preservation of open space under section 170(h)(4)(A)(iii), if the terms of the easement permit a degree of intrusion or future development that would interfere with the essential scenic quality of the land or with the governmental conservation policy that is being furthered by the donation. See § 1.170A-14(e)(2) for rules relating to inconsistent use.

(vi) Relationship of requirements—

(A) Clearly delineated governmental policy and significant public benefit. Although the requirements of "clearly delineated governmental policy" and "significant public benefit" must be met independently, for purposes of this section the two requirements may also be related. The more specific the governmental policy with respect to the particular site to be protected, the more likely the governmental decision, by itself, will tend to establish the significant public benefit associated with the donation. For example, while a statute in State X permitting preferential assessment for farmland is, by definition, governmental policy, it is distinguishable from a state statute, accompanied by appropriations, naming the X River as a valuable resource and articulating the legislative policy that the X River and the relatively natural quality of its surrounding be protected. On these facts, an open space easement on farmland in State X would have to demonstrate additional factors to establish "significant public benefit." The specificity of the legislative mandate to protect the X River, however, would by itself tend to establish the significant public benefit associated with an open space easement on land fronting the X River.

(B) Scenic enjoyment and significant public benefit. With respect to the relationship between the requirements of "scenic enjoyment" and "significant public benefit," since the degrees of scenic enjoyment offered by a variety of open space easements are subjective and not as easily delineated as are increasingly specific levels of governmental policy, the significant public benefit of preserving a scenic view must be independently established in all cases.

(C) Donations may satisfy more than one test. In some cases, open space easements may be both for scenic enjoyment and pursuant to a clearly delineated governmental policy. For example, the preservation of a particular scenic view identified as part of a scenic landscape inventory by a rigorous governmental review process will meet the tests of both paragraphs (d)(4)(i)(A) and (d)(4)(i)(B) of this section.

(5) Historic preservation—

(i) In general. The donation of a qualified real property interest to preserve an historically important land area or a certified historic structure will meet the conservation purposes test of this section. When restrictions to preserve a building or land area within a registered historic district permit future development on the site, a deduction will be allowed under this section only if the terms of the restrictions require that such development conform with appropriate local, state, or Federal standards for construction or rehabilitation within the district. See also, § 1.170A-14(h)(3)(ii).

243

(ii) Historically important land area. The term historically important land area includes:

(A) An independently significant land area including any related historic resources (for example, an archaeological site or a Civil War battlefield with related monuments, bridges, cannons, or houses) that meets the National Register Criteria for Evaluation in 36 CFR 60.4 (Pub.L. 89-665, 80 Stat. 915);

(B) Any land area within a registered historic district including any buildings on the land area that can reasonably be considered as contributing to the significance of the district; and

(C) Any land area (including related historic resources) adjacent to a property listed individually in the National Register of Historic Places (but not within a registered historic district) in a case where the physical or environmental features of the land area contribute to the historic or cultural integrity of the property.

(iii) Certified historic structure. The term certified historic structure, for purposes of this section, means any building, structure or land area which is—

(A) Listed in the National Register, or

(B) Located in a registered historic district (as defined in section 48(g)(3)(B)) and is certified by the Secretary of the Interior (pursuant to 36 CFR 67.4) to the Secretary of the Treasury as being of historic significance to the district.

A structure for purposes of this section means any structure, whether or not it is depreciable. Accordingly easements on private residences may qualify under this section. In addition, a structure would be considered to be a certified historic structure if it were certified either at the time the transfer was made or at the due date (including extensions) for filing the donor's return for the taxable year in which the contribution was made.

(iv) Access.

(A) In order for a conservation contribution described in section 170(h)(4)(A)(iv) and this paragraph (d)(5) to be deductible, some visual public access to the donated property is required. In the case of an historically important land area, the entire property need not be visible to the public for a donation to qualify under this section. However, the public benefit from the donation may be insufficient to qualify for a deduction if only a small portion of the property is so visible. Where the historic land area or certified historic structure which is the subject of the donation is not visible from a public way (e.g., the structure is hidden from view by a wall or shrubbery, the structure is too far from the public way, or interior characteristics and features of the structure are the subject of the easement), the terms of the easement must be such that the general public is given the opportunity on a regular basis to view the characteristics and features of the property which are preserved by the easement to the extent consistent with the nature and condition of the property.

(B) Factors to be considered in determining the type and amount of public access required under paragraph (d)(5)(iv)(A) of this section include the historical significance of the donated property, the nature of the features that are the subject of the easement, the remoteness or accessibility of the site of the donated property, the possibility of physical hazards to the public visiting the property (for example, an unoccupied structure in a dilapidated condition), the extent to which public access would be an unreasonable intrusion on any privacy interests of individuals living on the property, the degree to which public access would impair the preservation interests which are the subject of the donation, and the availability of opportunities for the public to view the property by means other than visits to the site.

(C) The amount of access afforded the public by the donation of an easement shall be determined with reference to the amount of access permitted by the terms of the easement which are established by the donor, rather than the amount of access actually provided by the donee organization. However, if the donor is aware of any facts indicating that the amount of access that the donee organization will provide is significantly less than the amount of access permitted under the terms of the easement, then the amount of access afforded the public shall be determined with reference to this lesser amount.

(v) Examples. The provisions of paragraph (d)(5)(iv) of this section may be illustrated by the following examples:

Example 1. A and his family live in a house in a certified historic district in the State of X. The entire house, including its interior, has architectural features representing classic Victorian period architecture. A donates an exterior and interior easement on the property to a qualified organization but continues to live in the house with his family. A's house is surrounded by a high stone wall which obscures the public's view of it from the street. Pursuant to the terms of the easement, the house may be opened to the public from 10:00 a.m. to 4:00 p.m. on one Sunday in May and one Sunday in November each year for house and garden tours. These tours are to be under the supervision of the donee and open to members of the general public upon payment of a small fee. In addition, under the terms of the easement, the donee organization is given the right to photograph the interior and exterior of the house and distribute such photographs to magazines, newsletters, or other publicly available publications. The terms of the easement also permit persons affiliated with educational organizations, professional architectural associations, and historical societies to make an appointment through the donee organization to study the property. The donor is not aware of any facts indicating that the public access to be provided by the donee organization will be significantly less than that permitted by the terms of the easement. The 2 opportunities for public visits per year, when combined with the ability of the general public to view the architectural characteristics and features that are the subject of the easement through photographs, the opportunity for scholarly study of the property, and the fact that the house is used as an occupied residence, will enable the donation to satisfy the requirement of public access.

Example 2. B owns an unoccupied farmhouse built in the 1840's and located on a property that is adjacent to a Civil War battlefield. During the Civil War the farmhouse was used as quarters for Union troops. The battlefield is visited year round by the general public. The condition of the farmhouse is such that the safety of visitors will not be jeopardized and opening it to the public will not result in significant deterioration. The farmhouse is not visible from the battlefield or any public way. It is accessible only by way of a private road owned by B. B donates a conservation easement on the farmhouse to a qualified organization. The terms of the easement provide that the donee organization may open the property (via B's road) to the general public on four weekends each year from 8:30 a.m. to 4:00 p.m. The donation does not meet the public access requirement because the farmhouse is safe, unoccupied, and easily accessible to the general public who have come to the site to visit Civil War historic land areas (and related resources), but will only be open to the public on four weekends each year. However, the donation would meet the public access requirement if the terms of the easement permitted the donee organization to open the property to the public every other weekend during the year and the donor is not aware of any facts indicating that the donee organization will provide significantly less access than that permitted.

(e) Exclusively for conservation purposes—

(1) In general. To meet the requirements of this section, a donation must be exclusively for conservation purposes. See paragraphs (c)(1) and (g)(1) through (g)(6)(ii) of this section. A deduction will not be denied under this section when incidental benefit inures to the donor merely as a result of conservation restrictions limiting the uses to which the donor's property may be put.

(2) Inconsistent use. Except as provided in paragraph (e)(4) of this section, a deduction will not be allowed if the contribution would accomplish one of the enumerated conservation purposes but would permit destruction of other significant conservation interests. For example, the preservation of farmland pursuant to a State program for flood prevention and control would not qualify under paragraph (d)(4) of this section if under the terms of the contribution a significant naturally occurring ecosystem could be injured or destroyed by the use of pesticides in the operation of the farm. However, this requirement is not intended to prohibit uses of the property, such as selective timber harvesting or selective farming if, under the circumstances, those uses do not impair significant conservation interests.

(3) Inconsistent use permitted. A use that is destructive of conservation interests will be permitted only if such use is necessary for the protection of the conservation interests that are the subject of the contribution. For example, a deduction for the donation of an easement to preserve an archaeological site that is listed on the National Register of Historic Places will not be disallowed if site excavation consistent with sound archaeological practices may impair a scenic view of which the land is a part. A donor may continue a pre-existing use of the property that does not conflict with the conservation purposes of the gift.

(f) Examples. The provisions of this section relating to conservation purposes may be illustrated by the following examples.

Example 1. State S contains many large tract forests that are desirable recreation and scenic areas for the general public. The forests' scenic values attract millions of people to the State. However, due to the increasing intensity of land development in State S, the continued existence of forestland parcels greater than 45 acres is threatened. J grants a perpetual easement on a 100-acre parcel of forestland that is part of one of the State's scenic areas to a qualifying organization. The easement imposes restrictions on the use of the parcel for the purpose of maintaining its scenic values. The restrictions include a requirement that the parcel be maintained forever as open space devoted exclusively to conservation purposes and wildlife protection, and that there be no commercial, industrial, residential, or other development use of such parcel. The law of State S recognizes a limited public right to enter private land, particularly for recreational pursuits, unless such land is posted or the landowner objects. The easement specifically restricts the landowner from posting the parcel, or from objecting, thereby maintaining public access to the parcel according to the custom of the State. J's parcel provides the opportunity for the public to enjoy the use of the property and appreciate its scenic values. Accordingly, J's donation qualifies for a deduction under this section.

Example 2. A qualified conservation organization owns Greenacre in fee as a nature preserve. Greenacre contains a high quality example of a tall grass prairie ecosystem. Farmacre, an operating farm, adjoins Greenacre and is a compatible buffer to the nature preserve. Conversion of Farmacre to a more intense use, such as a housing development, would adversely affect the continued use of Greenacre as a nature preserve because of human traffic generated by the development. The owner of Farmacre donates an easement preventing any future development on Farmacre to the qualified conservation organization for conservation purposes. Normal agricultural uses will be allowed on Farmacre. Accordingly, the donation qualifies for a deduction under this section.

Example 3. H owns Greenacre, a 900-acre parcel of woodland, rolling pasture, and orchards on the crest of a mountain. All of Greenacre is clearly visible from a nearby national park. Because of the strict enforcement of an applicable zoning plan, the highest and best use of Greenacre is as a subdivision of 40-acre tracts. H wishes to donate a scenic easement on Greenacre to a qualifying conservation organization, but H would like to reserve the right to subdivide Greenacre into 90-acre parcels with no more than one single-family home allowable on each parcel. Random building on the property, even as little as one home for each 90 acres, would destroy the scenic character of the view. Accordingly, no deduction would be allowable under this section.

Example 4. Assume the same facts as in example (3), except that not all of Greenacre is visible from the park and the deed of easement allows for limited cluster development of no more than five nine-acre clusters (with four houses on each cluster) located in areas generally not visible from the national park and subject to site and building plan approval by the donee organization in order to preserve the scenic view from the park. The donor and the donee have already identified sites where limited cluster development would not be visible from the park or would not impair the view. Owners of homes in the clusters will not have any rights with respect to the surrounding Greenacre property that are not also available to the general public. Accordingly, the donation qualifies for a deduction under this section.

Example 5. In order to protect State S's declining open space that is suited for agricultural use from increasing development pressure that has led to a marked decline in such open space, the Legislature of State S passed a statute authorizing the purchase of "agricultural land development rights" on open acreage. Agricultural land development rights allow the State to place agricultural preservation restrictions on land designated as worthy of protection in order to preserve open space and farm resources. Agricultural preservation restrictions prohibit or limit construction or placement of buildings except those used for agricultural purposes or dwellings used for family living by the farmer and his family and employees; removal of mineral substances in any manner that adversely affects the land's agricultural potential; or other uses detrimental to retention of the land for agricultural use. Money has been appropriated for this program and some landowners have in fact sold their "agricultural land development rights" to State S. K owns and operates a small dairy farm in State S located in an area designated by the Legislature as worthy of protection. K desires to preserve his farm for agricultural purposes in perpetuity. Rather than selling the development rights to State S, K grants to a qualified organization an agricultural preservation restriction on his property in the form of a conservation easement. K reserves to himself, his heirs and assigns the right to manage the farm consistent with sound agricultural and management practices. The preservation of K's land is pursuant to a clearly delineated governmental policy of preserving open space available for agricultural use, and will yield a significant public benefit by preserving open space against increasing development pressures.

248

(g) Enforceable in perpetuity—

(1) In general. In the case of any donation under this section, any interest in the property retained by the donor (and the donor's successors in interest) must be subject to legally enforceable restrictions (for example, by recordation in the land records of the jurisdiction in which the property is located) that will prevent uses of the retained interest inconsistent with the conservation purposes of the donation. In the case of a contribution of a remainder interest, the contribution will not qualify if the tenants, whether they are tenants for life or a term of years, can use the property in a manner that diminishes the conservation values which are intended to be protected by the contribution.

(2) Protection of a conservation purpose in case of donation of property subject to a mortgage. In the case of conservation contributions made after February 13, 1986, no deduction will be permitted under this section for an interest in property which is subject to a mortgage unless the mortgagee subordinates its rights in the property to the right of the qualified organization to enforce the conservation purposes of the gift in perpetuity. For conservation contributions made prior to February 14, 1986, the requirement of section 170 (h)(5)(A) is satisfied in the case of mortgaged property (with respect to which the mortgagee has not subordinated its rights) only if the donor can demonstrate that the conservation purpose is protected in perpetuity without subordination of the mortgagee's rights.

(3) Remote future event. A deduction shall not be disallowed under section 170(f)(3)(B)(iii) and this section merely because the interest which passes to, or is vested in, the donee organization may be defeated by the performance of some act or the happening of some event, if on the date of the gift it appears that the possibility that such act or event will occur is so remote as to be negligible. See paragraph (e) of

§ 1.170A-1. For example, a state's statutory requirement that use restrictions must be rerecorded every 30 years to remain enforceable shall not, by itself, render an easement nonperpetual.

(4) Retention of qualified mineral interest—

(i) In general. Except as otherwise provided in paragraph (g)(4)(ii) of this section, the requirements of this section are not met and no deduction shall be allowed in the case of a contribution of any interest when there is a retention by any person of a qualified mineral interest (as defined in paragraph (b)(1)(i) of this section) if at any time there may be extractions or removal of minerals by any surface mining method. Moreover, in the case of a qualified mineral interest gift, the requirement that the conservation purposes be protected in perpetuity is not satisfied if any method of mining that is inconsistent with the particular conservation purposes of a contribution is permitted at any time. See also § 1.170A-14(e)(2). However, a deduction under this section will not be denied in the case of certain methods of mining that may have limited, localized impact on the real property but that are not irremediably destructive of significant conservation interests. For example, a deduction will not be denied in a case where production facilities are concealed or compatible with existing topography and landscape and when surface alteration is to be restored to its original state.

(ii) Exception for qualified conservation contributions after July 1984.

(A) A contribution made after July 18, 1984, of a qualified real property interest described in section 170(h)(2)(A) shall not be disqualified under the first sentence of paragraph (g)(4)(i) of this section if the following requirements are satisfied:

(1) The ownership of the surface estate and mineral interest were separated before June 13, 1976, and remain so separated up to and including the time of the contribution.

(2) The present owner of the mineral interest is not a person whose relationship to the owner of the surface estate is described at the time of the contribution in section 267(b) or section 707(b), and

(3) The probability of extraction or removal of minerals by any surface mining method is so remote as to be negligible.

Whether the probability of extraction or removal of minerals by surface mining is so remote as to be negligible is a question of fact and is to be made on a case by case basis. Relevant factors to be considered in determining if the probability of extraction or removal of minerals by surface mining is so remote as to be negligible include: Geological, geophysical or economic data showing the absence of mineral reserves on the property, or the lack of commercial feasibility at the time of the contribution of surface mining the mineral interest.

(B) If the ownership of the surface estate and mineral interest first became separated after June 12, 1976, no deduction is permitted for a contribution under this section unless surface mining on the property is completely prohibited.

(iii) Examples. The provisions of paragraph (g)(4)(i) and (ii) of this section may be illustrated by the following examples:

Example 1. K owns 5,000 acres of bottomland hardwood property along a major watershed system in the southern part of the United States. Agencies within the Department of the Interior have determined that southern bottomland hardwoods are a rapidly diminishing resource and a critical ecosystem in the south because of the intense pressure to cut the trees and convert the land to agricultural use. These agencies have further determined (and have indicated in correspondence with K) that bottomland hardwoods provide a superb habitat for numerous species and play an important role in controlling floods and purifying rivers. K donates to a qualified organization his entire interest in this property other than his interest in the gas and oil deposits that have been identified under K's property. K covenants and can ensure that, although drilling for gas and oil on the property may have some temporary localized impact on the real property, the drilling will not interfere with the overall conservation purpose of the gift, which is to protect the unique bottomland hardwood ecosystem. Accordingly, the donation qualifies for a deduction under this section.

Example 2. Assume the same facts as in Example 1, except that in 1979, K sells the mineral interest to A, an unrelated person, in an arm's-length transaction, subject to a recorded prohibition on the removal of any minerals by any surface mining method and a recorded prohibition against any mining technique that will harm the bottomland hardwood ecosystem. After the sale to A, K donates a qualified real property interest to a qualified organization to protect the bottomland hardwood ecosystem. Since at the time of the transfer, surface mining and any mining technique that will harm the bottomland hardwood ecosystem are completely prohibited, the donation qualifies for a deduction under this section.

(5) Protection of conservation purpose where taxpayer reserves certain rights—

(i) Documentation. In the case of a donation made after February 13, 1986, of any qualified real property interest when the donor reserves rights the exercise of which may impair the conservation interests associated with the property, for a deduction to be allowable under this section the donor must make available to the donee, prior to the time the donation is made, documentation sufficient to establish the condition of the property at the time of the gift. Such documentation is designed to protect the conservation interests associated with the property, which although protected in perpetuity by the easement, could be adversely affected by the exercise of the reserved rights. Such documentation may include:

(A) The appropriate survey maps from the United States Geological Survey, showing the property line and other contiguous or nearby protected areas;

(B) A map of the area drawn to scale showing all existing man-made improvements or incursions (such as roads, buildings, fences, or gravel pits), vegetation and identification of flora and fauna (including, for example, rare species locations, animal breeding and roosting areas, and migration routes), land use history (including present uses and recent past disturbances), and distinct natural features (such as large trees and aquatic areas);

(C) An aerial photograph of the property at an appropriate scale taken as close as possible to the date the donation is made; and

(D) On-site photographs taken at appropriate locations on the property. If the terms of the donation contain restrictions with regard to a particular natural resource to be protected, such as water quality or air quality, the condition of the resource at or near the time of the gift must be established. The documentation, including the maps and photographs, must be accompanied by a statement signed by the donor and a representative of the donee clearly referencing the documentation and in substance saying "This natural resources inventory is an accurate representation of [the protected property] at the time of the transfer."

(ii) Donee's right to inspection and legal remedies. In the case of any donation referred to in paragraph (g)(5)(i) of this section, the donor must agree to notify the donee, in writing, before exercising any reserved right, e.g. the right to extract certain minerals which may have an adverse impact on the conservation interests associated with the qualified real property interest. The terms of the donation must provide a right of the donee to enter the property at reasonable times for the purpose of inspecting the property to determine if there is compliance with the terms of the donation. Additionally, the terms of the donation must provide a right of the donee to enforce the conservation restrictions by appropriate legal proceedings, including but not limited to, the right to require the restoration of the property to its condition at the time of the donation.

(6) Extinguishment.

(i) In general. If a subsequent unexpected change in the conditions surrounding the property that is the subject of a donation under this paragraph can make impossible or impractical the continued use of the property for conservation purposes, the conservation purpose can nonetheless be treated as protected in perpetuity if the restrictions are extinguished by judicial proceeding and all of the donee's proceeds (determined under paragraph (g)(6)(ii) of this section) from a subsequent sale or exchange of the property are used by the donee organization in a manner consistent with the conservation purposes of the original contribution.

(ii) Proceeds. In case of a donation made after February 13, 1986, for a deduction to be allowed under this section, at the time of the gift the donor must agree that the donation of the perpetual conservation restriction gives rise to a property right, immediately vested in the donee organization, with a fair market value that is at least equal to the proportionate value that the perpetual conservation restriction at the time of the gift, bears to the value of the property as a whole at that time. See § 1.170A-14(h)(3)(iii) relating to the allocation of basis. For purposes of this paragraph (g)(6)(ii), that proportionate value of the donee's property rights shall remain constant. Accordingly, when a change in conditions give rise to the extinguishment of a perpetual conservation restriction under paragraph (g)(6)(i) of this section, the donee organization, on a subsequent sale, exchange, or involuntary conversion of the subject property, must be entitled to a portion of the proceeds at least equal to that proportionate value of the perpetual conservation restriction, unless state law provides that the donor is entitled to the full proceeds from the conversion without regard to the terms of the prior perpetual conservation restriction.

(h) Valuation—

(1) Entire interest of donor other than qualified mineral interest. The value of the contribution under section 170 in the case of a contribution of a taxpayer's entire interest in property other than a qualified mineral interest is the fair market value of the surface rights in the property contributed. The value of the contribution shall be computed without regard to the mineral rights. See paragraph (h)(4), example (1), of this section.

(2) Remainder interest in real property. In the case of a contribution of any remainder interest in real property, section 170(f)(4) provides that in determining the value of such interest for purposes of section 170, depreciation and depletion of such property shall be taken into account. See § 1.170A-12. In the case of the contribution of a remainder interest for conservation purposes, the current fair market value of the property (against which the limitations of § 1.170A-12 are applied) must take into account any pre-existing or contemporaneously recorded rights limiting, for conservation purposes, the use to which the subject property may be put.

(3) Perpetual conservation restriction—

(i) In general. The value of the contribution under section 170 in the case of a charitable contribution of a perpetual conservation restriction is the fair market value of the perpetual conservation restriction at the time of the contribution. See § 1.170A-7(c). If there is a substantial record of sales of easements comparable to the donated easement (such as purchases pursuant to a governmental program), the fair market value of the donated easement is based on the sales prices of such comparable easements. If no substantial record of market-place sales is available to use as a meaningful or valid comparison, as a general rule (but not necessarily in all cases) the fair market value of a perpetual conservation restriction is equal to the difference between the fair market value of the property it encumbers before the granting of the restriction and the fair market value of the encumbered property after the granting of the restriction. The amount of the deduction in the case of a charitable contribution of a perpetual conservation restriction covering a portion of the contiguous property owned by a donor and the donor's family (as defined in section 267(c)(4)) is the difference between the fair market value of the entire contiguous parcel of property before and after the granting of the restriction. If the granting of a perpetual conservation restriction after January 14, 1986, has the effect of increasing the value of any other property owned by the donor or a related person, the amount of the deduction for the conservation contribution shall be reduced by the amount of the increase in the value of the other property, whether or not such property is contiguous. If, as a result of the donation of a perpetual conservation restriction, the donor or a related person receives, or can reasonably expect to receive, financial or economic benefits that are greater than those that will inure to the general public from the transfer, no deduction is allowable under this section. However, if the donor or a related person receives, or can reasonably expect to receive, a financial or economic benefit that is substantial, but it is clearly shown that the benefit is less than the amount of the transfer, then a deduction under this section is allowable for the excess of the amount transferred over the amount of the financial or economic benefit received or reasonably expected to be received by the donor or the related person. For purposes of this paragraph (h)(3)((i), related person shall have the same meaning as in either section 267(b) or section 707(b). (See Example 10 of paragraph (h)(4) of this section.)

(ii) Fair market value of property before and after restriction. If before and after valuation is used, the fair market value of the property before contribution of the conservation restriction must take into account not only the current use of the property but also an objective assessment of how immediate or remote the likelihood is that the property, absent the restriction, would in fact be developed, as well as any effect from zoning, conservation, or historic preservation laws that already restrict the property's potential highest and best use. Further, there may be instances where the grant of a conservation restriction may have no material effect on the value of the property or may in fact serve to enhance, rather than reduce, the value of property. In such instances no deduction would be allowable. In the case of a conservation restriction that allows for any development, however limited, on the property to be protected, the fair market value of the property after contribution of the restriction must take into account the effect of the development. In the case of a conservation easement such as an easement on a certified historic structure, the fair market value of the property after contribution of the restriction must take into account the amount of access permitted by the terms of the easement. Additionally, if before and after valuation is used, an appraisal of the property after contribution of the restriction must take into account the effect of restrictions that will result in a reduction of the potential fair market value represented by highest and best use but will, nevertheless, permit uses of the property that will increase its fair market value above that represented by the property's current use. The value of a perpetual conservation restriction shall not be reduced by reason of the existence of restrictions on transfer designed solely to ensure that the conservation restriction will be dedicated to conservation purposes. See § 1.170A-14 (c)(3).

(iii) Allocation of basis. In the case of the donation of a qualified real property interest for conservation purposes, the basis of the property retained by the donor must be adjusted by the elimination of that part of the total basis of the property that is properly allocable to the qualified real property interest granted. The amount of the basis that is allocable to the qualified real property interest shall bear the same ratio to the total basis of the property as the fair market value of the qualified real property interest bears to the fair market value of the property before the granting of the qualified real property interest. When a taxpayer donates to a qualifying conservation organization an easement on a structure with respect to which deductions are taken for depreciation, the reduction required by this paragraph (h)(3)(ii) in the basis of the property retained by the taxpayer must be allocated between the structure and the underlying land.

(4) Examples. The provisions of this section may be illustrated by the following examples. In examples illustrating the value or deductibility of donations, the applicable restrictions and limitations of § 1.170A-4, with respect to reduction in amount of charitable contributions of certain appreciated property, and § 1.170A-8, with respect to limitations on charitable deductions by individuals must also be taken into account.

Example 1. A owns Goldacre, a property adjacent to a state park. A wants to donate Goldacre to the state to be used as part of the park, but A wants to reserve a qualified mineral interest in the property, to exploit currently and to devise at death. The fair market value of the surface rights in Goldacre is $200,000 and the fair market value of the mineral rights in [sic] $100,000. In order to ensure that the quality of the park will not be degraded, restrictions must be imposed on the right to extract the minerals that reduce the fair market value of the mineral rights to $80,000. Under this section; the value of the contribution is $200,000 (the value of the surface rights).

Example 2. In 1984 B, who is 62, donates a remainder interest in Greenacre to a qualifying organization for conservation purposes. Greenacre is a tract of 200 acres of undeveloped woodland that is valued at $200,000 at its highest and best use. Under § 1.170A-12(b), the value of a remainder interest in real property following one life is determined under § 25.2512-5 of this chapter (Gift Tax Regulations).

(See § 25.2512-5A of this chapter with respect to the valuation of annuities, interests for life or term of years, and remainder or reversionary interests transferred before May 1, 1999.) Accordingly, the value of the remainder interest, and thus the amount eligible for an income tax deduction under section 170(f), is $55,996 ($200,000 × .27998).

Example 3. Assume the same facts as in example 2, except that Greenacre is B's 200-acre estate with a home built during the colonial period. Some of the acreage around the home is cleared; the balance of Greenacre, except for access roads, is wooded and undeveloped. See section 170(f)(3)(B)(i). However, B would like Greenacre to be maintained in its current state after his death, so he donates a remainder interest in Greenacre to a qualifying organization for conservation purposes pursuant to section 170 (f)(3)(B)(iii) and (h)(2)(B). At the time of the gift the land has a value of $200,000 and the house has a value of $100,000. The value of the remainder interest, and thus the amount eligible for an income tax deduction under section 170(f), is computed pursuant to § 1.170A-12. See § 1.170A-12(b)(3).

Example 4. Assume the same facts as in Example 2, except that at age 62 instead of donating a remainder interest B donates an easement in Greenacre to a qualifying organization for conservation purposes. The fair market value of Greenacre after the donation is reduced to $110,000. Accordingly, the value of the easement, and thus the amount eligible for a deduction under section 170(f), is $90,000 ($200,000 less $110,000).

Example 5. Assume the same facts as in Example 4, and assume that three years later, at age 65, B decides to donate a remainder interest in Greenacre to a qualifying organization for conservation purposes. Increasing real estate values in the area have raised the fair market value of Greenacre (subject to the easement) to $130,000. Accordingly, the value of the remainder interest, and thus the amount eligible for a deduction under section 170(f), is $41,639 ($130,000 × .32030).

Example 6. Assume the same facts as in Example 2, except that at the time of the donation of a remainder interest in Greenacre, B also donates an easement to a different qualifying organization for conservation purposes. Based on all the facts and circumstances, the value of the easement is determined to be $100,000. Therefore, the value of the property after the easement is $100,000 and the value of the remainder interest, and thus the amount eligible for deduction under section 170(f), is $27,998 ($100,000 × .27998).

Example 7. C owns Greenacre, a 200-acre estate containing a house built during the colonial period. At its highest and best use, for home development, the fair market value of Greenacre is $300,000. C donates an easement (to maintain the house and Greenacre in their current state) to a qualifying organization for conservation purposes. The fair market value of Greenacre after the donation is reduced to $125,000. Accordingly, the value of the easement and the amount eligible for a deduction under section 170(f) is $175,000 ($300,000 less $125,000).

Example 8. Assume the same facts as in Example 7 and assume that three years later, C decides to donate a remainder interest in Greenacre to a qualifying organization for conservation purposes. Increasing real estate values in the area have raised the fair market value of Greenacre to $180,000. Assume that because of the perpetual easement prohibiting any development of the land, the value of the house is $120,000 and the value of the land is $60,000. The value of the remainder interest, and thus the amount eligible for an income tax deduction under section 170(f), is computed pursuant to § 1.170A-12. See § 1.170A-12(b)(3).

Example 9. D owns property with a basis of $20,000 and a fair market value of $80,000. D donates to a qualifying organization an easement for conservation purposes that is determined under this section to have a fair market value of $60,000. The amount of basis allocable to the easement is $15,000 ($60,000/ $80,000=$15,000/$20,000). Accordingly, the basis of the property is reduced to $5,000 ($20,000 minus $15,000).

Example 10. E owns 10 one-acre lots that are currently woods and parkland. The fair market value of each of E's lots is $15,000 and the basis of each lot is $3,000. E grants to the county a perpetual easement for conservation purposes to use and maintain eight of the acres as a public park and to restrict any future development on those eight acres. As a result of the restrictions, the value of the eight acres is reduced to $1,000 an acre. However, by perpetually restricting development on this portion of the land, E has ensured that the two remaining acres will always be bordered by parkland, thus increasing their fair market value to $22,500 each. If the eight acres represented all of E's land, the fair market value of the easement would be $112,000, an amount equal to the fair market value of the land before the granting of the easement (8x$15,000=$120,000) minus the fair market value of the encumbered land after the granting of the easement (8x$1,000=$8,000). However, because the easement only covered a portion of the taxpayer's contiguous land, the amount of the deduction under section 170 is reduced to $97,000 ($150,000-$53,000), that is, the difference between the fair market value of the entire tract of land before ($150,000) and after ((8x$1,000)+(2x $22,500)) the granting of the easement.

Example 11. Assume the same facts as in example (10). Since the easement covers a portion of E's land, only the basis of that portion is adjusted. Therefore, the amount of basis allocable to the easement is $22,400 ((8x$3,000) ×($112,000/$120,000)). Accordingly, the basis of the eight acres encumbered by the easement is reduced to $1,600 ($24,000-$22,400), or $200 for each acre. The basis of the two remaining acres is not affected by the donation.

Example 12. F owns and uses as professional offices a two-story building that lies within a registered historic district. F's building is an outstanding example of period architecture with a fair market value of $125,000. Restricted to its current use, which is the highest and best use of the property without making changes to the facade, the building and lot would have a fair market value of $100,000, of which $80,000 would be allocable to the building and $20,000 would be allocable to the lot. F's basis in the property is $50,000, of which $40,000 is allocable to the building and $10,000 is allocable to the lot. F's neighborhood is a mix of residential and commercial uses, and it is possible that F (or another owner) could enlarge the building for more extensive commercial use, which is its highest and best use. However, this would require changes to the facade. F would like to donate to a qualifying preservation organization an easement restricting any changes to the facade and promising to maintain the facade in perpetuity. The donation would qualify for a deduction under this section. The fair market value of the easement is $25,000 (the fair market value of the property before the easement, $125,000, minus the fair market value of the property after the easement, $100,000). Pursuant to § 1.170A-14(h)(3)(iii), the basis allocable to the easement is $10,000 and the basis of the underlying property (building and lot) is reduced to $40,000.

(i) Substantiation requirement. If a taxpayer makes a qualified conservation contribution and claims a deduction, the taxpayer must maintain written records of the fair market value of the underlying property before and after the donation and the conservation purpose furthered by the donation and such information shall be stated in the taxpayer's income tax return if required by the return or its instructions. See also § 1.170A-13(c) (relating to substantiation requirements for deductions in excess of $5,000 for charitable contributions made after 1984), and section 6659 (relating to additions to tax in the case of valuation overstatements).

(j) Effective date. Except as otherwise provided in § 1.170A-14(g)(4)(ii), this section applies only to contributions made on or after December 18, 1980.

Uniform Conservation Easement Act

[Note that this is the act as proposed by the National Conference of Commissioners of Uniform State Laws. This appendix does not include comments from the commissioners, which might be useful in gaining a fuller understanding of their intent, if not the intent of states that have enacted the Act.]

Section
1. Definitions.
2. Creation, Conveyance, Acceptance and Duration.
3. Judicial Actions.
4. Validity.
5. Applicability.
6. Uniformity of Application and Construction.

1. [DEFINITIONS].

As used in this Act, unless the context otherwise requires:

(1) "Conservation easement" means a nonpossessory interest of a holder in real property imposing limitations or affirmative obligations the purposes of which include retaining or protecting natural, scenic, or open-space values of real property, assuring its availability for agricultural, forest, recreational, or open-space use, protecting natural resources, maintaining or enhancing air or water quality, or preserving the historical, architectural, archaeological, or cultural aspects of real property.

(2) "Holder" means:

(i) a governmental body empowered to hold an interest in real property under the laws of this State or the United States; or

(ii) a charitable corporation, charitable association, or charitable trust, the purposes or powers of which include retaining or protecting the natural, scenic, or open-space values of real property, assuring the availability of real property for agricultural, forest, recreational, or open-space use, protecting natural resources, maintaining or enhancing air or water quality, or preserving the historical, architectural, archaeological, or cultural aspects of real property.

(3) "Third-party right of enforcement" means a right provided in a conservation easement to enforce any of its terms granted to a governmental body, charitable corporation, charitable association, or charitable trust, which, although eligible to be a holder, is not a holder.

2. [CREATION, CONVEYANCE, ACCEPTANCE AND DURATION].

(a) Except as otherwise provided in this Act, a conservation easement may be created, conveyed, recorded, assigned, released, modified, terminated, or otherwise altered or affected in the same manner as other easements.

(b) No right or duty in favor of or against a holder and no right in favor of a person having a third-party right of enforcement arises under a conservation easement before its acceptance by the holder and a recordation of the acceptance.

260 (c) Except as provided in Section 3(b), a conservation easement is unlimited in duration unless the instrument creating it otherwise provides.

(d) An interest in real property in existence at the time a conservation easement is created is not impaired by it unless the owner of the interest is a party to the conservation easement or consents to it.

3. [JUDICIAL ACTIONS].

(a) An action affecting a conservation easement may be brought by:

(1) an owner of an interest in the real property burdened by the easement;

(2) a holder of the easement;

(3) a person having a third-party right of enforcement; or

(4) a person authorized by other law.

(b) This Act does not affect the power of a court to modify or terminate a conservation easement in accordance with the principles of law and equity.

4. [VALIDITY].

A conservation easement is valid even though:

(1) it is not appurtenant to an interest in real property;

(2) it can be or has been assigned to another holder;

(3) it is not of a character that has been recognized traditionally at common law;

(4) it imposes a negative burden;

(5) it imposes affirmative obligations upon the owner of an interest in the burdened property or upon the holder;

(6) the benefit does not touch or concern real property; or

(7) there is no privity of estate or of contract.

5. [APPLICABILITY].

(a) This Act applies to any interest created after its effective date which complies with this Act, whether designated as a conservation easement or as a covenant, equitable servitude, restriction, easement, or otherwise.

(b) This Act applies to any interest created before its effective date if it would have enforceable had it been created after its effective date unless retroactive application contravenes the constitution or laws of this State or the United States.

(c) This Act does not invalidate any interest, whether designated as a conservation or preservation easement or as a covenant, equitable servitude, restriction, easement, or otherwise, that is enforceable under other law of this State.

6. [UNIFORMITY OF APPLICATION AND CONSTRUCTION].
This Act shall be applied and construed to effectuate its general purpose to make uniform the laws with respect to the subject of the Act among states enacting it.

IRS Notice 2004-41: Charitable Contributions and Conservation Easements

Released: June 30, 2004

Published: July 12, 2004

Charitable contributions and conservation easements. This notice informs taxpayers that the Service will, in appropriate cases, reduce or disallow deductions claimed by taxpayers under section 170 of the Code for transfers in connection with conservation easements. This notice also informs participants in these transactions that they may be subject to other adverse tax consequences, including penalties, excise taxes, and loss of tax-exempt status, as appropriate.

The Internal Revenue Service is aware that taxpayers who (1) transfer an easement on real property to a charitable organization, or (2) make payments to a charitable organization in connection with a purchase of real property from the charitable organization, may be improperly claiming charitable contribution deductions under § 170 of the Internal Revenue Code. The purpose of this notice is to advise participants in these transactions that, in appropriate cases, the Service intends to disallow such deductions and may impose penalties and excise taxes. Furthermore, the Service may, in appropriate cases, challenge the tax-exempt status of a charitable organization that participates in these transactions. In addition, this notice advises promoters and appraisers that the Service intends to review promotions of transactions involving these improper deductions, and that the promoters and appraisers may be subject to penalties.

CONTRIBUTIONS OF CONSERVATION EASEMENTS

Section 170(a)(1) allows as a deduction, subject to certain limitations and restrictions, any charitable contribution (as defined in § 170(c)) that is made within the taxable year. Generally, to be deductible as a charitable contribution under § 170, a transfer to a charitable organization must be a gift of money or property without receipt or expectation of receipt of adequate consideration, made with charitable intent. See U.S. v. American Bar Endowment, 477 U.S. 105, 117-18 (1986); Hernandez v. Commissioner, 490 U.S. 680, 690 (1989); see also § 1.170A-1(h)(1) and (2) of the Income Tax Regulations.

Section 170(f)(3) provides generally that no charitable contribution deduction is allowed for a transfer to a charitable organization of less than the taxpayer's entire interest in property. Section 170(f)(3)(B)(iii) provides an exception to this rule in the case of a qualified conservation contribution.

A qualified conservation contribution is a contribution of a qualified real property interest to a qualified organization exclusively for certain conservation purposes. Section 170(h)(1), (2), (3), and (4); § 1.170A-14(a). A qualified real property interest includes a restriction (granted in perpetuity) on the use that may be made of the real property. Section 170(h)(2)(C); see also § 1.170A-14(b)(2). For purposes of this notice, qualified real property interests described in § 170(h)(2)(C) are referred to as conservation easements.

One of the permitted conservation purposes listed in § 170(h)(4) is the protection of a relatively natural habitat of fish, wildlife, or plants, or similar ecosystem. Section 170(h)(4)(A)(ii); see also § 1.170A-14(d)(1)(ii) and (3). Another of the permitted conservation purposes is the preservation of open space ("open space easement"), including farmland and forest land, for the scenic enjoyment of the general public or pursuant to a clearly delineated governmental conservation policy. However, if the public benefit of an open space easement is not significant, the charitable contribution deduction will be disallowed. See § 170(h)(4)(A)(iii); see also § 1.170A-14(d)(1)(iii) and (4)(iv), (v), and (vi). Section 170(h) and § 1.170A-14 contain many other requirements that must be satisfied for a contribution of a conservation easement to be allowed as a deduction.

A charitable contribution is allowed as a deduction only if substantiated in accordance with regulations prescribed by the Secretary. Section 170(a)(1) and (f)(8). Under § 170(f)(8), a taxpayer must substantiate its contributions of $250 or more by obtaining from the charitable organization a statement that includes (1) a description of any return benefit provided by the charitable organization, and (2) a good faith estimate of the benefit's fair market value. See § 1.170A-13 for additional substantiation requirements. In appropriate cases, the Service will disallow deductions for conservation easement transfers if the taxpayer fails to comply with the substantiation requirements. The Service is considering changes to forms to facilitate compliance with and enforcement of the substantiation requirements.

If all requirements of § 170 are satisfied and a deduction is allowed, the amount of the deduction may not exceed the fair market value of the contributed property (in this case, the contributed easement) on the date of the contribution (reduced by the fair market value of any consideration received by the taxpayer). See § 1.170A-1(c)(1), (h)(1) and (2). Fair market value is the price at which the contributed property would change hands between a willing buyer and a willing seller, neither being under any compulsion to buy or sell, and each having reasonable knowledge of relevant facts. Section 1.170A-1(c)(2). See § 1.170A-14(h)(3) and (4) for a discussion of valuation.

If the donor (or a related person) reasonably can expect to receive financial or economic benefits greater than those that will inure to the general public as a result of the donation of a conservation easement, no deduction is allowable. Section 1.170A-14(h)(3)(i). If the donation of a conservation easement has no material effect on the value of real property, or enhances rather than reduces the value of real property, no deduction is allowable. Section 1.170A-14(h)(3)(ii).

PURCHASES OF REAL PROPERTY FROM CHARITABLE ORGANIZATIONS

Some taxpayers are claiming inappropriate charitable contribution deductions under § 170 for cash payments or easement transfers to charitable organizations in connection with the taxpayers' purchases of real property.

In some of these questionable cases, the charitable organization purchases the property and places a conservation easement on the property. Then, the charitable organization sells the property subject to the easement to a buyer for a price that is substantially less than the price paid by the charitable organization for the property. As part of the sale, the buyer makes a second payment, designated as a "charitable contribution," to the charitable organization. The total of the payments from the buyer to the charitable organization fully reimburses the charitable organization for the cost of the property.

In appropriate cases, the Service will treat these transactions in accordance with their substance, rather than their form. Thus, the Service may treat the total of the buyer's payments to the charitable organization as the purchase price paid by the buyer for the property.

PENALTIES, EXCISE TAXES, AND TAX-EXEMPT STATUS

Taxpayers are advised that the Service intends to disallow all or part of any improper deductions and may impose penalties under § 6662.

The Service intends to assess excise taxes under § 4958 against any disqualified person who receives an excess benefit from a conservation easement transaction, and against any organization manager who knowingly participates in the transaction. In appropriate cases, the Service may challenge the tax-exempt status of the organization, based on the organization's operation for a substantial nonexempt purpose or impermissible private benefit.

In addition, the Service intends to review promotions of transactions involving improper deductions for conservation easements. Promoters, appraisers, and other persons involved in these transactions may be subject to penalties under § 6700, 6701, and 6694.

DRAFTING INFORMATION

The principal author of this notice is Patricia M. Zweibel of the Office of Associate Chief Counsel (Income Tax & Accounting). For further information regarding this notice, contact Ms. Zweibel at (202) 622-5020 (not a toll-free call).

Notice 2004-41, 2004-28 I.R.B. 31, 2004 WL 1462264 (IRS NOT)

IRS Ruling Relating to
S Corporations

[*Author's Note: Gains, losses and other deductions that accrue to an S corporation "pass through" to the corporation's shareholders. Where a pass through item is a deduction for a charitable contribution made by the corporation the law limits the shareholders' deduction for the contribution to the shareholders' adjusted basis in their stock in the corporation, plus the shareholders' pro-rata share of any corporate debt.*

    In essence, what the following ruling says is that there are two components to a charitable contribution of appreciated property, including a conservation easement: the donor's adjusted basis in the contributed property and the value of the contribution in excess of that adjusted basis. Under the 2006 Pension Protection Act provisions (now expired) pertaining to charitable contributions of appreciated property by an S corporation, that portion of such a contribution that represents the value of the contributed property in excess of the S corporation's adjusted basis may be deducted by the corporation's shareholders without regard to the shareholders' adjusted basis in their stock and in their share of the corporation's debt.

    However, shareholders' deductions for that portion of such contributions that represent the corporation's adjusted basis in the contributed property continue to be limited to the shareholders' adjusted basis in their stock plus any of their share of the corporation's debt. This Rule only pertains to contributions made by S corporations during calendar years 2006 and 2007.]

Rev. Rul. 2008-16

ISSUE

If an S corporation makes a charitable contribution of appreciated property in a taxable year beginning after December 31, 2005, and before January 1, 2008, what is the amount of the charitable contribution deduction that a shareholder may claim in circumstances where § 1366(d) of the Internal Revenue Code (Code) limits the shareholder's pro rata share of the S corporation's losses and deductions for the taxable year in which the property is contributed?

Appendix E

FACTS

Individual A is the sole shareholder of S Corporation X. At the beginning of X's 2007 taxable year, A has a basis of $50x in the X stock. During 2007, X makes a charitable contribution of unencumbered real property, with an adjusted basis of $100x and a fair market value of $190x, in a transaction that qualifies under § 170(c). The charitable contribution is not subject to the limitations of § 170(e)(1). In 2007, X has §1363 taxable income of $30x and a long-term capital loss of $25x.

LAW

Section 170(a) allows as a deduction any charitable contribution (as defined in § 170(c)) the payment of which is made during the taxable year. The deduction allowable by § 170(a) is subject to the limitations of § 170(b).

Section 1.170A-1(c)(1) of the Income Tax Regulations provides that if a charitable contribution is made in property other than money, the amount of the contribution is the fair market value of the property at the time of the contribution reduced as provided in § 170(e)(1) and § 1.170A-4(a), or § 170(e)(3) and § 1.170A-4A(c).

Section 1363(b)(2) provides that the taxable income of an S corporation shall be computed in the same manner as in the case of an individual, except that the deductions referred to in § 703(a)(2), including the deduction for charitable contributions provided in § 170, shall not be allowed to the corporation.

Section 1366(a)(1)(A) provides that, in determining the tax of a shareholder, there shall be taken into account the shareholder's pro rata share of the corporation's items of income, loss, deduction, or credit the separate treatment of which could affect the liability for tax of any shareholder. Section 1366(a)(1) provides further that the items referred to in § 1366(a)(1)(A) include amounts described in § 702(a)(4).

Section 702(a)(4) refers to charitable contributions (as defined in § 170(c)).

Section 1366(a)(1)(B) provides that, in determining the tax of a shareholder, there shall be taken into account the shareholder's pro rata share of any nonseparately computed income or loss.

Section 1366(d)(1) provides that the aggregate amount of losses and deductions taken into account by a shareholder under § 1366(a) for any taxable year shall not exceed the sum of (A) the adjusted basis of the shareholder's stock in the S corporation, and (B) the shareholder's adjusted basis of any indebtedness of the S corporation to the shareholder.

Section 1366(d)(2)(A) generally provides that any loss or deduction which is disallowed for any taxable year by reason of § 1366(d)(1) shall be treated as incurred by the corporation in the succeeding taxable year with respect to that shareholder.

Section 1.1366-1(a)(2)(i) and (iii) provides that each S corporation shareholder must take into account separately the shareholder's pro rata share of the S corporation's gains and losses from sales or exchanges of capital assets and the corporation's charitable contributions.

Section 1.1366-1(a)(3) provides that each shareholder must take into account separately the shareholder's pro rata share of the nonseparately computed income or loss of the S corporation.

Section 1.1366-1(b)(1) provides, in part, that the character of any item of income, loss, deduction, or credit described in § 1366(a)(1)(A) or (B) is determined for the S corporation and retains that character in the hands of the shareholder.

Section 1.1366-2(a)(4) generally provides that if a shareholder's pro rata share of the aggregate amount of losses and deductions exceeds the sum of the adjusted basis of the shareholder's stock in the corporation and the adjusted basis of any indebtedness of the corporation to the shareholder, then the limitation on losses and deductions under § 1366(d)(1) must be allocated among the shareholder's pro rata share of each loss or deduction. The amount of the limitation allocated to any loss or deduction is an amount that bears the same ratio to the amount of the limitation as the loss or deduction bears to the total of the losses and deductions.

Section 1367(a)(1)(B) provides that the basis of each shareholder's stock in an S corporation is increased for any period by any nonseparately computed income determined under § 1366(a)(1)(B).

Section 1367(a)(2)(B) provides that the basis of each shareholder's stock in an S corporation is decreased for any period (but not below zero) by the items of loss and deduction described in § 1366(a)(1)(A).

Section 1.1367-1(f) provides that increases in an S corporation shareholder's stock basis that are attributable to income items described in § 1367(a)(1)(B) are made before decreases in such basis that are attributable to items of loss or deduction described in § 1367(a)(2)(B).

Section 1203(a) of the Pension Protection Act of 2006 (Pension Act), P.L. 109-280, 120 Stat. 780 (2006), amended Code § 1367(a)(2) to provide that the decrease in shareholder basis under § 1367(a)(2)(B) by reason of a charitable contribution (as defined in § 170(c)) of property shall be the amount equal to the shareholder's pro rata share of the adjusted basis of such property. The Technical Explanation of the Pension Act, Technical Explanation of H.R. 4, "The Pension Protection Act of 2006," JCX-38-06 page 271, provides the following illustration of § 1203:

> Thus, for example, assume an S corporation with one individual shareholder makes a charitable contribution of stock with a basis of $200 and a fair market value of $500. The shareholder will be treated as having made a $500 charitable contribution (or a lesser amount if the special rules of section 170(e) apply), and will reduce the basis of the S corporation stock by $200. (Footnote 306: This example assumes that basis of the S corporation stock (before reduction) is at least $200.)

Section 3(b) of the Tax Technical Corrections Act of 2007 (Technical Corrections Act), P.L. 172, 121 Stat. 2473 (2007), added § 1366(d)(4), which concerns the application of the basis limitation rule of § 1366(d)(1) to charitable contributions of appreciated property by S corporations. Generally, under § 1366(d)(1), the amount of losses and deductions which a shareholder of an S corporation may take into account in any taxable year is limited to the shareholder's adjusted basis in his stock and indebtedness of the corporation. Section 1366(d)(4) provides that, in the case of a charitable contribution of property, § 1366(d)(1) shall not apply to the extent of the excess (if any) of (A) the shareholder's pro rata share of such contribution, over (B) the shareholder's pro rata share of the adjusted basis of such property. Thus, the basis limitation rule of § 1366(d)(1) does not apply to the amount of deductible appreciation in the contributed property. See Description of the Tax Technical Corrections Act of 2007, JCX-119-07, pages 2–3.

The Pension Act amendment to § 1367(a)(2) and the Technical Corrections Act amendment to § 1366(d) apply to charitable contributions made by S corporations in taxable years beginning after December 31, 2005, and before January 1, 2008. Charitable contributions made by S corporations in taxable years beginning after December 31, 2007, barring any statutory change, are subject to the law in existence prior to these amendments. The IRS and Treasury Department are considering issuing guidance on the treatment of charitable contributions made by S corporations in taxable years beginning after December 31, 2007.

ANALYSIS

Under the facts of this revenue ruling, X makes a charitable contribution of unencumbered real property with an adjusted basis of $100x and a fair market value of $190x in a transaction that qualifies under § 170(c). The charitable contribution is treated as a separately stated item of deduction that passes through to A and is deductible in computing A's individual tax liability. Section 1.1366-1(a)(2)(iii).

Pursuant to § 1.1367-1(f), A's $50x basis in the X stock is first increased by $30x under § 1367(a)(1)(B) to reflect A's share of X's taxable income. A's basis in the X stock is then decreased (but not below zero) by A's pro rata share of the sum of the adjusted basis of the contributed property ($100x) pursuant to the flush language of § 1367(a)(2) and by A's pro rata share of X's long-term capital loss ($25x) pursuant to § 1367(a)(2)(B). However, A's pro rata share of the aggregate amount of losses and deductions ($125x) exceeds A's basis in the X stock of $80x. Section 1366(d)(1), accordingly, will limit the allowable losses and deductions to A for X's 2007 tax year.

Pursuant to § 1366(d)(4), the basis limitation rule in § 1366(d)(1) does not apply to a contribution of appreciated property to the extent the shareholder's pro rata share of the contribution exceeds the shareholder's pro rata share of the adjusted basis of the contributed property. Accordingly, the basis limitation rule of § 1366(d)(1) does not apply to A's pro rata share of the amount of deductible appreciation in the contributed property ($90x).

Under § 1.1366-2(a)(4), when a shareholder has losses or deductions in excess of the sum of the shareholder's basis in the stock plus indebtedness of the S corporation to the shareholder, the limitation on losses must be allocated pro rata to each item of loss or deduction. In the case of a charitable contribution deduction, the limitation amount allocable to such deduction is determined by reference to the shareholder's pro rata share of the contributed property's adjusted basis pursuant to § 1366(d)(4).

In applying § 1.1366-2(a)(4), the amount of the limitation allocable to a charitable contribution deduction is an amount that bears the same ratio to the § 1366(d) limitation as the shareholder's pro rata share of the contributed property's adjusted basis bears to the total of the shareholder's pro rata share of the corporation's losses and deductions (excluding the charitable contribution deduction attributable to the shareholder's pro rata share of the fair market value of the contributed property over the contributed property's tax basis).

Accordingly, the amount of the limitation allocable to A's share of X's charitable contribution deduction is determined by multiplying A's basis in the X stock ($80x) by a fraction, the numerator of which is $100x (the contributed property's adjusted basis) and the denominator of which is $125x (the total of the capital loss and the contributed property's adjusted basis). Thus, $64x is allocated to the charitable contribution deduction. The remaining $16x is allocated to the capital loss.

Accordingly, in 2007, the amount of the charitable contribution deduction that A may claim is $154x. This amount is comprised of A's pro rata share of the property's appreciation ($90x) plus the amount of the loss limitation allocated to A's pro rata share of the contributed property's adjusted basis ($64x). Under § 1367(a)(2)(B), A's basis in the X stock is reduced to 0 to reflect the $16x reduction in basis attributable to the capital loss and the $64x reduction in basis attributable to the charitable contribution deduction. Pursuant to § 1366(d)(2), the disallowed portion of the charitable contribution deduction ($36x) and the capital loss ($9x) shall be treated as incurred by X in the succeeding taxable year with respect to A.

HOLDING

If an S corporation makes a charitable contribution of appreciated property during a taxable year beginning after December 31, 2005, and before January 1, 2008, the amount of the charitable contribution deduction the shareholder may claim may not exceed the sum of (i) the shareholder's pro rata share of the fair market value of the contributed property over the contributed property's adjusted tax basis, and (ii) the amount of the § 1366(d) loss limitation amount that is allocable to the contributed property's adjusted basis under § 1.1366-2(a)(4). Any disallowed portion of the charitable contribution retains its character and is treated as incurred by the corporation in the corporation's first succeeding taxable year, and subsequent taxable years, with respect to the shareholder.

DRAFTING INFORMATION

The principal author of this revenue ruling is Cynthia D. Morton of the Office of Associate Chief Counsel (Passthroughs & Special Industries). For further information regarding this revenue ruling, contact Cynthia D. Morton at (202) 622-3060 (not a tollfree call).

Glossary

Arm's-length transaction: A transaction in which the parties are not motivated by a personal relationship with each other, or influence other than the profit motive. For example, a transaction structured primarily to reduce one's tax liability is not an arm's-length transaction.

Assessed value: The percentage of the fair market value of land to which a tax rate is applied to determine the amount of real property tax.

Bargain sale: A bargain sale is the sale of property to a governmental agency or public charity for less than its fair market value, with the intent that the difference between the sales price and the fair market value be a charitable contribution. Sections 1011(b) and 170 of the *Internal Revenue Code* govern bargain sales.

Conveyance: The transfer of title to real property by gift, sale, contribution, exchange, or otherwise.

Fair market value: The value at which a piece of property would sell in an arm's-length transaction, in which the seller is under no compulsion to sell and the buyer is under no compulsion to buy.

Fee simple: A phrase from English law describing outright ownership of real property, as opposed to the ownership of an interest, such as a right-of-way, or easement, in real property. The "fee simple absolute" is ownership of all of the interests in real property (e.g., surface, subsurface, water, timber, air) without exception.

Form 990: The information return required by federal law to be filed by every public charity that is not "government affiliated." This form is required to be filed by all private land trusts.

Land trust: A publicly supported charity, one of whose purposes is land conservation.

Glossary

Public agency: A federal, state, or local government agency or the federal government; a state or local government itself. All public agencies are qualified to hold deductible conservation easements.

Public charity: A nonprofit organization (including corporations, trusts, community foundations, etc.) that is qualified as an "exempt organization" under section 501(c)(3) of the *Internal Revenue Code* and that meets the "public support test."

Quid pro quo transaction: As applied to conservation easements, a transaction in which the donor of a conservation easement receives a financial or regulatory benefit in exchange for contributing the easement that precludes the "charitable intent" necessary for allowance of any tax benefits.

Real property: Land and improvements on land.

Regulatory benefit: In the context of conservation easements, a benefit to a landowner in the form of governmental approval or permission for one or more uses of land.

Tax basis: Essentially, the amount one pays for real property. This amount may be adjusted up or down, resulting in an "adjusted basis" to reflect improvements, depreciation, charitable contributions, etc. Basis is used to determine the amount of tax the owner of real property must pay when he sells the property. Tax is imposed on the "gain on sale," which is the difference between sales price less costs of sale, and the basis, or adjusted basis if applicable. Basis also limits the amount of deduction allowed for the contribution of a conservation easement made during the first year the donor owns the property placed under easement.

Tax benefit: Any reduction in income, estate, or real property taxes resulting from either a tax deduction, a tax credit, or, in the case of real property taxes, a reduced assessment.

Tax credit: The reduction of a taxpayer's liability in an amount equal to some statutorily recognized payment or contribution. A credit directly reduces the amount of tax on a dollar-for-dollar basis, which makes it a much more powerful benefit than a tax deduction.

Tax deduction: The reduction of a taxpayer's income in an amount equal to some statutorily recognized payment or contribution. A deduction directly reduces the amount of a taxpayer's income against which tax is imposed.

Resources

The following is a very short list of the resources available to those interested in pursuing further some aspect of the material covered in this book. While there are few books on this material, there are many articles, particularly law review articles, many of which are excellent.

STATUTES
26 *United States Code* section 170—covers charitable contributions in general.

26 *United States Code* section 170(b)—covers limitations on charitable deductions.

26 *United States Code* section 170(b)(1)(A)(vi)—covers publicly supported exempt organizations.

26 *United States Code* section 170(b)(1)(E)—covers special limitations for qualified conservation contributions.

26 *United States Code* section 170(c)—defines charitable contributions.

26 *United States Code* section 170(d)—covers carryovers of excess contributions.

26 *United States Code* section 170(e)—covers limitations to basis for certain contributions.

26 *United States Code* section 170(f)(8)—covers substantiation and acknowledgment of contributions.

26 *United States Code* section 170(f)(11)(E)—new law; covers qualified appraisers and appraisals.

26 *United States Code* section 170(h)—covers contributions of conservation easements.

26 *United States Code* section 501—covers exempt organizations.

26 *United States Code* section 509—covers private foundations.

26 *United States Code* sections 641–685—cover trusts, estates, and beneficiaries.

26 *United States Code* sections 701–761—cover tax treatment of partners and partnerships.

26 *United States Code* section 1011(b)—covers bargain sales.

26 *United States Code* sections 1366–1368—cover tax treatment of S corporation shareholders.

Resources

26 *United States Code* sections 2001–2058- contain the federal estate tax provisions.

26 *United States Code* section 2031(c)—provides a partial exclusion from federal estate tax for land subject to a conservation easement.

26 *United States Code* section 2032A—provides for the special valuation of farms and ranches for estate tax purposes.

26 *United States Code* sections 2501–2524—contain the federal gift tax provisions.

26 *United States Code* section 2522(d)—provides a deduction from the federal gift tax for contribution of a conservation easement.

26 *United States Code* section 4958—covers excise taxes on excess benefit transactions.

26 *United States Code* section 6695A—provides a new penalty for overvaluation by appraisers.

REGULATIONS

26 *Code of Federal Regulations* section 1.170A-1—covers charitable contribution deductions in general.

26 *Code of Federal Regulations* section 1.170A-4—covers the limitation to basis for contributions of appreciated property held for one year or less.

26 *Code of Federal Regulations* section 1.170A-7—covers the prohibition against deductions for the contribution of "partial interests."

26 *Code of Federal Regulations* section 1.170A-8—covers limitations on the deduction of charitable contributions.

26 *Code of Federal Regulations* section 1.170A-9(e)—defines *publicly supported organizations* and the one-third public support test.

26 *Code of Federal Regulations* section 1.170A-11—covers limitations and carryover of charitable deductions by corporations.

26 *Code of Federal Regulations* section 1.170A-13—covers record keeping and return requirements for charitable deductions.

26 *Code of Federal Regulations* section 1.170A-14—covers conservation easements.

26 *Code of Federal Regulations* sections 53.4958-0–53.4958-8—cover excess benefit transactions and related excise taxes.

26 *Code of Federal Regulations* section 1.1366-2(a)(1)—covers the allocation of tax items between S corporation shareholders.

IRS ADMINISTRATIVE MATERIALS

Rev. Rul. 67-246—covers deductibility of a ticket to a charity ball.

Rev. Rul. 68-432—covers dual-purpose contributions.

Technical Advice Memorandum 9239002, 1992—covers quid pro quo transactions.

Notice 2004-41—covers conservation buyer transactions.

Notice 2006-96—provides guidance for appraisals of noncash charitable contributions under the new rules of the Pension Protection Act of 2006.

IRS AM (Chief Counsel Attorney Memorandum) 2007-002—covers federal tax treatment of state tax credits for conservation easement contributions.

UNIFORM LAWS

Uniform Conservation Easement Act
Uniform Trust Code

BOOKS

Appraising Easements: Guidelines for Valuation of Land Conservation and Historic Preservation Easements, 3rd ed., published by the Land Trust Alliance and the National Trust for Historic Preservation (1999).

The Conservation Easement Handbook, 2nd ed., Elizabeth Byers and Karin Marchetti Ponte, published by the Land Trust Alliance and the Trust for Public Land (2005).

The Federal Tax Law of Conservation Easements, Stephen J. Small, published by the Land Trust Alliance (1985, 2000). Details the history and status of federal tax law relating to conservation easements.

Field Guide to Conservation Finance, Story Clark, published by Island Press (2007).

The Law of Easements and Interests in Land, James W. Ely Jr. and Jon W. Bruce, published by Thomson/West (2007). Provides a general overview of all types of easements.

The Law of Trusts and Trustees, 3rd ed., George Gleason Bogert and Amy Morris Hess, published by Thomson/West (2005). Section 433, chapter 22, "The Cy Pres Power," Ronald Chester, George Gleason Bogert, and George Taylor Bogert, provides a description of the cy pres doctrine.

Preserving Family Lands, 3 vols., Steven J. Small, published by the Landowner Planning Center: vol. 1 (1998), vol. 2 (1997), and vol. 3 (2002). Covers the role of conservation easements in estate planning for family lands.

Standards and Practices, published by the Land Trust Alliance (2004).

Tax Benefits and Appraisals of Conservation Projects, Larry Kueter and Mark Weston, published by the Land Trust Alliance (2007). Part of the Land Trust Alliance's Standards and Practices curriculum.

Williston on Contracts, 4th ed., Richard A. Lord, published by Thomson/West (1990). Vol. 10, section 27:14, provides a discussion of the doctrine of "promissory estoppel."

ARTICLES

Blackie, Jeffrey A., "Conservation Easements and the Doctrine of Changed Conditions," *Hastings Law Journal* 40 (1989): 1187. Provides an analysis of the legal nature and development of conservation easements and the modification and termination of easements.

"Clay, Sand, or Gravel As 'Minerals' within Deed, Lease, or License," 95 ALR 2d 843 originally published by *American Law Reports* in 1984. Provides an extensive compilation of state law regarding the definition of the term *mineral*.

Dana, Andrew C., "Conservation Easement Terminations, Property Rights, and the Public Interest," draft prepared for Advanced Legal Roundtable on Extinguishment of Conservation Easements sponsored by the Land Trust Alliance (2005). Discusses the appropriateness of the application of the charitable trust doctrine to conservation easements.

Daniels, Tom, "The Purchase of Development Rights, Agricultural Preservation and other Land Use Policy Tools: The Pennsylvania Experience," *Journal of the American Planning Association* (1998), published by the State University of New York at Albany. Describes the use of the purchase of development rights in Pennsylvania by the former administrator of the Lancaster County purchase of development rights program.

Engel, J. Breting, "The Development, Status, and Viability of the Conservation Easement as a Private Land Conservation Tool in the Western United States," *Urban Lawyer* 39 (2007): 19, 33. Covers the history of conservation easements.

Resources

Greene, Duncan M., "Dynamic Conservation Easements: Facing the Problem of Perpetuity in Land Conservation," *Seattle University Law Review* 28 (2005): 883, 891. Explores the issue of permanent land conservation.

Hanly-Forde, Jason, George Homsy, Katherine Lieberknecht, and Remington Stone, "Transfer of Development Rights Programs," published online by Cornell University (2007); http://government.cce.cornell.edu/doc/html/Transfer%20of%20Development%20Rights%20Programs.htm. Describes how transferable development rights programs work.

Hutton, William T. "Easements as Public Support: The 'Zero-Value' Approach," chapter 12 of *The Conservation Easement Handbook* (2005), published by the Land Trust Alliance and the Trust for Public Land.

King, Mary Ann, and Sally K. Fairfax, "Public Accountability and Conservation Easements: Learning from the Uniform Conservation Easement Act Debates," *Natural Resources Journal* 46, no. 1 (2006): 65. Provides a history of the development of the Uniform Conservation Easement Act and commentary on the obligations of land trusts to manage easements.

Korngold, Gerald, "Privately Held Conservation Servitudes: A Policy Analysis in the Context of In Gross Real Covenants and Easements," *Texas Law Review* 63, no. 3 (1984): 433. Provides an analysis of the legal nature and development of conservation easements and the tension between permanent protection of land and economic imperatives.

Lindstrom, C. Timothy, "*Hicks v. Dowd*: The End of Perpetuity?" 8 Wyo. L. Rev., 25 (2008). Covers the charitable trust doctrine and its applicability to conservation easement terminations and amendments.

McLaughlin, Nancy A., "Amending Perpetual Conservation Easements: The Myrtle Grove Controversy," *University of Richmond Law Review* 40 (2006): 1031, 1075. Covers the National Trust's amendment of a conservation easement and the charitable trust doctrine's application to conservation easement amendments.

McLaughlin, Nancy A., "Rethinking the Perpetual Nature of Conservation Easements," *Harvard Environmental Law Review* 29 (2005): 422, 424. Covers the charitable trust doctrine and its applicability to conservation easement terminations and amendments.

Silverman, Mark J., "Recent Developments in the Step Transaction Doctrine," *Practising Law Institute Tax Law and Estate Planning Course Handbook*, vol. 779, p. 179 (2007). Summarizes and updates the status of the step transaction doctrine.

Wright, John B., and Rhonda Skaggs, "Purchase of Development Rights and Conservation Easements: Frequently Asked Questions," technical report published by the University of New Mexico Agricultural Experiment Station, College of Agriculture and Home Economics (2006). Describes the elements of a purchase-of-development-rights program.

LEGAL CASES

Commissioner v. Duberstein, 363 U.S. 278, 80 S.Ct. 1190 (1960). Addresses the motivation required for making a gift.

Glass v. Commissioner, 124 T.C. No. 16 (2005), *affirmed Glass v. C.I.R.*—F.3d—, 2006 WL 3740797 C.A.6 (2006). Addresses compliance with the "conservation purposes" requirements of the Code; in the case, a landowner protecting only a very minor portion of his property prevailed over the IRS at both the trial court and the appellate court levels.

Great Northern Nekoosa Corp. v. U.S., 38 Fed.Cl. 645 (1997). Addresses the prohibition against surface mining.

Hicks v. Dowd et al., 2007 WY 74 (2007). The first reported case in the United States to address the propriety of the termination of a conservation easement.

McDonald's Restaurants of Illinois, Inc. v. Commissioner, 688 F.2d 520 (7th Cir., 1982). Addresses the step transaction doctrine.

McLennan v. U.S., 23 Cl.Ct. 99 (1991), *affirmed* 994 F.2d 839 (1993). Addresses compliance with the conservation purposes test and whether a motivation to obtain a tax benefit precludes a charitable contribution.

Stubbs v. U.S., 428 F.2d 885 (1970). Addresses quid pro quo transactions.

Turner v. Commissioner, 126 T.C. No. 16 (2006). Involves a successful challenge by the IRS of a conservation easement on the grounds that no significant public benefit was provided by the easement, and that the easement failed to meet the conservation purposes requirements for protection of open space, habitat, or historic preservation.

United Cancer Council, Inc. v. Commissioner, 165 F.3d 1173 (7th Cir., 1999). Addresses the requirement that an exempt organization must operate primarily for its exempt purposes.

U.S. v. American Bar Endowment, 477 U.S. 105, 106 S.Ct. 2426 (1986). Addresses charitable contributions having a dual purpose.

Index

Index

Index

| Flip Switched. |

Amount   Billed.   ✓ Paid.
         CSB/